GUIDE TO WORKING ABROAD

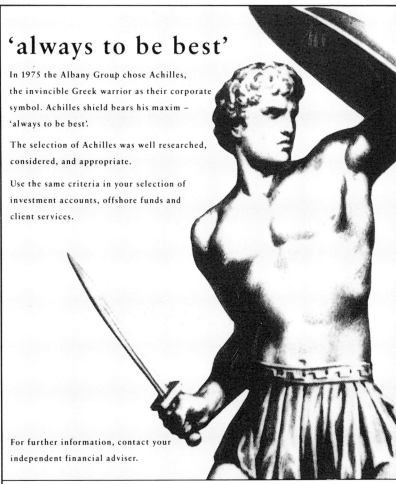

The Daily Telegraph
GUIDE TO WORKING ABROAD

FOURTEENTH
EDITION

Godfrey Golzen

KOGAN
PAGE

First published in 1977
Fourteenth edition 1991

Kogan Page Limited
120 Pentonville Road
London N1 9JN

British Library Cataloguing in Publication Data

A CIP record for this book is available from the British Library.

ISBN 0–7494–0406–X

Typeset by DP Photosetting, Aylesbury, Bucks
Printed and bound in Great Britain by
Clays Ltd, St Ives plc.

Acknowledgements

Many individuals and organisations have helped us with information and advice on various aspects of working and living abroad, and in updating information for this edition. We wish to extend our thanks to Margaret Stewart for her contributions to several previous editions; Tony Smith of International Training and Recruitment Link Ltd for writing the Introduction; Corinne Julius for writing the chapter on the education of expatriates' children and that on adapting to the culture shock; the Centre for International Briefing, Farnham Castle, Surrey; the Overseas Development Administration for information on the situation in developing countries; the European Council of International Schools; Innes Anderson of Anderson Sinclair & Co for detailed advice on the financial planning chapter; Colin Bexon of Hay-MSL Ltd for information on job opportunities; R J B Anderton of Anderton & Son for his help on the chapter on letting your home; Colin Warner of Ernst & Young for updating and suggesting various revisions to the chapter on taxation; Louis Conrad of the Conrad School of Languages and Sally Johnson of Berlitz for help on the section on learning a language; Keith Edmonds of Expats International; Joanna Knappert and Fabienne Brazzill of Employment Conditions Abroad Ltd; Cathie Connolly of International House; Tom Golzen; Helen Steadman; the Overseas Branch of the Department of Social Security; the members of foreign embassies and high commissions in London and of British embassies overseas who have helped in the revision of the text; and readers who have written in with criticisms, information and suggestions.

Contents

Further Information

Preface

Undoubtedly the most significant event since the last edition has been the invasion of Kuwait in August 1990, its subsequent looting by the Iraqis, and the huge build-up of coalition forces in Saudi Arabia that preceded the mercifully short Gulf War of January and February 1991. It is still too early to assess the impact that the aftermath of all this will have on expatriate job prospects, but British firms have been assured that they will get an appreciable share of the value of the contracts arising out of the cost of rebuilding Kuwait. That has been estimated at £50 billion.

Recruitment firms foresee a massive recruitment drive over the next 12 months for those with construction industry-related skills. If it happens on anything like the scale forecast, it will come as a great relief for one of the worst affected sectors of the UK economy, because the expectation is that the US contractors who will be getting the bulk of the work will also be recruiting a good deal of their managerial and professional workforce in the UK.

The UK will also benefit from another factor. Until the Gulf War, a high proportion of jobs in construction jobs at senior and middle level, particularly in Kuwait, were held by Palestinians. It would be an understatement to say that they are now out of favour there.

As far as the rest of the Middle East is concerned, the main opportunities are thought to be in Saudi Arabia. Though that country suffered very little damage from the War itself, the cleaning-up operation following the presence of 500,000 troops there will be massive. In other countries in the region the main effect of the end of crisis is that projects which have been on ice since August 1990 are coming back on stream.

The big question mark at the time of writing is Iraq itself. The rebuilding of that country's infrastructure would be a much larger undertaking than anything in Kuwait, but the general opinion is that nothing will happen while Saddam Hussein remains in power. Once he falls, there would probably be a massive reconstruction programme. It would have to be funded by the World Bank because Iraq, though potentially a rich country, is heavily in debt as a result of Hussein's military adventures.

How safe will Westerners be in a region where passions have run high in the last two years? An optimistic view of the situation is put forward by Ghassan Yazigi, MSL International's head of overseas recruitment. He is a Syrian and maintains there is no hostility to Westerners as individuals, even in countries that did not support the coalition or whose inhabitants were less than enthusiastic about the pro-coalition line taken by their governments. But he warns that expatriates will have to be more sensitive to local sensibilities and cultures than some of them have been in the past.

Further lessons that have emerged incidentally from the Gulf crisis are pointed out by Roger Steel, a solicitor with Frere Cholmeley:

- Employment contracts should include a *force majeure* clause, which means that the expatriate employee is excused from carrying out its conditions if there is reason to fear for his safety.
- Expatriates should have the right to get out of the country in an emergency, without seeking authority. Doubt about this may well have stopped some expatriates from leaving Kuwait following the Iraqi invasion.
- Ideally, the contract of employment should oblige the employer to cover the incidental costs of an early return home under the above circumstances. In particular, these should cover the legal cost of terminating the tenancy of people to whom you have let your UK home and possibly also the tax liability implications of coming back early – see Chapters 3 and 4.

However, many experts feel that in the long term the economic game has moved away from the Middle East.

In the past couple of years the changes in the pattern in jobs abroad noted in the last edition have become more pronounced. Except in information technology, specialist medicine and, in some countries, mining engineering, the availability of medium- and long-term jobs in the oil-producing countries of the Middle East has continued to decline, salaries have been at a virtual standstill and benefits have been cut back. However, low inflation and zero income tax rates still make employment in this region attractive. The tendency now is to offer short-term contracts and secondments to deal with specific trouble-shooting assignments – many of them associated with maintenance problems on buildings and plant installed too hastily in the boom years of the seventies. There seems little prospect of that situation changing.

The decline in oil prices has a good deal to do with the flatness of the Middle East economies but, in the view of recruitment experts, the real reason is that the global economic game has simply moved elsewhere to larger, more vigorous, less tradition-bound societies than those of the states around the Arabian Gulf and their neighbours. The big opportunities in jobs abroad now, they say, are as follows:

- Senior management and specialist technical posts with European and American firms setting up businesses on the rim of the Pacific Basin with their large, entrepreneurial and highly motivated workforce.

- With British and US companies who have woken up to the implications of the single European market after 1992. They are above all looking for people who can combine management and language skills. Previous experience as an expatriate is a plus point. 'We prefer someone who has worked in the country for which we're recruiting,' says one headhunter. 'But someone who's lived abroad at all has at least demonstrated the flexibility which is one of the qualities you need to make a success of an expatriate posting.'
- The single European market is part of a larger picture of 'globalisation' of the world economy, prompted to some extent by information technology and also by rapidly improving transport facilities. To give just one example, it is possible to transmit orders compiled by daily electronic point of sale (EPOS) readings to a factory in the Far East and have the goods made up and in the shops in Milan or London within a few days. These developments make it likely, in the view of some observers, that global transfers of managers and specialists will become as common as moves of executives to different offices or plants within countries.
- There may be a growth in opportunities in Eastern Europe as a consequence of the dramatic changes that took place there towards the end of 1989. The countries which seem likely to progress most rapidly in the direction of western style economics are East Germany, Czechoslovakia and Hungary. But just how far-reaching economic progress will be, it is too early to tell. 1990 was, on the whole, a disappointing year, although this may have been due to the recession in some Western countries and to the effects of the Gulf War.
- The last three years have seen a well-publicised wave of takeovers of US firms by foreign ones taking advantage of the weakness of the US dollar. British companies have been in the forefront of this trend, though other European countries have also been active here. This has opened the USA, previously something of a management closed shop, to non-American executives.

Standing in the way of free movement across countries, however, are continuing restrictions on the issue of work permits – except for citizens of member countries within the EC. In almost all countries, a work permit is necessary before you can take up a job, though these are generally issued readily through a local employer who can demonstrate that no suitable national is available. A local employer in this sense includes foreign firms with a local office or factory. It follows that the best approach is through an externally based firm or one that is recruiting outside the country. In most cases it is forbidden to visit a country on a tourist or visitor's permit, look for a job and then apply for a work permit.

Local employers in developing and newly industrialised countries

There has been a slow but perceptible shift towards local companies as well as governments becoming expatriate employers. This can present certain hazards in countries where the role of the employee is a lowly one by definition, irrespective of the seniority of the job, and where British expatriates are now quite often competing with qualified people from developing countries such as Pakistan, Egypt and Korea. It is important in those cases that acceptable contracts of employment are negotiated beforehand and that nothing vital should be left to verbal 'understandings'.

The growth of local employment has also had another effect of which readers should be aware. People going out to work for British or multinational firms could rely on them to come to their aid if they ran into personal difficulties with local laws (even if their case was not a particularly deserving one!) or to get them out of the country if political conditions made this necessary. Working for a foreign employer may make it necessary to rely for protection on British diplomatic channels. Their role has been much criticised – according to the Foreign Office this is because the limits of what British embassy and consular people can and cannot do has not been understood. Readers are advised to look at the guidance given on this in Chapter 8, as well as to take to heart the information that is provided on local business and social etiquette in the Middle and Far East. The instability of the international job market, on account of both economic and political factors, has had the effect of making overseas contract periods much shorter – sometimes by accident, sometimes by design. One only has to look at the way the events in Tiananmen Square in 1989 brought economic development in China to a standstill to appreciate that expatriates must bear in mind at least the possibility of an unexpected return home. The other internationally growing problem is crime, and page 132 contains a section on how best to deal with this personal risk.

Working abroad and career development

Since the late 1980s, one of the big changes that has been noted in the pattern of employment abroad is the shift away from its opportunist aspects, in which more money, a better climate and a higher standard of living were the main motivators, towards its place in managerial career development. A recent book, *The High Flyers* (Blackwell), points out that most chief executives have worked abroad at some point. The advantages of this are seen to be, first, exposure to responsibility across a wide range of management functions, usually at quite an early age, the development of overseas experience and contacts, and the chance to learn another language. A survey published in 1990 by the recruitment consultants MSL

International makes plain how that lesson has been absorbed. It showed that 96 per cent of a sample of high flying graduates included a spell of work abroad as one of their career aims.

However, those who are thinking of going abroad as part of a career development plan within the organisation to which they wish to return should make sure that such experience will be valued. There are firms where jobs abroad, intentionally or otherwise, are a kind of corporate Siberia. Signs, on the other hand, that this is a positive move are generally reckoned to be as follows:

- Proper briefing procedures on working and living aspects of the assignment before departure. Also, advice on personal finance and taxation aspects and what to do about UK property, dependants, school-age children etc while working abroad.
- A salary policy that fits coherently into the home salary and benefit structure, so that when you return it will be at the level you would have reached had you been progressing successfully within the home company.
- The existence of channels of communication for keeping in regular touch, not just on business matters, but on corporate affairs generally.
- Full exchange of views, up to contact at the most senior appropriate levels, while on home leave.
- A coherent policy for bringing back returnees into functions, posts and areas of responsibility where the experience is used properly.
- The presence within the company of managers in senior positions who have themselves worked abroad.

In fact, opportunities are increasing for students to work abroad, either before graduation or as an aspect of postgraduate fulfilment. *International Jobs – A Guide for UK and Overseas Students* is an excellent and inexpensive guide on this topic produced by the University of London Careers Advisory Service, 50 Gordon Square, London WC1H 0PQ.

Overseas salaries

The annual comparison of executive salaries in 18 industrialised or West European countries produced by Employment Conditions Abroad in 1990 reproduced on page 178, shows that though in purely monetary terms British salary levels are still languishing around the lower quartile, the purchasing power of UK managers' salaries has moved up two places since last year. It is now in the top half of the survey. It is this that is really the crucial issue in making salary comparisons. Many European salaries are 50 per cent and more above UK ones, but in some countries taxation and higher living costs level them out. However, the quality of life in some locations, such as Australia, would be regarded by many expatriates as outweighing direct cost of living factors.

A recent survey of global living costs by Business International, incidentally, shows Iran, Japan, Finland, Zaire, Sweden and Norway as the world's most expensive locations. Poland, India, Zimbabwe and Czechoslovakia are among the cheapest. London, by the way, ranks equal eleventh with Geneva.

European based employers' salary policies

A recent survey prepared by Organization Resources Counselors Inc looks at companies remuneration policies and practices for expatriate managers. It finds that the majority adopt what is called the 'balance sheet' concept of maintaining an equivalent purchasing power at the host location as the employee has at home by making up differences caused by housing, tax and living costs. In addition, they pay an annual premium, commonly around 15 per cent, of home salary for the hard-to-quantify extra costs that one incurs in living abroad. They do not, however, make up for the loss of a spouse income. Opportunities for wives to pick up work abroad or to continue with a professional career are variable and this is one of the points career couples need to check on before deciding to accept a post.

In addition to the annual premium, many companies also pay a hardship allowance, based on such factors as more or less favourable features of climate, health, culture, the availability of western-style goods and services, social life, housing, education and security risks to persons and property. According to ECA, Australia and New Zealand, Western Europe, Canada, the USA, South Africa and – somewhat surprisingly – Malta and several West Indies countries are the ones with the fewest hardship factors. The Middle East, some of the more turbulent African countries and China have the most.

The pattern of the book

In what is now its fourteenth edition, the general pattern of the book follows the formula which readers have in the past found helpful. Thus, while talking about salary benefits and tax levels in a way which will assist the reader to evaluate and compare jobs which he is applying for or has been offered, the book is equally concerned with giving brief descriptions of living and working conditions, compiled as far as possible from first-hand sources, in the countries that we have identified as being the principal areas of opportunity or interest (the two are unfortunately not necessarily the same thing) for expatriates.

Obviously, in a book of this nature the scope for going into detail is limited; so what we have done is, first, to answer what we believe are the main questions people raise about the general implications of going to work abroad: how it affects their status as UK taxpayers; what happens to their entitlement to UK welfare benefits; what to do about letting their home; what action to take about children's education, and so forth. Then, in the second part of the book, we have given surveys of various countries, which will enable readers to get some idea of what life there might be like. The information, now gathered largely from 1990–91 sources, is as up to date and accurate as we have been able to make it. At the same time we must issue the usual disclaimers about not being held responsible for errors, first, because even the reporting of facts can sometimes be a subjective business and, second, because inflation – a worldwide phenomenon – tends to date figures rather quickly. However, the slow-down in inflation to single figures in most countries, other than those with obvious political or economic problems, has meant that cost of living figures have not had to be drastically altered. Exchange rate fluctuations are a bigger problem. Because of these, any sterling figures given should be treated as being indicative rather than precise. You will obviously check with your bank what your pound is worth. (In countries with a dollar currency, the figures quoted are understood to be in local, not US, dollars.)

We should like to hear from anybody who has more current information or who has suggestions for including additional material or more country surveys, which may be incorporated in future editions.

We have also made some obvious, but intentional, omissions. One of these is the question of health which we feel is expertly covered for lay readers in an inexpensive and widely recommended book: *Preservation of Personal Health in Warm Climates*, available from the Ross Institute of Tropical Hygiene, Keppel Street, Gower Street, London WC1E 7HT, though we would add one piece of advice here: do not take any drugs with you to a Third World or developing country unless they are prescribed and labelled. A new service from the London School of Hygiene and Tropical Medicine called MASTA (Medical Advisory Service for Travellers Abroad) offers a tailor-made health brief to specific countries. Application forms are available from Boots the Chemist or can be obtained direct from MASTA (tel: 071-631 4408). There is, however, one major international health hazard that has come to the fore since earlier editions of this book: the problem of AIDS. It has reached epidemic proportions in some parts of Africa and is causing concern in many other countries, including the USA. It is no longer sufficient to warn expatriates against the dangers of homosexuality or even promiscuity. People can become infected through transfusions of infected blood or treatment with instruments that have not been properly sterilised. Expatriates are now advised to contact British embassies or high commissions, who keep registers of reliable blood donors among the expatriate community. It is also inadvisable in many countries to attend local doctors' or dentists' clinics unless they are known to enforce the highest standards of hygiene.

Those working in Saudi Arabia should note that they will have to produce a doctor's certificate to show that they are HIV negative. It has been pointed out that this can raise problems when applying for medical insurance. Even the answer 'yes' to the question 'Have you ever been HIV tested?' can raise the suspicion that your lifestyle exposes you to the rise of AIDS. Thus, if you have been HIV tested in connection with an assignment to Saudi Arabia, you should point this out if the question arises on medical insurance forms.

Social security is dealt with in a general chapter but the systems in individual countries are not covered in any detail. Benefits and contributions are constantly fluctuating and up-to-date information can be obtained from the appropriate embassies or high commissions, or from the Department of Social Security, Overseas Branch, Newcastle upon Tyne NE98 1YX.

We have cut lists of addresses to the minimum. The location of embassies and consulates can easily be established from the London telephone directory or the *London Diplomatic List* (available from HMSO), and prospective workers overseas should contact the legation's legal or labour counsellor or the embassy's information department.

London, June 1991 *Godfrey Golzen*

Part 1
General Aspects

Introduction

Tony Smith
Managing Director, International Training and Recruitment Link (ITRL) Limited

Job prospects for UK expatriates

The reputation of British expatriates is still very highly regarded abroad and their salary rates are very competitive against labour recruited from the USA and the other Western European states. In reality, US and European contractors frequently turn to the United Kingdom to recruit workers for their overseas projects at salary rates below those demanded by their own nationals. This type of contract is normally quite lucrative in salary terms for the UK national and has the added advantage that the contractor frequently provides good living and contract conditions.

The ability to earn significant salaries overseas, together with the chance to avoid UK taxes, sounds like Utopia. However, in reality, the expatriate worker is faced with a new set of problems. Many of these will be outside work and will cover his family and social life. Working abroad requires a substantial adjustment in attitudes towards work and life in general. The ability to adapt to the new environment is absolutely essential, together with a willingness to make the best of things as they are in the new surroundings. Attempting to change the new surroundings to a British way of life is bound to be frustrated and to result in the resentment of the host country.

Lucrative overseas employment can solve many problems and may seem like the answer to a prayer. But it also creates problems, which may result in broken marriages, ruined careers and delinquent children. In accepting a job overseas you are taking a substantial risk and you should calculate how big the risk is in your particular case. Very often you will find that there is a direct correlation between risk and salary. For example, working for a major company such as British Aerospace in Saudi Arabia carries much less risk than working for a Saudi company. The rate of pay offered will probably be very different, with the Saudi company offering much higher pay, but the security and facilities which British Aerospace provide would not be available. However, even working for British Aerospace will not stop or cure all the problems caused by working overseas. It will also not give workers immunity if they break the laws of the host country.

People work overseas for many different reasons and are motivated to do so by many different things. It is difficult to believe anyone who says that money is not one of the major incentives. The duration of overseas employment is also very varied. Some people just work a one- or two-year contract to pay off the mortgage, or to produce the capital to start a business. However, such short-term contracts are becoming less common, and usually tend to be taken up by 'permanent expatriates' – those people who have spent much of their working lives abroad.

Increasingly, a longer commitment – of five years or more – is required, and recruiters are keen to attract candidates who have not worked abroad before and who are looking for a change of emphasis. Frequently a lengthy period overseas is attractive, for those in their late 40s, as a final career move.

Career development is another common reason for working abroad and is particularly important and frequent for those working in multinational and international companies, government bodies, banks and organisations with large export markets.

An expatriate returning to the UK faces as many adjustments to life and work as he does in going out to an overseas job. Picking up the threads of a career in the UK can be extremely difficult and overseas experience is not always regarded favourably. Employers with no previous experience in overseas work themselves may think that you are returning from a very alien and low technology environment, and doubt your ability to cope with new technology and life in the UK.

As an international recruiting organisation, it is our task to find workers who can perform a specified job in an overseas environment. It is easy to find candidates who can do the job in a British environment but only a small proportion can survive and succeed overseas. Our second task is to ensure that any applicant we select is aware of all the problems and difficulties he is likely to encounter in the country he is going to work in. We do not want the candidate to be surprised by conditions when he arrives, and the last thing we want is a premature termination of contract. This is bad for the individual and may affect his future employment prospects. It is bad for the company since it is very disruptive and involves them in substantial replacement costs. It is bad for the agent since it undermines the confidence of the client and can also turn him totally against the idea of using British workers.

Given that you have decided, after careful consideration of your family and your career, to find work overseas, you will need to identify the best way of achieving this, and to decide in which overseas countries you wish to work. Working in the Middle East is very different from working in Africa, which is also poles apart from working in the USA, Europe or the Far East.

The overall number of jobs for UK expatriates has declined quite markedly in recent years and the jobs most affected are for unskilled, semi-skilled, skilled, clerical and administrative workers. Many of these types of job are now filled by workers from the Far East and the Indian subcontinent where wage rates are much lower. The same market forces have resulted in some of the more senior jobs which have traditionally been filled by Americans being switched to less costly British labour.

Back in the 1970s and early 1980s, the Middle East provided large numbers of jobs for UK expatriates, but demand dropped significantly after the 1986 oil price collapse. Then the invasion of Kuwait in the summer of 1990 led to a panic exodus of expatriates from many parts of the region. Some cautious recruitment activity resumed towards the end of the year, but most potential applicants were deterred, first by the threat of a Gulf War and then by the conflict itself.

Frequently, salaries are now only 10–20 per cent above current UK rates, but of course the ability to avoid tax and deductions from salary and the receipt of free accommodation and other benefits still make contracts financially attractive.

How to find work overseas

Having decided that you wish to work overseas you should:

1. Look at whether there are any opportunities for overseas employment within your own company. This has the advantage that a period of work overseas could be fitted into your overall career plan, which would alleviate any problems you would face in re-establishing yourself in the UK after your period of overseas work.
2. Look at British (and multinational) companies which can offer the chance to work overseas as part of your overall career development.
3. Look at foreign companies which are recruiting from the UK labour market. These fall into two categories: (a) foreign companies recruiting UK nationals to work in their own country; (b) foreign companies recruiting employees to work in other countries.
4. Assess the opportunities that exist with overseas government bodies, voluntary work overseas, overseas development aid programmes, United Nations and World Bank projects. These jobs are virtually always in the poorer and developing countries.
5. Since some jobs are never advertised and are filled by some agencies from their candidate registers, it is important to have your details on file with the major international recruitment agencies. Some welcome the receipt of résumés and application forms, but others are not interested and rely entirely on advertising to fill their jobs. There are a number of highly reputable and professional agencies specialising in overseas jobs and you can be sure that if they hold an employment agencies licence they are bound by rules which ensure proper service to clients and job-seekers.

Family considerations

Perhaps the most fundamental question an expatriate must resolve is whether he is going to take up a post on bachelor/unaccompanied status or whether he is looking for married/accompanied postings. Many people who apply for overseas jobs have not thought out the problems and have not reached a family agreement on the type of posting required. One of the major irritations affecting international recruiters is that some candidates apply for single status jobs and then at the final interview state they are only prepared to accept a married status situation. This results in a complete waste of time and money for both parties and is guaranteed to reduce your chances of getting employment through that agent.

Before you even decide to apply for an overseas job you must discuss and agree with your family the status of posting that you are prepared to take, the countries you would want to work in, and the minimum remuneration and benefits package you will accept. Only when you have decided these points are you in a position to start making job applications.

The following sections offer a brief outline of life and work in particular localities and may help you to identify which geographical area will suit you best.

North America

United States of America

The USA is a particularly popular location for expatriates, but very few applicants can hope to achieve their ambition to work there. It is only possible to recruit in job categories which cannot be filled indigenously. The most likely categories to succeed are highly qualified engineers, technicians and managers in high-technology fields. Even the offer of a job does not guarantee early entry into the USA. Permanent relocation can take 15–24 months to clear the US authorities. For those looking for short-duration employment there is a temporary visa programme which allows short-duration hire in areas of extreme demand such as electronic engineering and computing. Employment is for one year only although it is sometimes possible to get extensions up to a maximum period of three years.

In weighing up whether the USA suits your requirements you will find that it is not an area which allows you to make substantial savings, and that the increased salaries offered are easily disposed of through the many social and recreational facilities available. The USA is in many ways an easy place to settle in, since we speak the same language and our ways of life are also somewhat similar. If you decide that the USA is for you then you will need to be very patient and be prepared to wait up to two years to get there. Housing is not normally provided by employers and you will have to meet all living and housing costs out of your salary. Remember too that you may become eligible for the military draft and US tax, and it has been quite a shock to some expatriates to find 'Uncle Sam' and the 'IRS' interested in them.

Canada

Canada's way of life and standard of living are in many ways very similar to the USA's. However, there are quite significant differences, the most obvious being the dual language system of French and English. Expatriates relocating to Quebec province will find that knowledge of French is essential from a business point of view. Entry into Canada is a much easier and quicker process than into the USA with Canada accepting more than 10,000 UK nationals each year. There are two basic routes of entry. The first is 'employment authorisation', which is the entry of foreign workers into Canada who have first negotiated a job with a Canadian employer. The employer in turn obtains permission from his employment centre in Canada to offer the post to a foreign national. This permission is now given reluctantly and only if your employment would not adversely affect the job opportunities of Canadian residents. The second route is 'permanent residence', and this involves applying for an immigrant visa and meeting the requirements of the Canadian Immigration Act. Selection for this scheme works on a points systems and it is very helpful to have a job offer before applying.

There is a demand for engineers, accountants, computing staff, skilled tradesmen, industrial chemists, medical and nursing staff. Canada appears to be an easy country to settle in and well over a million UK nationals have emigrated there since 1945. But some people have found it hard there because of the harsh winter climate and the difficulty of finding new friends. A short holiday in Canada is probably a good way of deciding if Canada is for you and will give an opportunity to assess employment prospects.

Europe

The completion of the single market in 1992 is expected to herald much wider job mobility within the Community. It is anticipated that major companies will travel across national frontiers to fill key positions. It is felt that there will be a keen interest to attract Britons to mainland Europe since salaries in many EC countries are currently higher than in the UK. Many predict a substantial increase of job opportunities in sales and marketing.

The changes within Eastern European countries, allowing free travel and the right to work abroad, may have a significant impact. This could put pressure on some expatriate opportunities since the salary expectations of Eastern Europeans are substantially below those of workers in the UK and its EC partners.

Outside the Community the picture is very different. Nearly all the non-EC European countries exercise very strong control over work permits and immigration, and often the only way around these barriers is marriage to a national of the country concerned. This may seem rather a high price to pay for finding a job. Language is also a problem throughout most European countries and in nearly all cases a knowledge of the language of the country is essential. An exception to this is the case of short duration contracts for skilled tradesmen, particularly in Germany and the Netherlands. However, work in this area has seen many abuses by potential employers and agents, and anyone accepting these contracts would be well advised to check out the potential employer. This will avoid travelling across Europe only to find that no job exists or that it is a very different propositon from that which had been promised.

Middle East

There are still opportunities for British expatriates to work in the Middle East and more than 60 per cent of these vacancies are in oil rich Saudi Arabia. The demand comes from both the commercial and public sector, with contract conditions which range from the superb to the absolute rock bottom. In the past few years there have been delays and cancellations of many major projects in the Middle East, with a substantial reduction in expatriate opportunities although the demand for UK workers was less affected than for other nationals.

Saudi Arabia

There are jobs in British, US, German, French, Dutch and multinational and Saudi companies. Many expatriates live in self-contained compounds, some of which contain swimming pools, shops, squash courts, video, TV and other excellent facilities, including restaurants. Some of these compounds provide a very high standard of living and are suitable for families. But many compounds are bachelor only, and the conditions are very basic and much like an army camp. Most Saudi companies and other companies with small scale businesses and projects will provide accommodation in villas or apartments which are located in the community. Much of this accommodation is adequate and British expatriates can expect to get at least their own bedroom and shared commonroom facilities.

There is a strictly limited number of visas for wives and children, and these are normally available to staff who are qualified to at least HNC standard or where the employer can make out a special case. Whether you live in a compound, villa or apartment you will be bound by the following strict rules:

1. Women are generally not allowed to work.
2. Women are not allowed to drive.
3. Women cannot leave the house unless accompanied, even for simple things like shopping.
4. No alcohol is allowed.
5. No pork or pork products are allowed.

6. Social contact between men and women is extremely limited.
7. The normal working week is five and a half or six 10-hour days.

The effect of these rules may mean that a wife is a prisoner in the home for long periods and her life can be more difficult than her husband's. It demands a ready ability to amuse oneself for long periods. Rules in Saudi Arabia are rigidly enforced and it is foolish to break them, since penalties are very harsh by western standards.

Other countries in the Middle East

Other Middle Eastern countries also provide jobs for British workers, albeit a smaller volume. The most significant markets are Bahrain, Dubai, Abu Dhabi, Qatar, Oman and Sharjah. Kuwait could well be the biggest expatriate job market of all, following the Gulf War, but it may well remain a hardship post for some time. Conditions vary considerably and are generally more liberal than in Saudi Arabia. Bahrain and Dubai are the most popular locations in the Gulf with British expatriates, because life is easier and there are fewer restrictions. Rates of pay tend to reflect conditions, with Saudi Arabia paying highest and Bahrain at the lower end of the scale. All salaries in the Gulf States are free of local tax and there is free movement of currency to the United Kingdom or elsewhere. Opportunities throughout the Middle East generally provide the chance to make very significant savings.

North Africa

The countries in the area which offer the greatest number of opportunities are Libya, Egypt, Algeria and Tunisia. Algeria has a substantial number of British expatriates although French and North American nationals still fill many posts.

Libya provides the greatest number of jobs and these are mainly concerned with various facets of the Libyan oil industry.

Expatriates are generally well treated and are welcomed by the local population. The oil companies take very good care of their workers and there is no harassment of workers by the authorities. Work for oil companies is either head office based, and in this case is generally in a major city and offers married status contracts, or is desert based. Desert based posts are always bachelor status and all-found in terms of accommodation, food and recreational facilities, and involve rotational work cycles. Rotations range from 35 days on, 21 days off, to 90 days on with 21 days off. On each rotation round trip air tickets are provided. Salaries are paid offshore in US dollars or pounds sterling without deduction. Workers are normally safeguarded against any UK tax liability. These positions offer very high levels of savings.

Libya is a Moslem country, but it is much less strict than Saudi Arabia.

Women can go out unaccompanied, work and drive, and enjoy a reasonable social life.

Britain currently does not enjoy diplomatic relations with Libya and UK interests are taken care of by the British Interests Section of the Italian Embassy. One should realise that government help might be difficult to obtain in times of emergency.

Consumer goods are scarce and are very highly priced in Libya and all your needs are better bought outside the country. Fresh foods are freely available including meat (except pork), vegetables, fruit, bread, rice, sugar etc. Processed foods are hard to find and are expensive. The importation of liquor is prohibited.

The number of openings in Egypt have increased, particularly since the country started to receive greater US and foreign aid. There are also a small number of jobs available in Tunisia. In Algeria and Tunisia it is very useful to be able to speak French.

West Africa

The main country for expatriate recruitment in this area is Nigeria with far fewer opportunities in Ghana, Liberia, Sierra Leone and Cameroon. Cameroon used to rely almost entirely on French expatriates but an increasing number of British have been recruited. Local taxation tends to be punitive throughout the region. Nigeria recruits substantially from the UK and there has been no sign of this changing. The main requirements are in engineering and management. Work permits are difficult to obtain and applications have to be fully documented to prove the expertise of the individual. People taking up employment in Nigeria need to take care of both their property and themselves since there is a significant incidence of theft and aggravated robbery. Many companies provide employees with assistance to ensure their safety and security.

East Africa

The opportunities in this area have greatly diminished and Kenya is the only country offering significant prospects. It can provide a high standard of living and an attractive way of life, but taxes are high and remittances outside the country are restricted.

Central Africa

The prime opportunities in this area are to be found in Zambia, which recruits substantial numbers of UK expatriates for work in the copper belt. Zambia offers a pleasant way of life although certain commodities become scarce from time to time. At times personal security has been a problem. Salaries are only moderate, and annual remittances are not likely to exceed £6000 per annum. Zimbabwe is offering new opportunities for British expatriates, mostly on short-term contracts, although some longer-term (four- to five-year) contracts are available.

South Africa

There has always been a large number of opportunities in South Africa for British workers and there is potential for a significant increase in the number of jobs on offer.

The country enjoys a superb climate and living conditions for expatriates and it would be seen as an ideal place to work were it not for the volatile political and racial situation.

You must realise that if you work in South Africa and have a South African visa in your passport you will become *persona non grata* in many other countries in Africa and the Middle East.

Far East

The Far East is often thought to be an ideal location by potential expatriates: this is a quality-of-life rather than a financial judgement. Apart from opportunities in oil exploration, drilling and processing based in Indonesia, Brunei, Singapore and Hong Kong, the region has shown a decline in expatriate opportunities. Most countries now have restrictive employment and immigration regulations. Hong Kong probably offers the best opportunities, but jobs are necessarily short term, as uncertainty reigns about the colony's prospects once it returns to Chinese control in 1997.

The liberalisation of China and its rapid industrialisation was thought likely to generate substantial opportunities for British companies and British workers. However, so far very few jobs have been created and the Chinese have generally recruited expert consultants on short-term contracts to train and guide their own staff. The suppression of students in China in 1989 has made some companies reluctant to undertake projects in China, and there are few opportunities.

Australia

There are very few opportunities outside the formal emigration process. If you are interested in permanent relocation it is best to contact Australia House to find out which jobs are likely to get acceptance for immigration. Immigration policy encourages the entrepreneur willing to invest and set up a business which might provide more jobs.

South America and West Indies

There are very limited opportunities for British expatriates in South America. Invariably a fluent knowledge of Spanish or Portuguese (depending on precise location) is essential. Economically, South America falls mainly under US influence and turns more readily to the North American market for recruitment. However, the conflicts in Central America and the security problems of some South American countries have reduced the number of Americans willing to consider posts in the area. Living standards are high but so is inflation. In many locations theft is rife and precautions need to be taken to protect yourself and your property. The West Indies now offers few expatriate opportunities and these are keenly contested because of the good climate and living conditions.

Conclusion

You may think that the facts portrayed paint a rather gloomy picture of the opportunities available. However, the rewards can be high and work abroad usually offers the chance to make significant savings. The amount of your savings depends largely on the location chosen and your attitude to life abroad.

Perhaps the expatriate who finds life the most difficult is the married man with teenage children since in many countries secondary education is either unavailable or extremely expensive. The alternative of a UK boarding school is also expensive, and tends to break up the family unit.

We would strongly recommend that if you are seriously contemplating a job overseas you should research the job market very carefully. You should try to decide whether you have the ability to survive and succeed overseas and whether, where appropriate, your family can also adapt to the new life style. Once you have made this decision honestly you must identify the countries which offer the rewards and the conditions you require.

Chapter 1

The Overseas Job Market

It is difficult, if not impossible, to form any precise idea of the number of UK citizens currently working overseas. Despite the flood of manpower statistics which flows from Whitehall, there is no central register of expatriates. The broad trend can, however, be adduced by examining people's intentions, looking at the range of jobs on offer, and the numbers of applications for particular posts. The peak was probably reached in 1976. Thereafter, rising unemployment in many countries, political uncertainties in the Middle East and parts of Africa and perhaps more optimism about prospects at home combined to make people more cautious. Moreover, progressive reductions in UK tax rates tended to reduce financial incentives to work and live overseas.

Expatriate employment, though continuing to be an attractive prospect to UK job seekers, is no longer the Klondike it used to be. At present only the most intrepid and seasoned expatriates are prepared to take up Middle East postings, although when the dust from the Gulf War settles there may be renewed opportunities, particularly in connection with the rebuilding of Kuwait. Balance of trade and political problems have affected the expatriate job market in Africa and Latin America, though the Far East and Pacific have continued relatively stable. Compensating factors are a continuing demand in specific areas of employment, notably in the financial and retail service sectors and the growth in short-term contracts, previously referred to.

The shading off has been accompanied by a trend towards greater stability in salaries as well as some degree of uniformity in the remuneration packages being offered by different employers for comparable jobs as competition for expatriate labour diminishes. In many parts of the world remuneration in sterling terms has only risen by the level of UK inflation.

Opportunities have diminished more markedly at technician and supervisory levels, because of competition from qualified Third World personnel who are prepared to accept much lower salaries, and also because of the gradual emergence of skilled workers among local nationals as the fruits of training schemes come on stream. On the other hand, at more senior grades the relatively low level of British executive salaries by international standards continues to make UK managers an attractive proposition – especially those who are prepared to be reasonably flexible about working and living conditions. The typical American expatriate employee will often expect to take with him the standard of living associated with an executive life style in the US. Consequently, more senior jobs are going to British or European personnel.

Technicians

This term covers many grades of expatriate worker, from truck drivers and road builders to site supervisors and project directors. Many overseas companies, especially airlines and construction companies, recruit directly in the UK by advertising in UK newspapers. Examine all such offers carefully. Many companies will arrange for technicians going abroad to meet compatriots on leave, who can answer their questions.

However, this is one area where opportunities are now very limited indeed. Workers from countries such as Korea, the Philippines and Pakistan now predominate at this end of the labour market.

At the top end of the scale, the Malla Group at 173–175 Drummond Street, London NW1 3JD (tel: 071-388 2284) has a register of international experts on all subjects who are leased out on contract world wide.

The professionally qualified

The professions and qualifications most in demand overseas are medicine, agriculture and food, process engineering, finance, civil engineering and construction. In general, positions in these areas can best be found through the companies themselves or through management consultants and 'head hunters' (executive search consultants). Many consultants specialise in particular professions such as accountancy.

Some are on a small, specialist scale. An example of a big international multi-purpose agency is International Training and Recruitment Link Limited (51A Bryanston Street, London W1H 7DN; tel: 071-706 3646, and Barnwell House, Barnwell Drive, Cambridge CB5 8UJ; tel: 0223 212346). They are a major international training and recruitment agency specialising in executive, managerial, technical and scientific fields. They have a fully computerised candidate file, which is matched up with jobs as they are notified. They are particularly involved with construction, maintenance and operations, engineering, oil and petrochemicals, health care, hospitals and general, financial and commercial management. They also have a contract labour company which specialises in contracts lasting between one month and one year for engineers, technicians, managers and supervisors in the petrochemical and process industries. These contract staff provide cover during shutdowns and turnarounds, and also run on-the-job training programmes in maintenance and operations.

People with professional qualifications will obviously consult their appropriate professional association or trade union. In the medical profession, jobs are usually found through advertisements in the medical press. Applicants are advised to contact the British Medical Association to make sure that the terms and conditions offered conform with recommended standards, and also to make use of its personal advisory bureau which gives advice and information. Most intending emigrants would prefer to work in North America and Australasia, but opportunities are limited. The USA has virtually closed its doors to overseas doctors. Within the EC there is recognition of medical qualifications. Remuneration is highest in Germany and Denmark, followed by France, Belgium and Luxembourg, with the UK towards the bottom of the scale. But there is unlikely to be much of a 'brain drain' to Europe since there is already a surplus of doctors in training and the profession is becoming particularly overcrowded in Italy and Scandinavia.

The developing countries, by contrast, are in urgent need of doctors and nurses. The average doctor/patient ratio in these countries is about 1:10,000 compared with 1:750 in the UK; in some areas it is as high as 1:80,000, rural areas being almost completely neglected.

European Institute of Business Administration

For high flyers, a possible source of recruitment to overseas executive and managerial posts is the European Institute of Business Administration –

INSEAD. This centre, situated in beautiful surroundings on the edge of the forest of Fontainebleau, France, runs both a 10-month MBA programme and shorter executive development courses on every aspect of management. Holders of the MBA obtained after completion of the postgraduate programme (September to June and January to December) can find jobs through the career management service. The emphasis is on international business management. The curriculum vitae of each INSEAD graduate is circulated to several hundred national and multinational companies. The list of placements since the centre was founded in 1958 reads like a directory of international business. The largest number are employed within the EC, headed by France; there are several hundred in the UK and a number in the USA and in developing countries. Industry, banking and consultancy represent the largest sectors.

The majority of MBA students come as non-sponsored individuals. Various scholarships and loans are available. INSEAD is clearly a good investment for your future if you have the right background, eg if you are between 23 and 35 and have a university degree and some years' business experience (in exceptional cases these conditions are waived). Most of the teaching is in English, with some in French. So in addition to English, a fair knowledge of French is required. A third language is required for the MBA diploma; courses in German and Spanish are available.

Overseas Development Administration

Many types of experienced staff are needed in developing countries, and the UK government, chiefly through the Overseas Development Administration (ODA), plays its part in helping to meet this need. Naturally, every country aims to have its public services staffed eventually by its own nationals. However, there is a real need for the services of people from Britain until sufficient local specialists are available. ODA therefore wishes to encourage people with suitable qualifications and experience to serve overseas for limited periods as part of their professional careers.

Opportunities exist in various fields, eg agriculture, education, fisheries, accountancy, engineering, customs, mining, law, surveying, telecommunications and medicine.

Terms of employment

Staff are normally recruited for overseas service under one of the following arrangements:

Supplementation schemes. Under these schemes staff are in the direct employment of an overseas government or institution. They are paid by the overseas employer in the local currency at the local rate for the job, and they usually receive a terminal gratuity of up to 25 per cent of the basic salary. Overseas emoluments are subject to local income tax.

To bring the emoluments up to UK levels, the British government pays a tax free supplement in sterling. Tax free overseas allowances, designed to meet the additional cost of living overseas, will either be built into the supplement or paid in addition to it.

Technical cooperation. Staff are employed by the UK government and serve on loan to overseas governments. Their salary is paid by the British government and is subject to UK income tax; there is no terminal gratuity. An overseas allowance, which is reviewed from time to time and is tax free, is paid to meet the additional cost of serving overseas. Appointments are normally for two or three years but there are occasionally short-term specialist assignments.

Staff recruited under either the supplementation schemes or technical cooperation receive paid leave, free or subsidised accommodation and free family passages to and from the overseas post. Other benefits include education allowances and holiday visit passages to enable children at boarding school in Britain to visit their parents. Medical and dental treatment may be provided free of charge or, alternatively, the greater part of any necessary expenditure reimbursed. In many cases arrangements can be made for superannuation rights to be preserved.

Appointments are normally available only to British citizens and to citizens of the Republic of Ireland who have no close connections with the country for which they have applied.

UN and other international organisations

One of the ODA's functions is to help recruit British specialists for the field programmes of the United Nations and its specialised agencies; this is done through its International Recruitment Unit and about 1000 vacancies are reported each year. Currently there are virtually no career opportunities in the professional/technical field in the headquarters of the United Nations or its agencies, since it is considered desirable that there should be an equitable geographical distribution of posts and Britain is usually at the top of its desirable range. The main UK agencies with which the ODA deals are: the Department of Technical Cooperation and Development, the International Labour Office (ILO), the Food and Agriculture Organisation, the Industrial Development Organisation and the Economic, Social and Cultural Organisation. The ODA also assists the World Bank Group, Regional Development Banks and other international organisations with recruitment.

The types of job fall into four categories: advisory; teaching and training; surveys of minerals and natural resources; and 'cadre', operational and executive. Governments of developing countries look to the UN and its agencies to supply economists, statisticians and financial experts; teachers and training experts; geologists, mining engineers, seismologists and hydrologists; agriculturalists, agronomists, veterinary and fishery experts; and experts in housing, town planning, social welfare and community development, tourism, education administrators and lecturers, scientists, technologists and engineers, librarians and archivists, and experts in media and communications.

Most appointments to such posts are generally for one year, often extended, and there are also short-term assignments. Candidates are normally 35 and over, but age is no bar – some experts are in their 50s and 60s. The jobs attract good salaries and assignments of 12 months or longer are not subject to UK income tax. Subsistence allowances, or cost-of-living allowances, are paid in local currency and employees are assisted with education and medical treatment, very much on the pattern of the UK government schemes.

There are occasional vacancies for staff in the Brussels headquarters of the EC. These are advertised in the national press and in EC official publications and inquiries should be made direct to Brussels. Sometimes there are positions in the EC offices in developing countries, mainly for agricultural and economic specialists and civil engineers. Language qualifications are essential for any EC appointment.

Further information from: Overseas Development Administration, Abercrombie House, Eaglesham Road, East Kilbride, Glasgow G75 8EA (tel: 03552 41199).

The British Council

The British Council promotes Britain abroad. It provides access to British ideas, talents and experience in education and training, books and periodicals, the English language, the arts, science and technology.

It is represented in 87 countries, where it runs 143 offices, 116 libraries and 52 English language schools. The Council provides an unrivalled network of contacts with government departments, universities, embassies, professional bodies and business and industry in Britain and overseas.

The British Council is an independent and non-political organisation. In developing countries it has considerable responsibilities for the ODA in the field of educational aid, and in recent years it has become involved in the design and implementation of education projects funded by international lending agencies such as the World Bank.

The Council also acts as an agent for governments and other employers overseas in recruiting for contract teaching and educational advisory posts in ministries, universities, training colleges and secondary and primary schools. The Council usually guarantees the terms of such posts and may subsidise them. In these appointments it works closely with ODA. Teachers are also recruited on contract for the Council's network of English language schools.

Vacancies include advisers, headships and posts in universities; the majority are for subject specialists and require previous teaching experience. The subject most required is English language.

Appointments are on contract, usually for two years initially and often renewable by agreement. It is frequently possible to move from one contract appointment to another, but British teachers overseas will generally find that for pension reasons they must return to Britain after two or three such appointments.

Vacancies are advertised in *The Times Educational Supplement*, the *Guardian* and specialist journals. A booklet, *Teaching Overseas*, is published by the Council and is available on request from the Overseas Educational Appointments Department, The British Council, 65 Davies Street, London W1Y 2AA (tel: 071-930 8466).

The British Council periodically invites applications for entry into its Overseas Career Service. Global mobility, ie the willingness to serve anywhere in the world, is an absolute condition of appointment. Applications are particularly encouraged from persons with qualifications and experience in the following fields: science, engineering, agriculture, English language teaching, librarianship, information science, publishing, accountancy, education, media, management studies and the arts.

A booklet describing the Overseas Career Service is available from the Personnel Department (Recruitment) at the address above.

Teaching English as a foreign language

EFL teachers are in demand in both the private and public education sectors abroad. Public sector recruiting is usually done by the government concerned through the British Council; private recruitment varies from the highly reputable organisation (such as International House) to the distinctly dubious. Most EFL teachers have a degree and/or teaching qualification. An RSA (Royal Society of Arts) EFL qualification will also be required. A four-week RSA/UCLES (University of Cambridge Local Examination Syndicate) Certificate in TEFLA (Teaching English as a Foreign Language to Adults) is available at International House in London and Hastings, and at a number of other centres. The course may also be taken on a part-time basis. Experienced EFL teachers may gain a further qualification, the RSA Diploma in TEFLA (essential for more responsible posts). An annual guide to training courses is published by the *EFL Gazette*, address on page 37.

Apart from the checklist on page 170 (most of which does not apply), bear the following points in mind when applying for an EFL post abroad:

1. Will your travel expenses be paid? Some schools refund them on arrival or at the end of the contract.
2. Is accommodation provided? If so, is it free or is the rent deducted from your salary? Is your salary sufficient to meet the deduction? If you find your own accommodation, are you helped to find it, especially if your knowledge of the local language is modest? Does the school lend you money to help pay the accommodation agency's

fee and deposit? If the accommodation is provided, does it include hard or soft furnishing, so what should you bring with you?

3. Contracts and work permits. Will you have a contract, how long for, and will the school obtain the permits to legalise your position in the country?
4. Salary. Are you paid by the hour, week or month? If you are paid by the hour, is there a guaranteed minimum amount of teaching available for you? Do ensure that you can survive financially in the face of cancelled classes, bank strikes and numerous public holidays. Are there cost of living adjustments in countries with alarming inflation rates?

   Salaries are generally geared to local rates, but do make sure they are adequate. In sterling terms, one may earn a very low salary (in Rabat, for instance) yet enjoy a higher standard of living than a teacher earning double in Italy, or three times as much in Singapore.
5. How many hours are you expected to teach? Be wary of employers who expect you to teach more than about 25 hours a week (remember you need additional time to prepare lessons). What paid leisure time do you expect? This is variable, but two weeks at both Easter and Christmas is fairly common.
6. What type of student will you be teaching? Children or adults, those learning general English or English for special purposes (ESP)?
7. What levels will you be teaching and what course books are used? Will there be a director of studies to help you over initial difficulties and provide some form of in-service training?

A knowledge of the local language is an asset; in some situations, it is absolutely essential. Without it, one's social contacts are restricted to the English-speaking community which, in some areas, is virtually non-existent.

Locating the vacancies

1. International House recruits teachers only for its own and affiliated schools of which there are 89 in 19 countries. These schools abide by certain conditions:
   (a) There is a maximum of 25 hours' teaching per week
   (b) Holidays are paid
   (c) Travel expenses are refunded
   (d) Medical insurance is arranged
   (e) There is usually a director of studies or senior teacher
   (f) Students are tested before the class starts so there are no mixed level classes.

   Vacancies elsewhere can be seen on the IH notice board in the Teacher Selection Department, 106 Piccadilly, London W1V 9FL.
2. Advertisements appear in publications such as *The Times Educational Supplement* (Fridays), the *Guardian* (Tuesdays), and

the *EFL Gazette* (available from 10 Wrights Lane, London W8 6TA).

3. The British Council (Central Management of Direct Teaching Department) recruits EFL teachers for the British Council's Language Centres around the world. It can be contacted on 071-389 4913. British Council vacancies are also advertised in the press.
4. Agencies include:
   The Centre for British Teachers, Quality House, Quality Court, Chancery Lane, London WC2A 1HP (tel: 071-242 2982); they recruit for countries such as Malaysia and for private companies.
5. Specialist Language Services (Directory) Ltd, Cromwell House, 13 Ogleforth, York YO1 2JG (tel: 0904 36771). A minimum of two years' experience is called for; teachers are recruited for EFL and ESP (for engineers etc).

Opportunities for women

The Sex Discrimination Act makes it illegal to specify in an advertisement whether a British job is open to a man or woman, but no such restrictions apply to advertisements of overseas jobs. In practice, openings for career women in overseas countries are limited. Most European countries, theoretically at least, provide equal pay for equal work and apply the non-discrimination convention of the ILO. As in Britain, there is no discrimination in theory, but plenty in practice. It is difficult for women to get top-level jobs in industry and management in EC countries, though perhaps more usual in Sweden and in the USA. The number of women in senior business, managerial and technical positions is very small compared to the number of men in such positions. Many women do, however, work overseas as nurses, bilingual secretaries, interpreters, translators, teachers and nannies. Their salaries are usually above those paid in the UK and jobs are much sought after.

There is a constant and continuing demand for qualified British nurses. Their recruitment and placing is mainly handled by the Royal College of Nursing's International Department, which also gives advice to nurses who want to work abroad.

In many developing countries, and in parts of the Middle East, it might be difficult, if not impossible, for a woman to take up paid work. A woman who gave up her own career to accompany her husband overseas might find it difficult to get a job in her own right unless she was exceptionally qualified, say as a doctor.

Many wives in developing countries club together to run a crèche, nursery or kindergarten. As well as serving a useful purpose in themselves, such activities help to relieve the problem of boredom which is a frequent source of complaint among wives, particularly those whose children may be at school in the UK.

Secretarial jobs abroad are advertised in UK media and sometimes – for English-speaking secretaries – in foreign newspapers.

Au pair girls

Living-in jobs are available, particularly for young women, as au pairs, mothers' helps, domestics and housekeepers. They are mainly for those who wish to travel, enlarge their experience or learn another language.

Au pair girls have to be prepared to work hard during a minimum stay of six to 12 months; they are not treated as guests of the family. The minimum age in Spain is 18 years; other countries specify 17 years. A visa is needed for non-EC countries.

The girls live as family and have their own room. They get a fair amount of free time and pocket money of around £30 a week. The free time is largely intended for study purposes, and the usual thing is one day a week totally free, also two to four evenings. Au pairs must be prepared to do most kinds of housework and look after the children, including baby sitting, for five hours a day. If the children are small, the girl will probably keep their room and clothes clean; children of school age will need supervision and company and she may need to prepare their meals when parents are absent. She will be responsible for her own room. Experience with brothers and sisters is obviously valuable. Willingness to work, loyalty and a sense of responsibility are essential.

Mother's help/domestic is a full-time job, usually with one and a half days free and some evenings. In addition to room and meals, girls would get £55 a week or more, depending on ability, experience, free time and responsibilities. A work permit is required for a full-time post in most non-EC countries.

The girls pay their own outward fares. The salaries may sound small, but they are related to age and experience and, taken together with room and board, make up a tolerable sum when one considers that travelling time and expenses are not involved. The posts are richer in experience than savings, but can be very satisfying and offer a means of travel to the impecunious.

A *maid* or *cook/housekeeper* receives higher pay than a mother's help, depending on ability, age and experience.

Au pair agencies give advice and help, but it is the responsibility of the individual to make her own travel arrangements and obtain the necessary passport, visa and permits by application to the relevant embassy or consulate.

If you go abroad as an au pair, be prepared for loneliness at the start; you will miss your compatriots and companions of your own age. You will need to adapt to foreign household routines – the food, the hours etc. The sooner you learn the language, the easier things will be for you. Once you know the family schedules, check the availability of local language classes during your free time, as they will extend your social contacts outside the house. If you are a town person, consider carefully before accepting a post deep in the country. Suburbs tend to be a good compromise – prices are lower, the houses are more spacious, and there is less pressure on services, though the town is not far away.

If an au pair is unfortunate enough to be hospitalised, her pay will cease as the family will need to pay a replacement, so she should consider whether to take out insurance or how easy it would be to return home in an emergency.

Voluntary work

Those who are technically skilled or professionally qualified and would like to share their skills with developing countries could apply to VSO (Voluntary Service Overseas).

VSO has over 1000 volunteers working in more than 40 countries, in Africa, Asia, the Caribbean and the Pacific. The skills required by the Third World are constantly changing and VSO is increasingly looking for skilled medical, technical, agricultural, and business and social development volunteers as well as for qualified teachers. Volunteers are aged from 20 to 65, with the average age now 32.

Accommodation is free and volunteers receive the local rate of pay, plus fares and allowances towards equipment, and holidays. The minimum period of service is two years, but many volunteers stay longer.

Working and living conditions, particularly in more remote regions where the needs are most urgent, can be very basic. The rewards are not financial but personal, allowing the volunteer to learn and work within very different societies and cultures.

Working on a kibbutz

Kibbutzim are communal societies in Israel which produce crops or light industrial goods. Founded in 1909, there are now 250 of them, each with its own cultural and social life. Matters of principle relating to the general running of the kibbutz are discussed and decided at a weekly meeting of all the members.

Arrangements to work in a kibbutz are made by agencies. Applicants should be between 18 and 32 years of age, physically and mentally fit; expectant mothers and one-parent families are not eligible. Volunteers buy their own return tickets, or must have adequate funds for the return journey. Different kibbutzim require different minimum commitments, ranging from five weeks to four months. There are no wages – a small sum is paid to each member weekly as pocket money; toilet requisites, cigarettes and stationery are distributed regularly. Accommodation (two to four in a room), food, laundry, entertainment and medical care are all provided free.

Work starts early so that volunteers are mostly at leisure during the hottest part of the day; the working visitor is expected to put in eight hours daily, six days a week, in either agriculture, light industry or domestic service (dining room, laundry, kitchen). Sunday is a normal working day as the weekend starts at Friday lunch time. After four weeks there is a three-day free period. Kibbutzim arrange occasional excursions for their working volunteers.

Apply for information to: Kibbutz Representatives, 1A Accommodation Road, London NW11 8ED (tel: 081-458 9235).

Learning the language

The traditional picture of the Englishman who expects all foreigners to speak English or hopes to get by with schoolboy French has disappeared. In the modern world of fast-moving communications, language proficiency is an essential tool. It is true that English is the world's leading language for business and commerce and is taught in most schools as the second language. But, in many countries, knowledge of the indigenous language is essential and often a prerequisite of employment. It is vital where a job involves contact with local people, particularly in administration or industry where orders and instructions have to be given and understood. Even where a job is technical and does not involve direct communication, it is an advantage to be able to join in conversation and be more fully integrated with local society.

Anybody working in the EC should be proficient in French and/or German. In Spain and Latin America, Spanish is essential (except in Brazil where Portuguese is spoken). In the Third World, and in the Middle East, knowledge of indigenous languages is not so essential but it is useful to speak Arabic or Swahili, particularly in remoter areas. So the best thing you can do if you are going to work overseas is to learn one or more languages or brush up your existing knowledge.

The increasing demand for languages is being met in a number of ways. There is the 'do-it-yourself' approach which can include:

1. Learning at home, using Linguaphone courses or other self-study materials.
2. Hiring a private tutor: try to find a native speaker, who is prepared to conduct most of the lesson in the foreign language rather than waste valuable time talking about the language in English.
3. Open learning courses at your local college of further education or polytechnic. Many have established 'drop in' centres where you have access to a language laboratory, and possibly also computer-assisted learning, with back-up from a tutor when you need it. This form of learning can be very effective for those whose time is limited and who need a flexible programme of study.

You may prefer to attend a language class, and these are run by most local authority adult education institutes and colleges. However, learning on the basis of one or two sessions a week is not the most effective way of getting to grips with a foreign language – you will make a lot more progress on a more intensive course.

Private language schools generally offer intensive or 'crash' courses. Be careful to check the bona fides of a course before you enrol. An example of the type of tuition available is the Berlitz School of Languages, which aims to 'tailor-make our language programmes to suit every individual's language needs'. There are private lessons and private tuition 'crash' courses in basic languages – English, French, German, Italian, Portuguese and Spanish. Most comprehensive are the Total Immersion Courses (the name is a registered trademark), in which people are involved for nine hours a day, five days a week from two to six weeks speaking only the language they are learning. There are also group courses and arrangements can be made for in-company tuition.

Conrad Languages Ltd (Premier House, 77 Oxford Street, London W1R 1RB; tel: 071-434 0113) are specifically geared towards meeting the linguistic needs of business people. Technical and technological terms for specific industries are included. Languages include English, German, French, Spanish, Italian, Portuguese, Dutch, Arabic, Farsi, Chinese and Arabic. For those who want to learn a language in the shortest possible time there are intensive courses, as well as private tuition. The school also offers in-company courses, weekend 'brush up' courses and special tuition for executives, individually or in groups. For example, the school's research department produced a petroleum language course and trained a specialised tutor to teach on board tankers for a company in Venezuela. It has also arranged specialist courses for personnel of Shell, Esso and BP.

The most intensive course is the Language in Action course, which includes audio-visual sessions, group discussions and management simulations. It lasts from 9.00 am to 6.30 pm (including a working lunch) for one to six weeks.

Fees at these schools are high, but there is general agreement that it is a worthwhile investment. Administrators of language schools sometimes complain that too few companies attach real importance to language proficiency and often leave it too late for effective action.

As an alternative to a private language school, you (or your employer) might consider one of the government-funded 'language export centres'. They bring together universities, polytechnics and colleges, with the aim of providing language courses for local firms, as well as advice on exporting. For further information contact the Adult Training Promotions Unit, Room 2/2, Department of Education and Science, York Road, London SE1 9PH; tel 071-934 0888.

Other options include the foreign cultural institutes, such as the Alliance Française or the Goethe Institut, which run well-established courses, and organisations running courses abroad (nothing can beat learning a language in the country where it is spoken). Courses abroad are advertised in *The Times* and the *Guardian*.

Further information and advice are available from CILT (the Centre for Information on Language Teaching and Research), Regent's College, Inner Circle, Regent's Park, London NW1 4NS; tel: 071-486 8221.

Chapter 2

Finding a Job Abroad

How do you set about trying to find a job abroad? The immediate and most effective answer will come as a surprise to some: you look in the UK papers, not only the nationals and the Sundays, but also the specialist press of your profession or occupation and in career newspapers such as *Graduate Post*. Graduates can look in annual career directories, such as *Graduate Opportunities*, for details of overseas employers. It stands to reason that any employer wishing to recruit UK personnel will advertise in the UK press, but there is also another good reason why the 'overseas vacancies' pages are worth scanning: they give a very good indication of going rates of salary and benefits in particular parts of the world. Indeed, even if you have been made an offer without having replied to an advertisement, it is worth looking closely at these pages over a few issues to make sure that the remuneration package being put to you is in line with market rates.

However, if you are actually looking for a job, do not just confine your reading to the ads. It is worth reading any news and features that relate to the countries you are interested in. Not only will news of general or specific development – a new type of industry opening up, for instance – give you background information that might be very useful in an interview, but it might also in itself be a source of job leads. Indeed, if you can read the papers in the language of the country you would like to work in, so much the better. They will go into potential job-lead information in more depth, apart from the fact that they also contain job advertisements. How useful these are likely to be to the British job seeker depends somewhat on the country in which the paper is published. In the Far East, for instance, employers would almost exclusively be looking for locals when advertising in a local paper. But in the EC, a response from a suitably qualified EC national might well produce a positive result. Indeed in some European countries, notably Germany, there is a trend towards taking on British people for overseas jobs. Quite a number of European countries are involved in projects in the Middle East and in other resource-rich countries where English is the dominant language. In those cases they are beginning to think in terms of putting some UK nationals on location as well as their own people.

Apart from the major newspapers, some countries have also developed

their equivalent of career publications. Two monthly publications containing a directory of job vacancies in Germany are *Markt* and *Chance*. *Markt* is published by VVF, Huttenstrasse 10, Wiesbaden W6200. *Chance* is published by Unicom Verlag, Rathausplatz 5, Bochum W4630. There are also a number of news sheets which are advertised from time to time, but some of them, it must be said, are fly-by-night operations and you would be ill-advised to part with your money without seeing a sample copy or to subscribe for more than six months at a time. The *Connaught Executive Bulletin* does, however, appear to be a fairly well-established operation. Available from Connaught Publishing Ltd, 32 Savile Row, London W1X 1AG, it comes out weekly.

Possible sources of job information are, of course, legion and they change constantly. Apart from keeping a close watch on the papers, as good a move as any is to get in touch with trade associations connected to the country in which you are interested or local Chambers of Commerce there. They will not be able to give you any job leads as such, unless you are very lucky, but they can usually give you lists of firms or other organisations which have a particularly close connection with the UK. Preliminary leads of this nature are quite essential if you are going to a country to look for a job on spec, though except in the EC you should never state this as your intention when entering a country. In most places now you need to have a job offer from a local employer in order to get a work permit, so you should always state that you are entering as a visitor, whatever your subsequent intention might be. It must be said, however, that some countries do not permit turning a visitor's visa into a work permit – that is something you will have to check on, discreetly, before you go.

In general, however, going abroad on spec to find a job is not a good idea. Even in the EC, where it is permitted, some job seekers have had unhappy experiences unless they are in 'hot' areas such as electronics. By far the best plan is to get interviews lined up before you go or at least to get some expressions of interest from potential employers – they will probably not commit themselves to more than that from a distance, even if there is a job possibility. To do more might put them under an embarrassing moral obligation when you turn up on their doorstep, having spent a lot of time and money to get there.

Writing on spec letters to potential employers is a subject that is well covered in other books: for instance, in two by the author of this one, *Changing Your Job After 35* (Kogan Page) and *Jobs in a Jobless World* (F Muller). In essence what you have to do is address yourself to something that you have identified as being the employer's need or possible need – this is where researching the background and looking for job leads comes into play. For instance, if you have read in *Der Spiegel* or in *Frankfurter Allgemeine Zeitung* of a German firm being awarded a large contract in the Middle East, it is likely that they will respond in some way, provided your letter demonstrates that you have relevant experience. Even if they intend

advertising the job, the fact that you have taken an intelligent interest in their activities will count in your favour. It is rarely worth while advertising in the situations wanted column though writing to headhunters is a good move, especially if you are qualified to work in one of the fields in current demand: electronic engineering, financial services and retailing. Letters should be kept short and your CV should not exceed two pages – highlighting and quantifying achievements, rather than just listing posts you have held. With technical jobs you may have to show that your knowledge of the field is up to date with current developments, especially in areas where things are changing rapidly.

When a job is actually advertised, the interview will probably be in London, or your fares will be paid if you are called upon to travel abroad. Here again, the rules for replying to an advertisement are no different from those relating to UK employers: read the text carefully and frame your reply and organise your CV in such a way as to show you meet the essential requirements of the job. As one Canadian employer put it recently, paraphrasing, no doubt, John F Kennedy's much quoted presidential address, 'The question to ask is not what I can gain from moving to your company, but what your company (or organisation or school) can gain from me.'

Chapter 3

UK Taxation Aspects of Working Abroad

It is essential for anyone going to work abroad to seek advice on the tax implications of such a move. Your normal accountant or bank manager may not be sufficiently well versed in these matters, unless they have a good deal of experience in them, though most larger professional firms and bigger bank branches will be dealing with at least some expatriate clients. At the same time you should acquaint yourself at least with the basic principles of your tax position as an expatriate. Like most things concerned with tax, the concepts, although in some ways simple, are richly overlaid with confusion.

Range of taxes

First of all you should remember that the word 'tax' embraces many different ways in which the UK tax man can put his hand in your pocket. For the expatriate it can include:

- Tax on income arising in the UK
- Tax on income arising overseas
- Capital gains tax
- Inheritance tax.

In addition, the expatriate needs to consider the tax laws of the country in which he has chosen to live.

Double taxation agreement

A great many countries (your local tax office can give you a list of them) have a tax treaty with the UK. Since most, though not all, countries have some sort of income tax system you will fall within it if you stay there long enough; and you may be taxed there on income arising in the UK (from their point of view these would be foreign earnings). So that you are not taxed twice on the same income, ie in the UK and in your country of residence, the tax treaty would either say which country has the right to tax a particular source of income or will set out how you are able to set off the tax due in one country against that due in another.

This double taxation relief works both ways. If you are living in the UK and have foreign earnings which are taxed in the country where they arise you can set off the foreign tax against your UK tax assessment. Note, though, that you should set off tax against tax, not ask the UK tax people to assess your liability on your foreign earnings net of tax paid abroad. For instance, supposing you have earned £1000 abroad on which you paid £200 in local tax. If you declare your foreign earnings in the UK as being £800 your UK tax on this, assuming you pay the basic rate of 25 per cent, would be assessed as £200 so you only net £600 after paying two lots of tax. On the other hand, if you declare your earnings at £1000 you will be assessed at £250 against which you can set off the £200 you have already paid overseas. On this basis you will net £750, having met both sets of tax obligations.

Residence

In using the innocuous word 'residence' in the previous section we have touched on one of the key concepts in the whole business of the taxation of foreign earnings. To a large extent the amount of hold the tax man has over you depends in logic, as well as in justice and common sense, on where you are physically present during a tax year – known as 'residence' in the trade. The problem is how, having decided to leave this country for good or for a long period, do you establish that you are no longer resident here? The answer is simple, though buried in mumbo-jumbo.

If you work full time abroad for a period which includes at least one complete tax year (that is one running from 6 April to 5 April not just any 12-month period) in which all except incidental duties are performed outside the UK, you will be regarded as no longer resident in this country provided your visits to the UK do not exceed 182 days in any one tax year or an average of 90 days per annum.

If you are in full-time employment abroad the fact that you may maintain a house or flat here for your own use will not preclude you from being treated as a non-resident. However, if you perform duties of your overseas employment in the UK which are more than incidental and you maintain accommodation here for your use, you will be regarded as remaining resident for UK tax purposes.

So, what are the advantages of being not resident? A non-resident is not liable to UK tax on any income arising outside the UK. This includes earnings from overseas employment even if those earnings are paid in the UK or are sent back here. Any income arising in the UK, such as the profit from letting your UK home while you are away or investment income arising in the UK, would potentially still be subject to UK tax. However, following a change in UK law which took effect from 6 April 1990, a British subject who is not resident in the UK is still entitled to claim his full personal allowances which can be set against any income arising in the UK.

Apart from the fact that once non-residence has been established your income outside the UK is no longer liable to UK tax, another benefit of your new-found status is that you may be able to get a tax rebate on some of the PAYE tax which you paid in the tax year in which you left. This is because you would probably not have had the full benefit of the personal allowances included in your PAYE tax code. The form on which you claim any repayment is a P85, which is also used to inform the Inland Revenue of your departure for overseas.

There is, however, another and potentially more significant benefit in becoming resident abroad. You will not be liable to capital gains tax on transactions conducted in the UK or elsewhere between the date of your original departure and the date of your permanent return provided you keep that status for at least 36 months. You do become liable for capital gains tax on disposal made after your return so it is essential to realise capital gains while you are still non-resident.

Those who are non-resident for a period of less than 36 months are also not liable to capital gains tax but only on transactions made up to 5 April preceding their return. Capital gains made in the tax year of their return to the UK are, however, taxable. In other words they could be in the position of paying capital gains tax on transactions conducted while they are actually non-resident. The way to avoid this is to realise capital gains in the tax year before the tax year of your return.

Failing to become non-resident

The situation becomes more difficult if you fail to become non-resident. This may happen because your employer abroad starts sending you to the UK for regular and frequent visits. If these are business visits the Inland Revenue may not regard them as being incidental to your overseas employment. It is generally accepted that visits to the UK for reasons such as reporting on progress or receiving fresh instructions and undergoing periods of training may be regarded as incidental. However, if an important part of your duties overseas requires you to come to the UK to perform those duties the Inland Revenue may decide that you are not in full-time employment abroad.

Another more likely pitfall is this: supposing you take a tax free job in a country and then decide to quit before you have completed a full tax year abroad and you return to the UK. You would then be potentially liable for UK tax on your world wide income including your earnings, even though these were advertised as being free of tax. In other words, such earnings are only tax free provided you stay long enough out of the UK tax network.

You might say, of course, that if your income is derived from overseas sources and you are effectively, if not technically, resident abroad, what can the tax man do if you break one of the conditions to be treated as not resident? The answer is: not a great deal until you eventually return to this country to live here. Then you will have to fill in a form about the purpose and length of your visits to the UK while you were living abroad and you

would then be liable for arrears of tax found to be due.

However, if you fail to become non-resident, although you are potentially liable to tax on your world wide income, there is a special tax relief due which is commonly called 'the 100 per cent deduction'. This tax relief is available to people who work abroad for a period of at least 365 days irrespective of whether or not it covers a complete tax year. During that time you are allowed to visit the UK but no single visit should exceed 62 days and at any time you visit the UK the period spent there must not exceed one-sixth of the total number of days in the period up to that date. If the overseas employment is for a period shorter than 365 days or if it ends prematurely, it may from a UK tax point of view be worth tacking on an overseas holiday to bring you up to the qualifying period. Note, though, that this 100 per cent deduction only extends to earnings from employment. It does not apply to interest earned in the UK or to rental income or dividends and you will also remain liable to capital tax in the UK on gains made during that period though there is an exemption on the first £5500.

Husbands and wives

The residence status of a husband and of a wife are determined quite separately and, with the advent of independent taxation, a wife is subject to tax on her own income. For this purpose money that you give or send to your wife is not treated as income in her hands.

MIRAS

Basic rate tax relief on the interest on the first £30,000 of a qualifying mortgage is usually given under the MIRAS system. MIRAS stands for Mortgage Interest Relief At Source. Under MIRAS the borrower deducts from his mortgage interest payments an amount equal to tax at the basic rate of 25 per cent. The lender is reimbursed by the Inland Revenue with the amount the borrower has deducted. This has taken the place of the formal system of adjusting the PAYE code of the person concerned to make the income tax allowance on mortgage interest.

Curiously enough, expatriates, in certain limited circumstances, can also deduct the 25 per cent from their mortgage interest repayments on their main UK home even when they are not paying UK tax because they are not resident here. In effect, the Exchequer is making eligible expatriates a present of 25 per cent of their mortgage interest payments. However, the conditions for MIRAS as far as expatriates are concerned are quite narrow and it will only apply if you can tell the Inspector of Taxes that you intend to return to live in the mortgaged property within four years of the date of your original departure. However, the full implications of MIRAS are fairly technical and you should seek advice from your accountant or your building society about them.

Pension arrangements

An important consideration when going to work overseas is the impact that this may have on your pension arrangements. If you are sent abroad by your UK employer, you may continue to participate in your employer's pension scheme without regard to your residence status, provided the Inland Revenue agree.

If you have your own personal pension plan the contributions you can make are a fixed percentage of what the tax man calls net relevant earnings. If you are not resident and exempt from tax on your overseas earnings, these will not be classed as relevant earnings and it may well be that you would not be able to make any contributions.

It may be that you can join the pension plan of your overseas employer and, provided you are not resident in the UK, there would be no UK tax implications on contributions into that plan. You should, however, bear in mind that 90 per cent of the pension deriving from such funds is taxed when you return to the UK. In other words, it is treated slightly more favourably than UK based pension schemes.

Pension arrangements are complicated and you are strongly advised to take advice before entering into any arrangements.

Returning to the UK

As well as seeking advice when you go to work abroad, it is also necessary when you are planning to return here. Along with the weather, the tax man will be there to extend his doubtful welcome because once you return to the UK permanently, you become resident and ordinarily resident from the date of your arrival.

The only aspect of this situation which falls into the category of good news is the fact that a full year's personal allowances and reliefs will be granted, even though you may have been resident in the UK for only part of that year. The obvious implication of this is that the timing of your return is important: if you arrive at the beginning of the tax year the concession will be worthless; if you arrive too late in the tax year you may not have enough UK income to set your allowances off against. Somewhere in the middle of the tax year would be ideal if you can arrange it that way.

It is sometimes difficult to determine what is regarded as income derived from working abroad. The tax authorities now set out some fairly clear rules on the matter. For example, terminal leave and pre-arranged bonus pay are exempt from UK tax, provided they relate to a period when you have been exempt from tax even if they continue to be earned after you return to the UK.

You will also have to watch the position on UK bank deposit and building society accounts. Under a concession you can as a non-resident claim to have interest on these accounts paid gross instead of having tax deducted at source. If you do so, however, you should remember that in the year you return to the UK the concession will be withdrawn from the date you become resident and the tax man will calculate the tax due on the interest paid gross up to that date. The way to prevent this is to close the UK account in the tax year before you return and place the money in an offshore bank account which pays interest gross. If the offshore account is then closed shortly before you return to the UK, the interest earned on that account would be tax free.

If you have any assets which are showing a potential capital gain you should consider disposing of them during a period when you are exempt from capital gains tax. If the asset is showing a loss, however, it may be better to dispose of it when you are subject to capital gains tax so that you can have the credit for that loss.

Very often the problem for returning expatriates is that they are not sure whether they are going to stay permanently in the UK or not. It may depend on whether they manage to get a satisfactory job here, or they may have acquired a taste for the expatriate life and have come back for a trial period to see whether that taste is irreversible. It should, therefore, be noted that the treatment of temporary visitors (six months or less) is more favourable than that extended to those who have decided to become resident and ordinarily resident here. If you are unclear about your future plans you should make this fact plain to your financial consultant so that he can advise you on how best to mitigate and avoid your UK tax burden.

Domicile

At the start of this chapter reference is made to inheritance tax. For the purpose of inheritance tax, it is not the residence status of the individual which determines liability, but the person's domicile. Although ordinary English usage indicates otherwise, in tax terminology those two words 'residence' and 'domicile' do not mean the same thing.

Inheritance tax, the tax that replaced capital transfer tax, is in some ways similar to the old concept of death duties in that a charge is made on the transfer of assets at death up to a maximum of 40 per cent. On the other hand, no charge is made on the transfer of assets between individuals provided these have been made more than seven years before death. In effect, it is a penalty on hanging on to one's assets for too long!

The liability to inheritance tax continues unless you are not only resident but also domiciled abroad. This means, in effect, that you have made a permanent home there and demonstrated the fact by, for instance, taking out citizenship, building up business or sending your children to school there while at the same time severing your ties with the UK. Once domicile is established in another country you would still have to wait three years before you can forget about inheritance tax. Even then it will continue to remain operative on assets you own in the UK.

Insuring your tax position

There have been a number of cases in recent years – Kuwait is the most notable example – where expatriates have had to pull out of a country for political reasons. This can have disastrous consequences for your tax position in the UK because, as we have stated earlier, you have to stay abroad for at least a year for your tax free salary to be regarded as such by the Inland Revenue in the UK. An imaginative policy offered by the Norwich Union, the Expatriates Contingent Tax Policy, enables you to insure against the consequences of expulsion, although it obviously does not cover the situation where a person is expelled for criminal activities or what are regarded as such in the country concerned: liquor offences in Moslem nations, for example. A similar type of cover is now available through Lloyds Bank, as part of a complete package which they have designed for expatriates.

Chapter 4

Financial Planning and the Expatriate

For most people, working abroad means a rise in income. For those in countries with a low rate of income tax, or, as is the case in some countries in the Middle East, without income tax, it may be the first chance they have had to accumulate a substantial amount of money, and this may indeed be the whole object of the exercise. Expatriates are therefore an obvious target for firms and individuals offering financial advice on such matters as tax, mortgages, insurance schemes, school fee funding, income building plans and stock and 'alternative' investments. Most of them are honest, but some are better than others, either in choosing investments wisely or in finding schemes that are most appropriate to the needs and circumstances of their client, or both. At any rate the expatriate with money to spend is nowadays faced with a wide variety of choices, ranging from enterprising local traders, proffering allegedly valuable antiques, and fly-by-night operators, selling real estate in inaccessible tropical swamps, to serious financial advisers and consultants. Assuming that you will have the sense to avoid the former, how do you choose independent financial consultants, what advice are they likely to give you and how do you evaluate it?

The selection of an adviser

Nowadays consultants travel widely and it should not be too difficult to make contact with them through advertisements, through one's own company's financial staff or, best of all, by word of mouth through friends of long standing. When the consultant meets you, he (we assume here that he will be male, though a number of women are moving into this field as well) will have to know a great deal about your financial circumstances to be able to produce a package that suits you. It is therefore important to spend some time before you meet resolving such questions as whether you are looking for income or capital appreciation, whether or not you plan to settle ultimately in the UK, whether you plan to retire early and so on.

Anderson Sinclair, a firm of consultants with long experience in advising expatriates, have devised a questionnaire which they go through with prospective clients and which helps to define the investment mix which would be right for them. Some of its salient points are:

(a) In what currency the salary is paid

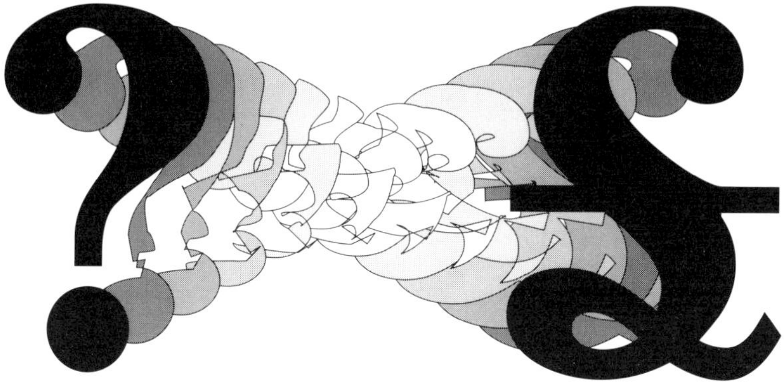

(b) Dates of departure from the UK and any visits there within the last three years
(c) When expecting to return permanently to the UK
(d) Mortgage commitments in the UK
(e) Whether intending to buy UK property
(f) Existing investment/life assurance/pension arrangements
(g) School fees provisions if/when not paid by employer
(h) Amount available for investment annually or as a lump sum
(i) Client's attitude to investment: interested, don't want to bother with it personally, speculative, conservative.

You should also be prepared to fire a few questions at your prospective adviser. Obviously you will want to know how much he is going to charge. You should also check on his experience and track record. In the case of investment advice, a past performance sheet of his recommendations over a three-year period should be requested. The results may not be conclusive – anybody can make money in a boom or lose it in a recession – but if you ask him to compare his performance with the *Financial Times* share index, this will at least give you some indication.

An extremely important development has been the passing of the Financial Services Act. This lays down strict rules for a variety of UK based providers of financial services. They are required to explain the full facts about any investment they recommend and also to make sure that it is appropriate to the client's financial circumstances. They may be required, for instance, to show that in the light of the client's circumstances, it is the best buy available. They will also have to keep much more detailed records than was the case in the past.

However, the Act does not cover firms which carry out their activities outside British jurisdiction. It follows, therefore, that those who do not want to comply with the laws will work from somewhere offshore. All the more reason to beware of some of the more exotic locations from which investments are sometimes marketed – but it should be noted that not even such respectable places as Frankfurt or Zurich will provide investor protection under the Act. In the absence of its safeguards there are one or two key questions which are worth asking anybody who approaches you with the offer of investment advice:

(a) Where is his company and/or the funds he represents principally based? Offices in unregulated tax havens like Andorra or Liechtenstein are often a bad sign. Connection with a reputable UK company is best.
(b) How often will you get a valuation of your holdings? It should be every six months.
(c) What are the charges and how are they arrived at?
(d) Assuming it is a limited company, not a sole trader or a partnership, when did the organisation the salesman represents last file a set of accounts? You do not have to be able to read accounts, but if they

have not filed any within the last couple of years that could be a bad sign.

(e) Does his organisation carry professional indemnity insurance? Note, however, this only protects you against negligence or criminal action – not against bad advice!

You should ask for written confirmation of anything you are told. That might not have a lot of legal force with a representative of a foreign based company, but it should deter the most blatant rogues. However, the passage of the Financial Services Act does mean that buying British is safest, if not necessarily best.

Investment

There are really only three types of objectives in investment: growth, income and growth with income. The choice of one main objective usually involves some sacrifice in regard to the other. A high degree of capital appreciation generally implies a lower level of income and vice versa. Growth with income is an ideal, but generally it means some growth with some income, not a maximisation of both. Ultimately, the objective is the preservation of capital in bad times and the increase of wealth in good ones, but your adviser cannot perform miracles. If he is lucky enough to catch the market in an upward phase he may be able to show quick results, but normally investment is a process that pays off over a longer period and through the course of varying market cycles.

Investment strategy

Following his preliminary meetings with you, your consultant should be able to formulate an investment strategy for you, based on your particular circumstances and such factors as the degree of risk that can be taken. The scheme he is most likely to recommend is that the bulk of your funds should be invested in an 'offshore fund'. Offshore funds are variants of the unit trust and are registered – with the government's blessing – in tax havens. They are usually managed from well-known financial centres such as New York, Hong Kong or London. They are particularly suitable for expatriates because the income is tax free and because they are outside foreign exchange controls. Though the latter have been suspended by the present government, there is no guarantee that they will not be reintroduced at some future date.

There are other reasons for considering offshore funds as a way of investing your money:

1. The spread of investments is world wide, thus protecting you in some measure from the fluctuations of individual national economies.
2. Their management is of high quality.
3. They follow closely the investment policy of institutions (ie pension

fund managers, insurance companies and major financial consultants) which now dominate stock markets and whose decisions therefore affect price movements.
4. Portfolio managers do a better job than private investors, who have a tendency to hold on to problem shares in the hope that they will pick up.

Investment possibilities through managed funds

There are many investment opportunities in the offshore fund markets, from specialised funds in individual countries to international ones spread across many industries. There are equally many ways of investing: regular investments, lump-sum purchase of units, periodic and irregular investments. It is also possible to invest in commodity markets and there are specialists trading in gold, silver, diamonds, sapphires and metals generally. Another innovation is the currency fund, which regulates holdings of foreign exchange and aims to predict fluctuations in exchange rates.

Your consultant should be able not only to inform you of the various schemes available, but also to advise on the degree of risk, the quality of management available and the combination of investments most likely to achieve your aims.

For those who prefer the safety of banks or building society deposits, there is now a concession to non-residents – interest is paid without tax being deducted at source. However, you will have to inform your bank about your non-resident status. A building society may also require you to open a separate, non-resident account.

You may still be assessed for income tax on any interest earned in the year of your return to the UK. For this reason, there are a number of advantages in taking up the facilities that UK banks offer non-residents to open an account in one of the established tax havens, notably the Channel Islands and the Isle of Man.

In all cases, though, there are important tax considerations before you return to the UK. You should discuss these with your adviser at least six months before then, so that the necessary plans can be drawn up.

Life assurance

Life assurance is also a form of investment in the sense that it provides financial protection for yourself and your family. As with other forms of investment, there are numerous possible options, many of them difficult for the layman to follow, and the temptation is to throw one's hand in and fall, metaphorically speaking, for the first smooth-talking young salesperson arriving on the doorstep with 'just the policy for you'. If you do, you are quite likely to end up paying more than you should for the wrong type of policy. Even if the representative comes from a reputable company,

this is by no means a guarantee that what you are being offered is a good buy. The difference in rates and profits between insurance companies is larger than you might think.

The right way to buy life assurance is through an independent professional adviser, outlining to him what you feel your needs are. In fact, even if you already have a policy, either on your own account or through your employer, there are a number of points you should check:

1. You should advise the company issuing the policy of a change of residence status.
2. You should check that your policy has no restrictions about overseas living.
3. You must ensure that you have set up a suitable system for paying premiums in your absence (eg via a banker's order).

Assuming, however, that you do not already have adequate life assurance, your adviser is likely to come up with one of four basic life assurance schemes:

1. Term assurance: this pays a fixed sum if you die within a specified time (eg before the age of 55).
2. Whole life: this pays a fixed sum irrespective of when you die.
3. Endowment: this gives you a sum of money at a fixed date, and is not only related to death. It is often used as a way of insuring mortgage payments; the mortgage is paid off when the policy matures.
4. Family income benefit: this gives an income after death and would usually be used to provide for your spouse and children. As a rule this would be taken out to give cover until all your children reach maturity.

All these policies may be taken out for a fixed sum and can be with or without profits. There may also be other variants, the most common of which is the facility to turn term assurance into an endowment policy. Your main concern, however, may be the degree of cover you require and this depends on the level of commitments that would be incurred by your family in the event of your death. A rule of thumb in most cases is that the capital sum provided should be five times the individual's annual income, combined with cover of between a half and three-quarters of annual salary until the children in the family reach maturity. You need not necessarily take out an insurance policy in sterling. There are foreign currency policies and, even though they are more expensive than sterling ones, for long-term expatriates in certain tax situations these may have aspects to recommend them. Again you will need professional advice in assessing your particular circumstances and choosing a scheme.

School fees planning

There are many schemes available for school fees planning. These schemes

aim to provide you with a tax-free income at a specified date for a predetermined length of time. They need not necessarily be used for educational purposes, and some readers may feel that if the employer is paying school fees, as is often the case, there is no need to take out such a policy. However, parents should bear in mind that it is highly advisable not to interrupt children's education, and taking out such a policy would obviously be a good way of ensuring that your child can go on with his education at the same school, even if your employment with that employer ended.

Pensions

One of the most important aspects of financial planning for expatriates relates to pensions. Most people will have been members of a UK scheme and will have been either 'contracted in' to or 'contracted out' of the government pension provisions. If your employer has contracted out – that is, made his own arrangements for you within the guidelines laid down by the government – you will normally retain the full benefits of the scheme, even if you are not resident in the UK. If he has contracted in, you will lose your right to the benefits once your contribution ceases. Private, contracted out schemes usually include a lump-sum death benefit as well as provision for benefits for disability.

This assumes that you are going to work abroad for a UK employer. If this is not the case, you will have to make your own arrangements with the help of your adviser, unless your employer abroad has a scheme of his own. Most multinationals do have such schemes, but they may have set up a pension fund in the country of residence and that country may have rules of its own and be subject to local legislation. Therefore, even if your employer is providing a scheme, you should ask for your adviser's comments on it.

People working overseas can now take a Jersey pension linked to a UK tax exempt pension fund. The contract is linked to the With Profit Fund of a select number of life offices. Termination benefits can be taken wholly in cash and free of any tax deduction in Jersey. Benefits can be taken at any age, and there is no limit imposed on contribution. The scheme is essentially for the benefit of those expatriates not planing to return and take up residence in the UK.

Returning to the UK

All aspects of pension and investment planning need to be reviewed if you are returning to the UK, or you may leave yourself open to tax problems that could easily have been avoided with good advice. You should therefore notify your financial consultant at least 12 months before the tax year of your return so that he can make arrangements to mitigate tax liabilities. The subject of tax is dealt with in more depth in Chapter 3.

Short-term contracts

Someone going abroad on a short-term contract of two years or less is in a somewhat different investment position from those who have committed themselves to longer spells or intend to remain working abroad. Certainly you should be very careful about taking on investment or pension plan schemes which require regular payments over periods longer than your contract. For instance, there was the case of a doctor in the Gulf on a two-year contract who was persuaded to invest £1500 a month in a unit-linked life assurance scheme with a 10-year duration. Clearly, on what he could reasonably expect to earn back in the UK, he had no hope of keeping up payments on that scale – yet to extricate himself from that commitment, once this became clear to him, cost six months' premiums: £9000!

In the opinion of some investment consultants, non-resident expatriates on short-term contracts might be best advised to put their savings deposit into a Channel Islands bank account. As not ordinarily resident non-residents they would not have to pay income tax on the interest up to the tax year of their return. Speculative investments tend to be risky on a short-term profit basis. When looking for longer-term profits, expatriates on two-year contracts or less are liable to be caught within the UK capital gains tax network unless they are able to realise their profits in the tax year before they return. If they endeavour to do so having regained UK resident status, they would be liable for CGT, even though the investment had initially been made when they were non-resident and not ordinarily resident.

Offshore insurance policies

The legislation relating to these has become increasingly complicated. Tax-mitigating benefits available through offshore insurance policies to those working abroad, but intending to return to the UK, have gradually been eroded by the Chancellor in his Finance Acts.

Since February 1988, the removal of certain technical tax avoidance devices available to expatriates no longer makes it possible for them to draw a tax-free income from life policies. These can, however, be encashed free of tax and financial advisers suggest taking out a large number of single policies (rather than one large one) and encashing them separately and in small numbers. This effectively creates a tax-free income.

There are also some other tax mitigating schemes related to offshore insurance policies. These are technically very complex. They are also subject to change as the Inland Revenue and financial experts play their cat and mouse game with tax loopholes. You should therefore check the latest position with an independent UK adviser before undertaking any offshore insurance commitment.

Chapter 5

Working Abroad and National Insurance

The desire to earn more money – and to pay less of it in tax and other deductions – looms large for many as a motive for going to work abroad. People who take this step are often temperamentally inclined to be strongly individualistic and self-reliant and as such many feel that they would rather fend for themselves when circumstances get difficult than rely on what they regard as 'state handouts'. Whatever the virtues of this attitude of mind may be, those who have it are more to be commended for their sense of independence than their commonsense. The fact is that during your working life in the UK you will have made compulsory National Insurance contributions and you are therefore eligible for benefits in the same way as if you had paid premiums into a private insurance scheme; drawing a state benefit you are entitled to is no more taking a handout than making an insurance claim.

National Insurance has another feature in common with private insurance: you lose your entitlement to benefit if you fail to keep up your contributions, though the circumstances under which this would happen are different from, and more gradual than in, the private sector. Furthermore, you cannot immediately reactivate your eligibility for benefits in full if, your payments having lapsed for a period of time, you return to this country and once again become liable to make contributions. For instance, in order to qualify in full for a UK retirement pension you must have paid the minimum contribution for each year for at least 90 per cent of your working life. In the case of other benefits too, in order to qualify to get them at the standard rate, there must be a record of your having made a certain level of contributions in the tax year governing that in which benefits are being claimed. The relevant conditions are set out in leaflet N1 38, available from the DSS, Overseas Branch, Newcastle upon Tyne NE98 1YX.

Liability for contributions while abroad

If your employer in the UK sends you to work in another European Community country or in a country with whom the UK has a reciprocal agreement (these are listed in leaflet NI 38) for a period not expected to exceed that which is specified in the EC regulations *or* the reciprocal agreement involved, you will normally continue to be subject to the UK social security scheme for that period and you will be required to pay Class 1 contributions as though you were in the UK. (The specified period can vary between one year where the EC regulations apply and up to five years depending upon the reciprocal agreement involved.) If your employment unexpectedly lasts longer than 'the specified period', then for certain countries you may remain insured under the UK scheme with the agreement of the authorities in the country in which you are working. Your employer will obtain a certificate for you from the Department of Social Security, Overseas Branch, confirming your continued liability under the UK scheme, which you should present to the foreign authorities if required to confirm your non-liability under their scheme.

If you are sent by your UK employer to an EC state or to a country with which there is a reciprocal agreement in circumstances other than the above, eg for an initial period expected to exceed 12 months or for a period of indefinite duration, then normally you will cease to be liable to pay UK contributions from the date you are posted and will instead become liable to pay into the scheme of the country you are working in.

If you are sent by your employer to a country other than those in the EC or with which there is a reciprocal agreement you will be liable to pay Class 1 contributions for the first 52 weeks of your posting provided your employer has a place of business in the UK, you were resident in the UK before you took up employment abroad and remain 'ordinarily resident' in the UK while you are abroad.

Making voluntary contributions

When your period of liability for Class 1 contributions ends, you may wish to pay voluntary Class 3 contributions to the UK scheme in order to protect your UK retirement/widow's pension entitlement. We will deal with the mechanics of this later, but at this stage it should be pointed out that if you are going abroad for a British-based firm you will be liable to make the same contributions as if you were employed in this country up to a maximum earnings level of £350 per week. Your proportion of this contribution will be deducted from your salary, as if you were still working in the UK. Payment of these contributions for the first 52 weeks of your employment abroad will make you eligible to receive sickness or unemployment benefit and, in the case of a woman, maternity allowance, under the usual conditions applicable to those benefits, on your return to the UK – even though this may be some years later – because Class 1 contributions will be deemed to have been paid in the tax year(s) relevant to your claim. This is subject to the proviso that you remained 'ordinarily resident' in the UK during your absence. If you did not intend to sever your connection with the UK when you went abroad, continuing ordinary residence will usually be accepted. To establish ordinary residence you may need to show that you maintained a home or accommodation in the

UK or stored your furniture in the UK during your absence. To maintain entitlement to other benefits, however, it will usually be necessary to pay Class 3 contributions after the Class 1 period has expired although this may not be necessary for the balance of the year – April to April – in which Class 1 liability ceased. The Overseas Branch of the DSS at Newcastle upon Tyne can advise you about this. Remember always to quote your National Insurance number when you write.

Class 1 contributions are not payable at all in respect of employment abroad if your employer has no place of business in the UK. However, if you work for an overseas government or an international agency such as the UN, you will be able to pay your share of the Class 1 contribution for the first 52 weeks of your employment abroad and so qualify on return to the UK for the benefits named in the previous paragraph.

You may, of course, have been a self-employed person paying the Class 2 rate of £5.15 a week. These contributions also imply a more limited rate of benefit – unemployment and injury or death caused by an industrial accident or prescribed disease are excluded – but like Class 3 contributions, they can also be paid voluntarily while you are abroad. However, you *need not* pay Class 2 contributions just because you were self-employed before you went abroad. You can go to the voluntary Class 3 rate, but if you want to qualify for sickness and invalidity benefit when you return to the UK to resume your self-employed career, you must remember to switch back to Class 2 payments for the two tax years governing the benefit year in which you are due to return. Thus for the sake of a few pence a week, it is obviously not worth switching to the Class 3 rate if you intend to go on being self-employed when you come back to this country.

These rates and conditions apply, of course, as much to women as to men. The right of married women to pay reduced rate contributions is being phased out. If you get married while working abroad you should write to the same DSS address as above for leaflet NI 1 which explains in more detail your National Insurance position as a married woman.

Leaflet NI 38, which has been mentioned earlier, contains a form at the back (CF 83) which should be filled in when you want to start making voluntary payments. You can pay by annual lump sum, by arranging for someone in the UK to make regular payments for you, or through direct debit.

Class 2 contributions can be paid up to the end of the sixth tax year following the one in which they were due. Class 3 contributions must be paid by the end of the sixth year following the one in which they were due. However, although you have six years in which to pay there is a limited period in which to pay at the relevant year's contribution rates. The Overseas Contributions Group of the DSS at Newcastle upon Tyne can advise you about this. Whatever method you choose it is important that your contributions are paid on time. For further information see leaflet NI 48 – *Unpaid and late paid contributions.*

Getting NI benefits abroad

Thus far we have only mentioned the range of benefits available to you once you return to the UK. But is there any way you can become eligible for benefits while still abroad? Generally, the answer is that you can only receive retirement pensions and widows' benefits, but there are important exceptions in the case of EC countries and some others – a full list is given in leaflet NI 38 – with which the UK has reciprocal agreements. How those agreements affect you varies somewhat from country to country, but in essence they mean that the contributions you have paid in the UK count, for benefit purposes, as if you had paid them in the reciprocal agreement country, and vice versa. This is usually advantageous if you do become eligible for benefit while abroad because in relation to the cost of living – or even in absolute terms – UK benefits are lower than many foreign ones. You will, in general, have to pay contributions to the scheme of the country you are working in, so by the same token if you are going to a country with which the UK has a reciprocal agreement, you will have to decide if you want to pay voluntary contributions to the UK in order to draw benefits when you return here. The DSS Overseas Branch can advise you on this. If you have not yet come under the scheme of a foreign country and are paying Class 1, 2 or 3 contributions to the UK while working abroad then, if you think you are eligible for benefit, you should write to the DSS Overseas Branch immediately the contingency governing your claim arises. One important point to bear in mind in this case, though, is that if benefit can be paid, you will only get paid at the UK rate, not that of similar welfare schemes of the country in which you are living. In many cases the latter may be much more generous than UK rates; furthermore, UK rates may bear very little relationship to the cost of living abroad.

In this connection it is also worth pointing out that the UK is by no means the top of the world league table when it comes to the percentage of the pay packet taken up by contributions to social services. In many of the EC countries, in particular, it is significantly higher. This is an important detail to discuss with a prospective employer, because the 'social wage' and what you have to put in to get it obviously has a bearing on the real value of the remuneration package you are being offered.

Working abroad and the NHS

In one important instance UK benefits are actually more generous than those of many other countries. We refer here to the UK National Health Service. But medical expenses incurred abroad are definitely not refunded by the NHS, which is only available to people living in this country; so, contrary to popular belief, you will no longer be able to get free NHS treatment in this country once you become permanently resident abroad. Many overseas countries do have reciprocal health agreements with the UK – once again a list is given in leaflet NI 38 – but the services they provide are not exactly comparable with those of the British NHS. The range of treatment provided free of charge varies considerably and it may be advisable to take out private health insurance to cover eventualities where free medical attention is not, or is only partially, available. You will have to make sure that you take abroad with you – to those countries where reciprocal arrangements do exist – the necessary documents that will enable you to transfer to local health schemes. Leaflets giving information on the procedures you need to observe in order to do this, both in the case of temporary spells and permanent residence abroad, are available from the addresses shown on pages 15 and 16 of NI 38.

Child benefit while working abroad

There are various situations which, in different ways, affect your entitlement to receive child benefit while working abroad.

1. If you go abroad permanently, taking your children with you, your child benefits cease from the date of your departure. When you arrive in the new country you can only rely on that country's family benefit. But in some rare cases where you go to a country with which Great Britain has a reciprocal agreement child benefit may be paid until you qualify for benefit from the other country's scheme.
2. If you go to work in another EC country you will generally be insured under its social security legislation and so entitled to the local family allowances. If you are insured under another EC scheme but leave your children behind in Great Britain, you may still be entitled to family allowances from the EC country in which you are insured. If you remain insured under the Great Britain scheme child benefit may still be payable whether your children are in Great Britain or with you. If your children are not with you, you would have to maintain them by at least the weekly rate of child benefit after the first 56 days. If your children live with you but your spouse or partner is insured under another EC scheme, you will be entitled to local family allowances. However, you may be paid a 'supplement' equal to the difference between the local rate and the Great Britain rate of benefit if the Great Britain rate is higher.
3. If you have been sent abroad to work temporarily, for a period of not more than eight weeks, and you return within that time, benefit will continue to be paid whether or not you take your children with you. Child benefit orders cannot be cashed outside Great Britain, but you will be able to cash them when you return, provided each order is cashed within three months of the date stamped on it. Alternatively, you can nominate someone in this country to draw child benefit on your behalf. After eight weeks of temporary absence, your eligibility for Great Britain child benefit ceases unless you happen to be in one of the reciprocal agreement countries, in which case you fall under the provisions of the first paragraph.

4. You can also continue to be eligible for Great Britain child benefit, even after eight weeks of absence, if in the relevant tax year at least half your earnings from the employment which took you abroad are liable to United Kingdom income tax. However, in this case your entitlement cannot be decided until your tax liability has been assessed.
5. If a child is born abroad within eight weeks of the mother's departure from Great Britain and she is abroad only temporarily, child benefit may be paid from then until the end of the eight-week period of absence. If you wish to claim in these circumstances you should write to the DSS, Child Benefit Centre (Washington), PO Box 1, Newcastle upon Tyne NE88 1AA, quoting your child benefit number if you are already getting child benefit for another child.
6. Special rules exist in respect of serving members of the forces and civil servants; persons falling into these categories should consult their paying officer or Establishments Division.

Full details of these schemes, including the form CH181(TO) which you have to fill in before your departure, are set out in leaflet CH 6, available from your local DSS office. Alternatively, you can get a copy by writing to DSS Information Division, Leaflet Unit, Block 4, Government Buildings, Honeypot Lane, Stanmore, Middlesex HA7 1AY.

Unemployment benefits for overseas job hunters

Under EC law you can now go job seeking for up to three months in most EC countries, provided you actually register for work there. While you are in the other country, you can continue drawing UK unemployment benefit via the employment services of the country you are in.*

You should inform your local unemployment benefit office *in writing* of your intention, and obtain from them leaflet UBL 22, well in advance of your departure. The Overseas Branch of the DSS will then issue the form either to you or the employment services of the EC country in which you will be seeking work. If the form is sent to you, you should take it with you when registering for work in the other EC country.

In practice, many EC countries have blocked this progressive move by putting obstacles in the way over such matters as residence permits – France is particularly bad in this respect – because the UK is not alone among Community countries in having an unemployment problem. The good news is that if you do succeed in getting a job in an EC country, in some states not only are wages and salaries higher but so also are unemployment benefits. If you are unlucky enough to lose your 'new' job

* Although Spain and Portugal joined the EC in 1986 they will not be relaxing restrictions on employing nationals of the EC states without a work permit until 1993. At present it is not possible for UK nationals to claim exportable unemployment benefit from the UK in either of these countries.

after working for more than a month in an EC country, you may become eligible for unemployment benefits which are very much higher than those in the UK.

Some Jobcentres now handle vacancies in the EC and can give further details on relevant legislation and social welfare provisions. The Employment Department, formerly known as the Training Agency issues a useful leaflet on these matters, called *Working Abroad.*

UK pension schemes and the expatriate

UK pension schemes have been affected by changes in the state provisions introduced in July 1988. Many pension experts think that employees of companies contracted in to the state scheme, known as SERPS, might be better advised to set up a personal pension scheme which the new legislation now allows them to do, on an individual basis. The value of such a step would depend on a wide variety of circumstances, such as age, whether the expatriate has taxable income in the UK, and if the employer has a contracted out pension scheme, just how good its benefits are. The issues are very complicated and you should seek advice from a reputable financial management firm with experience of expatriate problems.

Chapter 6

Expatriate Medical Insurance

Most of the countries that expatriates go to do not operate a national health service like that of the UK. It comes as something of a shock to find oneself paying £50 or more for a routine visit to a doctor or dentist and the costs of hospitalisation can be such as to wipe out the savings of months, or even years. In places like the EC, South Africa, Australia or other developed commonwealth countries there are established local methods of medical insurance, and in many cases the cost of this is included in the remuneration package. If not, then it is certainly a matter which should be clarified while you are negotiating the job offer.

As far as OPEC and similar resource-rich economies are concerned, some of these countries do have state medical schemes, and as a matter of fact their hospitals are, in many cases, better equipped than our increasingly run down institutions. They are, however, established primarily for the benefit of local nationals, which means that customs and culture of medical care are different from that which most westerners are used to. For this reason, most expatriates in those countries arrange for attention in private hospitals which, needless to say, tends to be very expensive indeed. Medical insurance for anyone going to these places is therefore essential and a number of plans have now been developed specifically for expatriates. The table on pages 90–93 provides a comparison of these schemes as from May 1991 and, as can be seen, there are some that are apparently better than others. However, the insurance business is fiercely competitive and it is quite likely that at any given point in the year the pattern of advantage will change. If you are paying your own insurance it is vital to ask your broker for a complete list of all the plans that are available, so that you can make a comparison between them. It is also worth finding out how long they take to settle claims.

It is also important to be sure that the scheme covers medical attention irrespective of the circumstances which caused it to be necessary. A case has recently been reported where an expatriate was seriously injured by an assault from a lunatic while at home, only to discover that his medical insurance did not cover injuries sustained outside his workplace. Another point to watch, though it does not strictly speaking come under medical insurance, is personal accident cover and consequential loss of earnings.

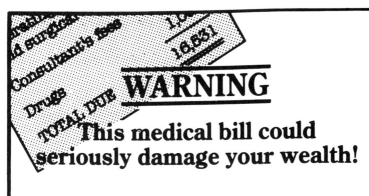

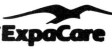

Such a policy is available from Europea and it is worth checking whether your cover extends to that eventuality.

It is also necessary, when it comes to making claims – and particularly when requesting repatriation for urgent treatment – that the local practitioner should be credible from the point of view of the insurers. It is a good idea to make yourself known to him at an early stage after your arrival and to notify your insurers about his identity. You should also carry the name of your insurers with you or at least keep it in some convenient place. Europea, one of the firms listed in the following survey, does in fact issue a kind of credit card to its policy holders against which treatment is available from its register of approved practitioners.

Another firm which issues its clients with a card is International SOS Assistance, whose Medical Security Passport enables the holder, or those looking after him or her, to call for medical assistance from six centres throughout the world. They specialise in medical repatriation and are used for this purpose by BUPA. As they point out, it is only of limited use to have cover for repatriation unless it can be implemented easily.

Checklist

1. Does the scheme cover all eventualities?
2. Are the scheme's benefits realistic in the light of local costs?
3. Can you make claims immediately or is there an initial indemnity period during which claims are disallowed? (Some insurers insist on this to protect themselves from claims caused by 'pre-existing medical conditions'.)
4. Is there a clause providing for emergency repatriation by air or air ambulance if suitable treatment is not available locally? If so, who decides what constitutes an emergency and/or adequate local treatment?
5. Is the insurer's nearest office accessible personally or by telephone? (For instance, it is very difficult to get in touch with London if you are in Indonesia.)
6. What is the length of the insurer's settlement period for claims?
7. Is there a discount for members of professional or other associations?
8. Does the policy continue to apply, partly or fully, while you are back in the UK?
9. Note comments on AIDS and HIV testing in the Preface, page 15.

Wherever you work or retire, you don't have to go without BUPA.
You never know where or when illness or injury will strike. It might be a snakebite in the Sahara, dehydration in Delhi or a collision on the Costa.
But wherever illness hits you BUPA can provide the right support.
If you can be treated locally we'll help you meet the often high costs involved.
If not, we'll make all the arrangements to transport you to a suitable place for the treatment you need. And we'll meet the costs.
So you'll soon be back on your feet, with no worries about the bills.
We've devised two schemes for expatriates, BUPA International Lifeline and now, Senior Lifeline. This means you can join right up to the age of 74.
For more details, send the coupon below.
When it comes to overseas healthcare, you'll find BUPA goes to the ends of the Earth to help.
To: BUPA International Sales Office, Provident House, Essex Street, London WC2R 3AX. Please send me details of:
BUPA International Lifeline (18-64 years) ☐
Senior Lifeline (65-74 years) ☐
Name ________ O/L30/2029/INT
Address ________
Country ________ Nationality ________
Telephone no. ________
Tick box for details about forming a company scheme ☐
BUPA International Lifeline

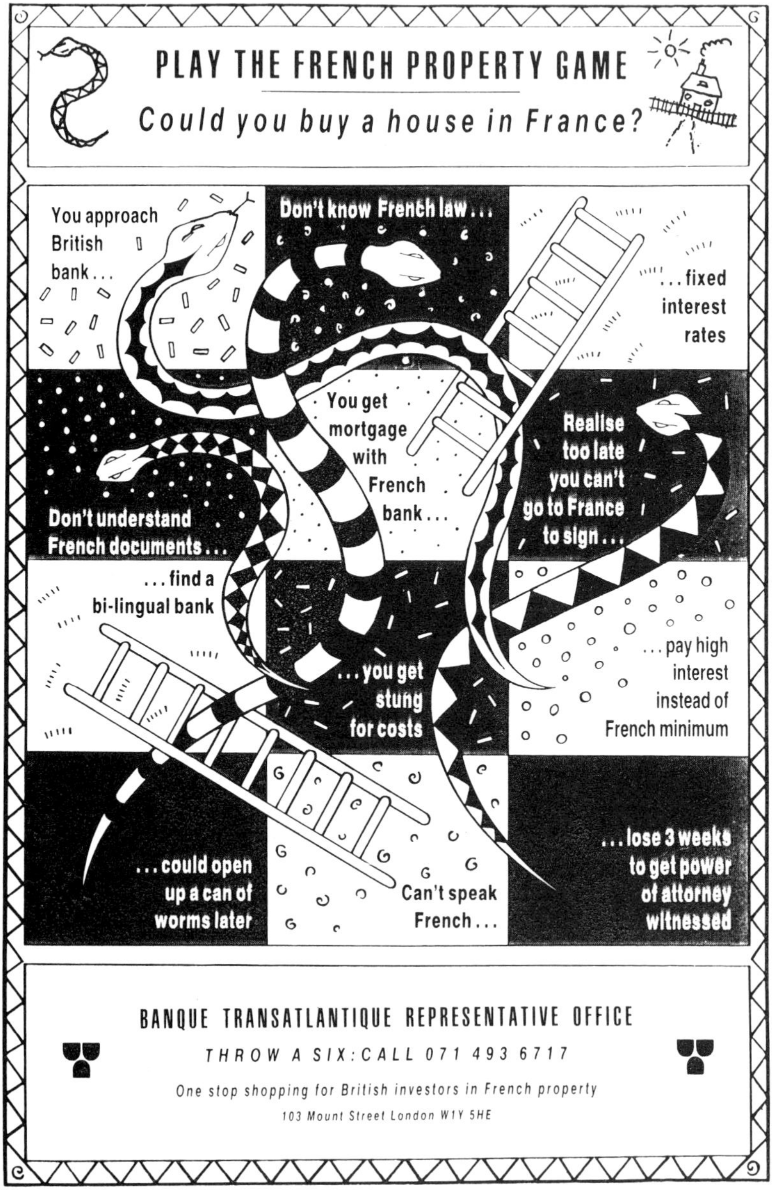
PLAY THE FRENCH PROPERTY GAME
Could you buy a house in France?
You approach British bank . . .
Don't know French law . . .
. . . fixed interest rates
You get mortgage with French bank . . .
Realise too late you can't go to France to sign . . .
Don't understand French documents . . .
. . . find a bi-lingual bank
. . . you get stung for costs
. . . pay high interest instead of French minimum
. . . could open up a can of worms later
Can't speak French . . .
. . . lose 3 weeks to get power of attorney witnessed
BANQUE TRANSATLANTIQUE REPRESENTATIVE OFFICE
THROW A SIX: CALL 071 493 6717
One stop shopping for British investors in French property
103 Mount Street London W1Y 5HE

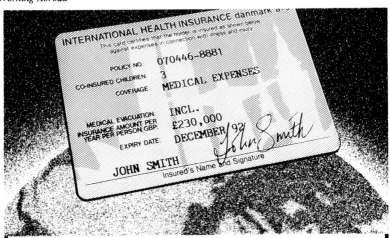

A Survey of Current Expatriate Medical Schemes

Benefits	*Private Patients Plan International Health Plan*	*BUPA International Senior Lifeline* (Typical Scheme)
Overall maximum	£100,000	£100,000
Hospital accommodationn	Full refund	Full refund
Home nursing	Full refund up to 14 days	£600/full refund, depending on circumstances
Surgeons' and anaesthetists' fees	Full refund	Full refund
Operating theatre fees	Full refund	Full refund
Hospital (non-surgical) treatment	Full refund (outpatients £1000)	Full refund
GP treatment	£1000 per annum. £20 excess on each visit to GP	£15 per visit (max 6 visits per annum)
Maternity care	Complications only (full refund) Normal childbirth available on corporate groups >10 employees	—

BUPA International Lifeline (Typical Scheme)	*Exeter Hospital Aid Society* (Middle range)	*Europea – IMG Ltd Expatriate Health Care*
£100,000	None	Single status £250,000. Husband/wife or single parent family £350,000 (max £250,000 per person, per occurrence). Family status £500,000 (£250,000 per person, per occurrence).
Full refund	£650 per week (Europe), £545 per week (outside Europe)	Unlimited cover up to maximum above.
—	£200 per week (10 weeks max.)	As above
Full refund	£1000 per operation* plus £300 for anaesthetists' fees	As above
Full refund	£400 per operation*	As above
Full refund (outpatients £1000)	Various inpatient charges are covered up to specified limits (outpatients £1000 per annum)	As above
—	Optional extra	As above
Complications only	Complications only	Up to £1000
	*Plus additional grant of up to 100% for complex major operations	

A Survey of Current Expatriate Medical Schemes

Benefits	*Private Patients Plan International Health Plan*	*BUPA International Senior Lifeline* (Typical Scheme)
Emergency dental treatment	£20 excess for out-patient treatment. No excess for emergency in-patient treatment.	—
Emergency evacuation/ repatriation	£35,000	No overall maximum
Premium	Varies according to age and area. Middle range:	Varies according to age. (No cover for USA and Canada.)
Key S = single M = married F = family	*Europe* Adult: £310 Child: £135 *World excl. North America* Adult: £385 Child: £170	50–65: £662 65–70: £765 70+: £978 75+: £1473
	1. Higher premiums apply for the USA and Canada. Rates quoted are for individuals. Company paid groups are lower.	

BUPA International Lifeline (Typical Scheme)	*Exeter Hospital Aid Society* (Middle range)	*Europea – IMG Ltd Expatriate Health Care*
—	—	Single status £500 Husband and wife/ single parent family £650 Family £750
No overall maximum	Not covered	Unlimited cover up to maximum above
Varies according to age. (Higher premiums for USA and Canada.) Under 50 range:		Varies according to area
Adult: £348 Child: £116	S: £540 F: £749	S: from £340 M: from £495 Child: from £70

2. Individual cover only.

Chapter 7

Letting and Insuring Your Home While Abroad

Most home owners going to live abroad for a limited period will be looking for a tenant to live in their house or flat while they are away. There is, of course, an obvious alternative, which is to sell, but then there is the question of storage of your effects – the average storage charge for the contents of a typical three-bedroomed house will be £50–£60 per week – and, more to the point, the fact that when you do return to this country you will have no place of your own to go to. Even if you do not intend to return to the house you lived in when you come back, it is generally advisable to retain ownership because your house represents a more or less inflation-indexed asset.

The case for letting, as opposed to leaving your home empty, hardly needs to be put today when squatting, vandalism and high interest rates are constantly in the headlines. The Government, recognising the difficulties for owners leaving their homes and wishing to encourage the private landlord, has introduced the Housing Act 1988 which came into force on 15 January 1989. This Act simplifies the many provisions of the various Rent and Housing Acts from 1965 to 1987, but even in early 1991 when this chapter was written there is still considerable doubt in the legal profession as there is little or no case law at the present time. The principal reason for the doubt in lawyers' minds is the choice provided for landlords between an assured tenancy and an assured shorthold tenancy. It is not possible here to define the various differences between these two forms of tenancy, but there are specific areas of which the owner-occupier needs to be aware. However, lettings to large companies where the occupier is a genuine employee being housed by the company temporarily are excluded from the Act. It should be noted that a letting to a member of the Diplomatic Corps who has immunity is inadvisable, as the individual would be outside the jurisdiction of British courts. It is essential, therefore, for the owner to obtain legal advice before deciding which form of tenancy to opt for.

Assured tenancies

1. An assured tenancy may be for a fixed term or periodic, ie month to month.
2. The tenant must be an individual, not a limited company.

3. The tenant must occupy the house or flat as his only or principal home.
4. There are various terms which should be provided in the agreement and in particular a provision for the rent to be increased by notice in writing.

The benefits of an assured tenancy are as follows: there is very little rent control; there is no restriction on the initial rent; premiums can be taken (although this is unlikely to be a marketable facility); rents can be increased during the tenancy, provided there is a term in the agreement; and even where not so provided the landlord may serve notice under the Act to increase the rent. In this latter instance, the tenant may go to the Rent Assessment Committee who must fix the rent at a 'market' figure, not at the previous imposition of what was perhaps unfortunately called a 'fair' rent.

Possession of the property can still be obtained by virtue of former owner-occupation and the service of the appropriate notice on the tenant before the commencement of the tenancy. Additional provisions for a mandatory possession order have been included in the new Act, such as three months' arrears of rent, and there are a number of discretionary grounds on which possession can be granted, even if the owner does not wish to return to the house. However, there is one specific disadvantage with the Act if the owner is unfortunate enough to have a tenant who refuses to leave when he wishes to reoccupy. This is the provision under the Act where the owner is obliged to serve two months' notice advising the tenant that he requires possession and on what ground(s) prior to any proceedings being commenced. This undoubtedly will extend the period needed before a possession order is granted by the Court and owners would be well advised to take out one of the various insurance policies now available to cover hotel costs, legal fees, etc and as a minimum to make sure that either alternative accommodation is temporarily available in the event of a return home earlier than expected or the tenancy is terminated well before the projected date of return.

Assured shorthold tenancies

1. These must be for a minimum term of six months without provision for a break clause, although after this period there can be two months' notice provided.
2. A notice must be served in the specified form at least four or five working days before the commencement of the agreement.
3. The tenant may apply to the Rent Assessment Committee during the period of the tenancy to fix the rental at a 'market' figure. However, on the expiry of the original term, the owner is entitled to require the tenant to pay a higher rental and the tenant is not entitled to go back to the Rent Assessment Committee. It is therefore preferable to have relatively short lease periods.
4. Two months' notice has to be served that the landlord requires possession before or on the day the fixed term comes to an end and, if the tenant refuses to leave, the Courts must grant possession, after the expiry of the notice.

As must now be obvious to the reader, the new rules do nothing to encourage the owner to attempt to let the property or manage his home himself while away, and the need for an experienced property management firm becomes even more important than in the past. A solicitor might be an alternative but, although more versed in the legal technicalities than a managing agent, he will not be in a position to market the house to the best advantage (if at all) and solicitors' practices do not usually have staff experienced in property management, able to carry out inspections, deal with repairs, arrange inventories and to handle the many and various problems that often arise.

Having retained a solicitor to ensure that you have the correct form of tenancy, you now need to find an experienced and reliable estate agent (ideally, he should be a member of the Royal Institution of Chartered Surveyors, the Incorporated Society of Valuers and Auctioneers or the National Association of Estate Agents) specialising in property management who will be well versed in both the legal and financial aspects of the property market.

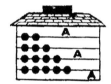

Property management

Property management is a rather specialised branch of estate agency and you should check carefully that the agent you go to can give you the service you need, that he is not just an accommodation broker, and that he is equipped to handle the letting, collection of rental and management of your property, as well as the more common kinds of agency work. Your solicitor should be able to advise you here, but to some extent you will have to rely on your own judgement of how ready and satisfactory the agent's answers are to the sort of questions you are going to want to ask him. There are several specialised firms well equipped to deal with your affairs. One such firm is Anderton & Son of Croydon, which supplied much of the information upon which this chapter is based. They deal with much of the southern commuting area serving London, from Ewell eastwards to Chislehurst, and also with country properties as far out as Sevenoaks and westwards to Dorking.

In the first place the agent you instruct should have a clear idea of the kind of tenant you can expect for your property, and preferably be able to show you that he does have people on his books who are looking for rented accommodation of this kind. Obviously the rental and the tenant you can expect will vary with what you have to offer. A normal family house in a good area should attract someone like the executive of a multinational company who is in a similar, but reverse, position to your own: that is, a man working here on a contract basis for a limited period of time who may well provide a stable tenancy for the whole or a substantial part of your absence. A smaller house or flat would be more likely to attract a younger person who only wants the property for a limited period or who, at any rate, might be reluctant to accept a long-term commitment because of the possibility of a change in professional circumstances or marital status. Equally, if you are only going to be away for a shortish period like six to 12 months, you are going to be rather lucky to find a tenant whose needs exactly overlap with your absence. You would probably have to accept a slightly shorter period than your exact stay abroad.

For your part you should bear in mind that tenants, unlike house purchasers, are usually only interested in a property with almost immediate possession, but you should give the agent, wherever possible, at least two or three months' warning of your departure in order that interest may be built up by advertising, mailing out details, etc over a period of time.

Rent

How much rent you can expect will also vary with what you have to offer and where it is, but the point to bear in mind is that rents are not usually subject to bargaining like a house price. Bargaining, if there is to be any, is more likely to occur over the terms of the lease which are set out below.

Do not, therefore, ask for an unrealistically high figure in the expectation that the tenant will regard this as a starting point for negotiation.

Your agent, if he knows his job, will be able to advise you on the rental you should ask, though if you have not had previous dealings with him it might be advisable to have your solicitor check out his figures or to ask the agent to give you some instances of rentals being charged for similar accommodation. On the other hand, an offer which is a bit less than you had hoped for, but from a good tenant, might be worth taking in preference to a better one from somebody who, for various reasons, looks more doubtful.

Terms of agreement

A property management agent should have, or be able to produce fairly quickly, a draft agreement to cover the specific situation of the overseas landlord. You should show this to your solicitor and how well it is drafted will again be a pointer to how effective the agent concerned is likely to be. The document should cover at least the following points:

1. The intervals of payment – monthly or quarterly – and the length of lease.
2. A prohibition from assigning the lease without your express permission; likewise from keeping animals on the premises or using them for other than residential purposes.
3. An undertaking by the tenant to make good any damage, other than fair wear and tear, to fixtures, fittings and furniture and to maintain the garden.
4. An undertaking by the tenant to pay for telephone and other services from the commencement of the lease.
5. An undertaking to allow the landlord, or his agent, regular access to the property for inspection and repair; and two months before the expiry of the lease to allow him to take other prospective tenants or purchasers round the property.
6. A clause stating that the lease is terminated if any of the other clauses are broken although the wording has to be carefully drafted to avoid invalidating the agreement.
7. What you, as landlord, are responsible for in the way of repairs: usually the maintenance of the structure and furnishings of the property together with anything left in the property (eg the central heating boiler). You can exclude some items, such as the television, from your responsibility, but generally the tenant is only liable for specific damage to items left in the house and not for their general maintenance.
8. Any special restrictions you want to impose: if, for example, your house is full of valuable antiques you may wish to specify 'no small children'.

9. The conditions under which the tenancy can be terminated prior to its full period having run and without any breach having taken place.
10. Notice must be served under Schedule 2, Ground 1 of the Housing Act 1988 which notifies the tenant that you are an owner-occupier within the meaning of the Housing Act. This gives the landlord and those members of his family who occupied the house before it was let the right to re-occupy it when the lease expires or is terminated.

Although the agreement is probably the central document in the transactions involved in letting your house, it does not bring to an end all the things you have to think about. For instance, there is the important matter of the contents insurance. Letting your home to a third party is probably not covered in your policy and you will have to notify your insurers (and the people who hold your mortgage) that this is what you are doing. At the same time you would be wise to check that the contents insurance covers the full value of what you have left in the house. This check could be combined with making a proper inventory of the contents which is in any case essential before tenants move into a furnished property. Making an exact inventory is quite a time-consuming business and you should bear in mind that it will also have to be checked at the end of the lease, when you may not be there. There are several firms that provide a specialist inventory service at both ends of the lease, covering dilapidations as well as items actually missing, for quite a modest charge which, incidentally, is deductible from the tax due from the letting. Any good property management agent should be able to put you on to one of them.

Equally, finding the tenant and getting his signature on the agreement marks the beginning rather than the end of the property management firm's responsibilities. Broadly, these fall under two headings: the collection of rental and the management of the property. The rent is collected from the tenant, usually on a standing order basis, under the terms – monthly or quarterly – as set out in the agreement; and, in the event of persistent non-payment, the agent will instruct solicitors on your behalf to issue a county court summons.

What can you expect from the agent?

Management is a more complex subject but an experienced property management agent should be able to supply you with a list of the services that he can undertake. It is, therefore, also a checklist of the kind of eventualities that may crop up in your absence which, broadly speaking, relate to the collection of rent, the payment of charges such as service charges and insurance, arrangements for repairs to the fabric of the building and its contents, garden maintenance or when forwarding mail.

Thus, apart from the basic business of collecting the rent, the agent can

also pay, on your behalf, any charges on the property (eg ground rent, water rates and insurance) that your contract with the tenant does not specify should be paid by him. There may also be annual maintenance agreements to pay in respect of items like central heating plant and the washing machine.

Then there is the question of what to do about repairs. As we have indicated earlier, whatever you manage to get the tenant to agree to take care of under the terms of the lease, there are certain responsibilities for maintenance and repair that you have to accept by virtue of your status as a landlord. If repairs are necessary, you will simply have to trust the agent to obtain fair prices for you.

On the other hand, except in the case of essential repairs which affect the tenant's legal rights of enjoyment of the property, you can ask your agent to provide estimates for having the work carried out, so that your approval must be obtained before the job is put in hand. Bear in mind, though, that in certain parts of the world the postal system may not be all that reliable. You may, therefore, find it a good idea to put a clause in the management contract giving the agent freedom to proceed with the best estimate if he does not hear from you within a specified period. For the same reason it is also wise to ask the agent to send you a formal acknowledgement of receipt of any special or new instructions you have given him. An example of this might be an instruction to inspect the property at regular intervals.

Depending on how many concessions you have to make to the tenant to get him to sign the lease, there may be other articles for which repair and maintenance remain your responsibility. These may include washing machines, TV and the deep-freeze. Such responsibilities should be set out in the management contract and you should give the agent the details of any guarantees or maintenance contracts relating to them and photocopies of the actual documents for reference. If no such arrangements apply, you should list the manufacturers' names and the model number and age of each item so that the agent can get the manufacturer to send the repair people along equipped with the right spares.

It is very important that a third party, other than you and the tenant, should be in possession of all this information, particularly when there is likely to be more than one tenancy during your absence; and it is a competent management agent, rather than friends, relatives or even a solicitor, who will be best equipped in this case to find new tenants, to check their references, to draw up new agreements and supervise the hand-over of the tenancy.

Costs and tax

The costs of all these services vary according to the nature of the package you need. The professional societies already mentioned recommend charges, which would be applicable in most circumstances. For example, letting and collection is usually 10 per cent of annual rental. In the case of

management services, expect to find additional charges made (usually 5 to 7 per cent of the annual rent). These are reasonable fees for the quite considerable headaches involved. We have shown enough of them here to indicate that not only is it virtually impossible to administer a tenancy yourself from a distance, but also that these are not matters to be left to an amateur – friend or relative – however well intentioned. In real terms the agent's charges may be reduced because they are deductible against the tax levied in the UK against rental income.

Expatriates letting their houses also derive a further benefit in respect of capital gains tax. Generally, if you let your principal residence, when you come to sell it you can claim exemption from CGT only for those years in which you lived in it yourself. However, if you let it because you are absent abroad this does not apply, provided you come back to live in the house before you sell it.

Finally, in this context, it is worth pointing out that some building societies are now prepared to consider giving mortgages to expatriates for the purchase of a property in the UK *and* to allow them to lease that property for the period of their stay overseas. Up to 90 per cent of the purchase price is available at normal building society rates of interest.

This is an attractive proposition for expatriates, particularly for young executives and professional people who have not yet bought a home in the UK but are earning a substantial income in, say, the Middle East, and for older expatriates perhaps thinking of a retirement home in the UK.

Some agencies supply details of the building societies offering this facility, or you could approach a society directly and explain your position. Should you buy a house as an expatriate and then let it until you return, the earlier recommendation that you leave the management of the property to an experienced and competent agent still applies.

There are, however, two problems. If a UK property is bought purely as an investment, you would have to time its sale carefully to avoid liability to CGT – see Chapter 3. The other is that if you are letting it in the mean time you have to be careful not to disclose your intention to sell it beforehand. Otherwise it could weaken your case for repossession under the Rent Act.

Taxation is too complex a subject and varies considerably in its effects on the individual, preventing any practical advice being offered other than to stress the necessity of employing the services of an accountant in your absence. Changes in the Budget allow the use of personal allowances against property income, subject to some restriction, while the Revenue have tightened up the method and timing and collection of tax due in each year, with stiffer penalties for late payment, and refusal to accept postponements except on specific grounds. Should you have an agent collecting the rent, whether this is a professional firm or a friend, he will be liable to pay tax on your behalf and, without an indemnity from a UK based employer or a chartered accountant, may be obliged to deduct tax from each monthly or quarterly rental payment, to enable payment of the

amount requested by the Revenue on 1 January.

Similar liabilities now fall on an agent collecting the rental in respect of the Community Charge. The owner will be responsible jointly with his agent to meet the standard charge if the property is empty, or where the property is let for less than six months to an individual. In these cases expect the agent to retain sufficient money to meet this commitment on your behalf.

Insurance

One important point that is often overlooked by people who let their house or flat is the necessity of notifying the insurers that a change of occupancy has taken place. Insurance policies only cover occupancy by the insured, not his tenants, though it can be extended to do so on payment of what is usually only a small premium.

What worries insurance companies much more is if the house is left unoccupied for any length of time. If you look at your policy you will see that it lapses if you leave your house empty for more than 30 days or so – a point that is sometimes forgotten by people who go away on extended holidays. If you are going abroad and leave the house empty – maybe because you have not yet succeeded in finding a tenant – the insurers will usually insist that you turn off the main services and that the premises are inspected regularly by a qualified person. That means someone like a letting agent, not a relative or friend who cannot be relied on 100 per cent. Even if you have let the house without an agent, it may still be advisable to get one to look after the place. A situation could easily occur where the tenant moves out, leaving the place empty and without satisfactory steps having been taken from an insurance point of view. Furthermore, if the worst happens and the house is broken into or damaged, it is imperative that the insurers are notified right away. The effects of damage can be made worse unless they are rapidly attended to, and insurers do not hold themselves responsible for anything that happens between the time the insured eventuality occurs and the time they are notified of it. For instance, if your house is broken into and, a few days later, vandals get in through a broken point of entry and cause further damage, you would not be covered for that second incident unless the insurers had been notified of the first break-in.

Valuable contents are best put into storage and insured there: Pickfords, for instance, charge a premium of 7½ per cent of the storage charge. For very high value items, safe deposit boxes are becoming popular, but from an everyday point of view, the important thing is to make sure you are insured for full values. If you insure contents for £15,000 and the insurer's assessors value them at £20,000 you will only get three-quarters of your claim. To keep insured values in line with rising costs, an index-linked policy would be the best buy for anyone contemplating a long stay abroad. A policy specially written for expatriates is available from the Europea

Group: the Expatriates UK Home Owners Insurance Contract. They also offer expatriate motor insurance on private cars being used overseas.

Insuring at full value, incidentally, is equally important when it comes to insuring contents and personal belongings in your residence abroad. Many items will cost much more locally if you have to replace them than they did at the time they were originally bought. It is possible to effect such insurance in the UK, but from the point of getting claims settled quickly it is better to insure in the country concerned, where possible.

Finally, but most important, you should insure against legal and hotel costs when letting your house. Although in principle the legal instruments for quick repossession exist, events have shown that a bloody-minded tenant with a committed lawyer can spin things out to his or her advantage for almost an indefinite period. Premiums, which can be offset against rental income, are in the region of £50 a year. A typical policy covering legal costs is the DAS Homeowners Legal Protection Policy.

Chapter 8

Moving Out, Settling In and Coming Home

What to take

Whatever agonising variables you feed into your mental computer about what and what not to take, you will certainly find that in the end you are left with two basic choices – either to take very little other than clothes, books, favourite possessions and whatever small items you and your family need to feel at home – or to take virtually everything.

It clearly depends on where you are going, how long you are going for, and who you are going to work for. If you are taking up an appointment in a sophisticated European capital or in North America, obviously you will not need the same kind of things as you would in a developing country, say in Africa or Asia, where everything tends to be scarce and expensive. If you are going to a tropical country, or the Middle East, clothes and equipment will be very different from what you will need in a temperate or northern area.

As a rule, travelling reasonably light is the best course of action. Even if you are going to be away for a long time, it seldom pays to take large items of household equipment, such as sofas, beds or wardrobes; the cost of shipping bulky items is very high. In any case, it can take quite a long time to clear them through customs when they arrive, so you will either have to send them ahead or find yourself arriving in a new place without any furniture.

Such situations are apt to be inconvenient and will probably result in your having to buy some things simply to tide you over. Clothes, bedlinen, crockery, kitchen equipment and so forth are cheap to transport – shipping companies usually convey some baggage free of charge – and usually expensive to replace at the other end. Furthermore, these items lend themselves to being sent ahead, and you can usually make do, or borrow, in the mean time.

Antiques are always worth taking, since they are vastly expensive in most places outside the UK, but remember that old furniture and pictures can be sensitive to climatic change. Such problems may also exist with electric equipment, and your record player or food mixer may have to go through costly adaptations to fit in with foreign voltages. Records, tapes and musical instruments deteriorate in hot climates. There can also be

problems over import controls, though most authorities have special dispensations for personal possessions.

As far as household equipment is concerned, much depends on the terms of your contract. Most commercial firms in developing countries will provide a fully furnished house or apartment (possibly also a car). Fully furnished means that everything, down to the last lampshade, is provided and you only need your personal effects. National governments and public corporations usually supply 'hard furnished' accommodation. Hard furnished is what it implies. Only the bare necessities such as tables and chairs and a bed are provided, and you will need to supply curtains, cushions, linen, loose covers, cutlery, crockery and kitchen gear. Often you can buy these things from an outgoing tenant or returning expatriate, but you have to be on the spot for this.

It is strongly recommended that where a married couple are going out to a developing country the husband should travel out alone in advance, unless furnished accommodation is assured, and only send for the family when this has been fixed up. It may mean staying in a hotel or hostel for a time, but it is worth the inconvenience to be able to learn the ropes at first hand and decide what will be needed from home. Some companies arrange for both husband and wife to go out in advance for a 'reconnaissance' visit.

In some cases, especially if the contract is a short-term one, in a difficult country, it is recommended that the husband should go out alone, leaving his wife and family in the UK. This may sound heartless, but it does minimise the upheaval and avoids disrupting the children's education.

If you are going to a tropical country where conditions are difficult, you may not be able to buy such items as a deep freeze, food mixer, sewing machine, hairdryer and electric iron except in the main centres. A portable electric fan is useful if the house is not air conditioned. An electric kettle is a must and so is a torch. There may be power cuts, so stock up with candles.

If you have very young children with you, take prams, carrycot, pushchair and plenty of toys. Camping equipment, eg tents and sleeping bags, may be useful, and so may gardening tools, as many houses have quite large gardens. Take golf clubs, tennis rackets, photographic equipment etc, since these leisure and luxury goods may be unobtainable or very expensive overseas, though this will again depend very much on where you go.

Stock up with cosmetics and toiletries, drugs and medicines since everything in this line is expensive and difficult to obtain. Find out the voltage and type of electric plug in use and, before you go if possible, check with the appliance manufacturer about any adaptations.

Don't rely on somebody sending you something from home. Postage is exorbitant, mails are slow and the contents liable to be pilfered. It may be possible to get your children, or your neighbour's children, to bring things out when they come on leave from school.

Removal

The best way to handle the question of actual removal is to consult one of the big removal firms. Overseas removal is not a job you should take on yourself, nor is it a good thing on which to try to save money. Moving abroad is a very different proposition from moving in this country and, in choosing your remover, it is better to ask for a good name than a good quote. The bigger removers are well informed about living conditions in overseas countries – check, though, that any printed literature they give you is fully up to date.

Removers are knowledgeable about what you can and should take with you, and most have agents at ports of entry who can help with the sometimes interminable business of clearing your belongings through customs. Another advantage of a 'name' remover is that they can generally get a better insurance deal than a smaller firm. You should, incidentally, increase your insurance to cover replacement costs at the other end. If you cannot get any specific information about this, an increase of 50 to 80 per cent over UK values will serve as a rough guideline.

An alternative to using one of the 'big names' is to contact one of the specialist consortia of overseas removal companies such as 'Omni'. These are made up of hand picked, privately owned companies specialising in overseas removals. As a team, members provide the strength and capacity of a large international concern; individually they are able to provide a local, personal service that many customers prefer.

All members conform to standards of service which are the same for members all over the world. So a remover operating out of the UK will provide the same level of service as his counterparts in Italy, for instance. Using the consortium method is rather like using a removal company with branch offices all over the world.

In the last few years there has been extensive publicity over the sudden demise of overseas removal companies, which – having received payment in advance – have left their customers' belongings either in the warehouse or, worse still, languishing in an overseas country. This usually resulted in families having to pay twice over for their household effects to be delivered, and many who could not afford to pay again had to abandon their belongings altogether.

Protection against this sort of disaster is now available through the Advance Payments Guarantee Scheme operated by the Overseas Group of the British Association of Removers. The Scheme provides that customers who have paid removal charges in advance to a firm participating in the Scheme are guaranteed that in the event of the removal company ceasing to trade, their belongings will either be delivered at no further cost, or they will be refunded the cost of the removal charges.

It should not be assumed that all removers are in the Scheme. The safeguard provided by the Scheme is available only through members of the BAR Overseas Group. The guarantee is underwritten by a mutual insurance company set up by the industry.

The British Association of Removers itself will be happy to supply readers of this publication with leaflets giving advice on moving abroad and brochures on the Advance Payments Guarantee Scheme. The Association also provides a list of companies participating in the Scheme. Readers should send a 9 in × 4 in sae to the British Association of Removers, 3 Churchill Court, 58 Station Road, North Harrow, Middlesex.

Removal costs vary according to the distance to be covered, the method of transportation (land, sea or air), the terms of the arrangement (delivery to port or home, packed or unpacked), and a range of other factors. Customers should obtain *written* estimates from several companies. Beware of firms which quote on the basis of approximate measures. Be specific, understand exactly the terms of the arrangement and obtain a written agreement, so that you have what amounts to a contract with which to resist 'surcharges' imposed at the point of disembarkation.

Some people like to pack their own things. If so, it is best to use tea-chests which are stout but light and can be strengthened by steel bands to withstand rough handling and exposure. It is essential to make a list of contents and advisable to see that your cases or boxes are readily identifiable for when you collect them at the other end. Smaller goods can be taken with you, up to the 20 kg allowable limit. Some things may be carried as hand luggage, depending on how full the plane is. But on all these points, be guided by the experts.

Pets often pose a problem. In some countries, a bill of health from the UK Ministry of Agriculture, Fisheries and Food is required, and the authorities must be notified in advance so that they can examine the animal before landing. When you come back to the UK, your pet will have to be placed in quarantine. The best course is to go to a firm which specialises in moving animals, such as Spratt's Animal Shipping Service or Par Air Services (Livestock) Ltd. They provide a door-to-door service, look after pets during the journey, and handle all the veterinary and customs formalities.

Choice of removers checklist

1. The remover should provide a free estimate and a written quote.
2. Does the quote specify *professional* packing under your general supervision?
3. How will fragile items, furniture and articles be packed?
4. What insurance cover is offered? If there is any excess (ie a minimum figure below which you will not be reimbursed) what is it?
5. Can the removers immediately provide the name and address of the port agents at your destination?
6. Will they deliver to your residence at the other end, or will you have to arrange clearance yourself?
7. What proportion of their current business is in overseas removals?

VAT

You will almost certainly find that some of the things you want are cheaper to buy here, even allowing for shipping charges. You should make sure that you take full advantage of the various VAT export schemes under which a UK resident going abroad for at least 12 months can escape having to pay VAT altogether. There are two schemes, one for cars and one for other goods.

Cars

You have to purchase your car (which need not be a British make) from the manufacturer or the sole selling agent. He will give you a form VAT 411 to fill in, which requires you to fulfil certain conditions:

1. You have to undertake to go abroad for at least 12 months, though you may bring the vehicle back for temporary visits; if so, you must take the registration document for production to Customs and Excise.
2. You have to take the car abroad within six months of buying it, though you may use it here up to that time.

HOW TO ORGANISE YOUR INTERNATIONAL REMOVAL

The first steps you should take are to determine which of your household furniture and personal possessions you wish to take with you to your new home, and which you are going to leave behind, perhaps in storage until you return.

It is often useful to find out something about the kind of property available at your destination. Is it likely to have fitted wardrobes? Do UK electrical appliances work in the country you are moving to? If not can they be adapted and if so how much will this cost? The answers to these kind of questions can help you reach a decision. What is the value of items of furniture at your destination? If the item is expensive to buy new at your destination and the secondhand value in the UK is not good then it makes sense to take it with you. As a general rule furniture that has been purchased within the last five years, and all types of antique furniture are well worth taking with you as their value overseas is often greater than it is here.

When you have decided which items are going with you then it's time to phone your removal company and arrange for their representative to come to your home to survey your household effects. During the survey the representative will compile an inventory of the items that you wish to take with you, assess the packing requirement and estimate the weight and volume of your possessions. The weight and volume will be crucial to the overall price paid and is usually expressed in Cubic Feet/Lbs or Cubic Metres/Kilos.

Once the remover has completed the survey a cost estimate for the removal of your possessions can be prepared.

An international removal is comprised of three important steps. Firstly there is the packing of your possessions (the origin service) which involves carefully ensuring that all items are wrapped in protective materials and all small articles eg glassware, are boxed in sturdy export cartons and cases. For delicate items of furniture, eg a grandfather clock, a special custom built crate may also have to be made. Once the packing has been completed your possessions can then be loaded and for surface transportation this will be either into a removal van or a 20ft or 40ft steel container. For air transportation, and for some surface destinations the loading will be into a wooden case, often referred to as a lift van. A lift van gives additional protection to high value possessions and is constructed so that it can fit neatly inside either a removal van or a steel container.

The second step to be carried out is the transportation which will either be by road, sea or air. The remover will select the most appropriate vehicle, ship or aeroplane according to the route and your final destination.

Once the transportation has been completed and your possessions have arrived at their destination the third step (the destination service) can begin. The remover will, through his colleague at your destination, arrange customs clearance, delivery and unpacking of your effects into your new home.

In other words the reverse of the packing services at origin will take place during the destination service.

Many of the leading international removers are shareholders in OMNI, Overseas Moving Network Incorporated, which is a consortium of the leading removers of the World welded together into a tight knit organisation designed to give high quality service at many worldwide locations. If you choose to move with an OMNI remover then smoothness and quality should be the passowrds of your relocation. John Mason International, with offices in London, Liverpool and Manchester, are one of the leading OMNI members in the United Kingdom.

3. You have to take delivery yourself and, until you have had it abroad for more than 12 months, no other person may use it (unless it is a person who is also going abroad for 12 months or is resident abroad). You must not sell it in the UK before then.

After you have had it abroad for 12 months, you can re-import the car and not pay VAT on it. But if you have to return here permanently before the 12 months are up, you will have to pay some VAT retroactively – all of it, if you return within three months. If the car is found to be in the UK after the date for its export shown in the registration document (ie six months from purchase date), you will have to pay VAT and car tax in full and it will also be liable to forfeiture. This applies even if failure to export the vehicle is due to circumstances beyond your control (eg theft or destruction). Therefore, while the car is still in the UK, before export, it is essential to insure it for its full value.

Other goods

Two different procedures apply if you want to claim back VAT on goods you are buying in the UK to take abroad for a period of more than 12 months. It depends on whether or not you are going to a Common Market country. If so, the constraints, governed by EC rules, are such that you would have to be exceptionally economy-minded to want to go through with all the bother involved in getting back the 17.5 per cent VAT you have paid.

The situation is somewhat better if you are going outside the EC because there is usually no limit on the size and value of the goods you can bring into the country of your destination. In that case it may be worth while getting your purchases zero rated (ie sold to you free of VAT) as exports. However, they have to be shipped for you – you cannot take delivery of them in this country – and a fair bit of documentation is involved, both for you and the retailer. You may not find it worth your while unless you are making fairly large purchases and only in one or two shops. In that case you should ask the retailer to advise you on the procedures for filling out form VAT 408.

Taking a car abroad

British people tend to prefer right-hand drive or automatic and will therefore consider buying their car here and taking it with them. First check at the embassy of the country you propose to live in that private car imports are permitted.

Probably the best way to plan this is to make a list of what you will want your car to do. The road surfaces may be less good than those you are used to, so you may consider taking a good secondhand car rather than a brand new one. You will not then be so worried about driving through very narrow streets. In some places drivers actually park by shunting the cars ahead and behind!

If you buy a new car in the UK before going abroad, you can use it here for six months, run it in and have your first service before you take it overseas. Check the servicing facilities in the area where you plan to live. It would be unwise to take a car abroad if the nearest dealer service is 70 miles away. This factor may well limit your choice.

A big car will be expensive with petrol and difficult to park. If you will be living in an apartment and there is no garage, the car will usually be left in the street and possibly for long periods at that. Consider carefully the security of your car and what you may have in it. Choose a model with locking wheel nuts and high quality locks so that it is hard to get into without smashing the windows. Radio thefts are prevalent in some countries; therefore you may wish to consider a demountable radio.

Should you decide to take a small car to a hot country, always buy one with a sun roof because the smaller cars carry no air conditioning.

People moving to Spain, for example, will often choose diesel cars because the fuel is half the price of petrol and easily available. Lead-free petrol is now available in many countries and you should check whether your engine will take this quality. Some engines need minor adaptation.

Taking your existing car abroad

If you take the car you own at present abroad for longer than 12 months, this is regarded as a permanent export and the procedure is described in leaflet V526, obtainable from your local Vehicle Licensing Office.

The following procedure applies to exports from England, Scotland, Wales and the Isles of Scilly only, not to Northern Ireland or the Isle of Man where cars are registered separately.

Complete section 2 on the back of the Vehicle Registration Document, entering the proposed date of export, and send the document to your local Vehicle Licensing Office or to the Driver and Vehicle Licensing Centre. This should be done well in advance of your departure.

You will receive back a Certificate of Export (V561) which in effect confirms your vehicle registration.

A different procedure applies in Northern Ireland as vehicles are registered locally; it is necessary to register and license a car taken *to* Northern Ireland permanently as soon as the current British tax disc expires, if not before. The Certificate of Export mentioned above will still be necessary.

Motoring services in Europe

The International Touring Alliance has its headquarters in Geneva, and driving clubs through Europe are affiliated to it, including the Automobile Association. These clubs provide a wide range of services to each other's members travelling abroad, so membership of one is worthwhile.

Customs

Regulations and procedures vary. Most customs authorities allow you to take in used things for your personal use and often let people, eg newly married couples, bring in new things duty free. Wherever possible keep receipts to show to the customs officials.

In most places, you are allowed to take in 'household and used personal effects', including refrigerators, radios, TV receivers and minor electrical appliances, but duties on new items of this kind are usually fairly steep. There are bans everywhere on guns, plants and drugs. Many Middle East and North African countries operate a boycott list, so do not take anything made in Israel or South Africa. Duty free wines, spirits and tobacco up to a certain amount - check with the airline - are normally allowed, except in most Middle East countries.

Removal checklist

Don't forget to tell the following organisations that you are moving abroad:

Your bank.

Income Tax Office. Notify the Inland Revenue giving the exact date of departure.

National Insurance/DSS benefits, allowances, pension. Send your full name, date of birth, National Insurance number, details of country to which you are moving and duration of your stay to the DSS Overseas Group, Newcastle upon Tyne NE98 1YX.

Vehicle licence. If you are taking your vehicle abroad for longer than a year this is regarded as a 'permanent export'. In this case you should return your existing (new style) registration document to the Vehicle Licensing Centre, Swansea SA99 1AB, filling in the 'permanent export' section. Alternatively, you can apply to your local Vehicle Licensing Office for the necessary forms.

Driving licence. You will probably want to retain your British driving licence. Many countries recognise it as valid and a list of those which do not is available from the AA.

International driving licence. An international driving licence is obtainable from the AA (even if you are not a member) and is valid for one year. The licence is not valid in the country where it is issued so you must obtain it before leaving the UK. Most countries require residents to hold a local driving licence so check whether this is the case on taking up your new residence.

Motor insurance. Notify your insurers of the date of your departure - your insurance should be cancelled from that date and you should

As your lifestyle changes, so will your travelling needs. This is particularly true when it comes to choosing luggage. Ultimately this will depend on how long you will be working abroad, your mode of travel and the amount of travelling you are likely to do when you reach your destination.

As a rule of thumb, refer to that old adage "you get what you pay for". If you buy cheaply you can't expect anything to last forever. Leading luggage company Delsey say you should be prepared to spend a minimum of £65 for a good quality 27 inch (70 cm) rigid or soft case and £30 for a spacious and durable soft bag.

Cases and travel bags come in a number of fabrics. Hardsided fabrics to look out for are ABS (acrylo nitryl butadiene styrene) and polypropylene, which is similar to the substance used for car bumpers. The most popular and durable choice on the soft side is nylon and 400 denier or more is the best.

Also remember to check out guarantees and hardware when buying new luggage. Delsey, for example, offer a five year guarantee on all rigid luggage. When it comes to hardware, look out for zips which should be nylon and locks which should be recessed so they can't be torn open by accidental catching. Wheels should also be recessed and handles should "flick-back" and then lie flat.

When you are planning to work abroad, you should work out your wardrobe very carefully. The climate will be the crux of your choice and if you opt for clothes that mix and match you will get the maximum use from them.

It is a good idea to make a list of everything you will need to take, including a mini list of "essentials" for your journey. This will govern the number of bags and cases you will need. Think over the list for a good few days in case you remember something else or realise you can leave some items behind. Finally, how about asking well travelled friends and colleagues for a few tips.

★

Delsey Luggage, Units 3 & 4, Armstrong Way, Great Western Industrial Park, Southall, Middx UB2 4NW. Tel: 081 571 6399.

obtain a refund for the rest of the insurance period. Ask your insurance company for a letter outlining your no-claims record to show to your new insurer.

Life and other insurances. Notify the companies concerned or your insurance broker if you use one.

Dentist. Let him know you are moving. As a matter of courtesy, it will save posting useless check-up reminders.

Private health insurance. Notify subscriber records department.

Gas – if you use it, notify your local gas showroom giving at least *48 hours'* notice. They will give you a standard form to fill in with details of the move and any current hire-purchase agreements. If appliances are to be removed they require as much notice as possible to arrange an appointment; there is a disconnection charge.

Electricity. Notify your local district office or showroom at least *48 hours* before moving. Arrangements are much the same as for gas.

Water. The local water board should also be notified at least *48 hours* before the move. Drain tanks and pipes if the house is to remain empty in winter.

Telephone. Notify your local telephone sales office as shown in the front of your directory at least *seven days* before the move.

Community charge. Notify the town hall. (See Chapter 7 for further details.)

Libraries. Return books and give in tickets to be cancelled.

Professional advisers such as solicitors, accountants, stockbrokers, insurance brokers etc. Make sure they have a forwarding address.

Stocks and shares. Write to the company registrar at the address on the last annual report or share certificates.

Organisations and clubs – any business, civic, social, cultural, sports or automobile club of which you are a member. For the AA write to Membership Subscriptions and Records, PO Box 50, Basingstoke, Hampshire and for the RAC write to RAC House, Lansdowne Road, East Croydon.

Credit card companies. Advise them that you are leaving the country.

HP companies. Notify the office where repayments are made. You will need to settle your account.

Local business accounts – department stores, newsagents, dairy, baker, chemist, dry cleaner, laundry, motor service station.

Publications. Cancel postal subscriptions to newspapers, magazines,

professional and trade journals, book and record clubs etc.

National Health Service. Return your NHS card to the Family Practitioners' Committee for your area, giving your date of departure, or hand it in to the immigration officer at your point of departure.

Pension schemes. If you have a 'frozen' or paid up pension from a previous employer notify the pension trust of your new address.

TV. If you have a rented set, make arrangements to return it.

Post Office. Notify day of departure and UK contact address.

Personal Giro – the Post Office have a special SAE for this.

Premium Bonds – anything rather than join the sad list of unclaimed prizes! Contact Bonds and Stocks Office, Lytham St Annes, Lancashire FY0 1YN to check the current position, because in a few countries, Premium Bond holdings may contravene their lottery laws.

Save As You Earn and National Savings Certificates. It is important to notify any permanent change of address, particularly for index-linked retirement issue certificates and SAYE contracts. Advise the Savings and Certificates and SAYE Office, Durham DH99 1NS, quoting the contract number(s).

National Savings Bank. Notify at Glasgow G58 1SB.

Your landlord. If you are a tenant, give the appropriate notice to quit.

Your tenants. If you are a landlord, that UK address you've organised will be needed.

Your employer. Give new address details, or a contact address, in writing.

Schools. Try to give your children's schools a term's notice that they will be leaving. If you wish your children's education to be continued in Britain, contact your local Education Authority or the Department of Education and Science, Elizabeth House, York Road, London SE1 7PH, for advice.

Make sure your *removers* have any temporary contact address and phone numbers for you, both in the UK and abroad, so that they can get in touch with you when the need arises. It is also useful for them if you can tell them when you expect to arrive in your new country.

Reproduced by courtesy of Pickfords Ltd.

Before you go

There are certain things you must see about before you actually leave. There are obvious chores, like cancelling milk and papers etc. Have a thorough medical check for yourself and your family before you go, including teeth and eyes. Some jobs, of course, depend on physical fitness. Make sure you have the necessary vaccination certificates and check the requirements. Most tropical countries need certificates against smallpox and possibly cholera and yellow fever; other vaccinations may be advisable. If you are going to the tropics, you should get *Preservation of Personal Health in Warm Climates* (Ross Institute of Tropical Hygiene, Keppel Street, Gower Street, London WC1E 7HT), which gives essential advice. Start taking anti-malaria tablets about a week before you leave and make sure you know about all the necessary precautions once you arrive.

In many Third World countries it is advisable to include a rabies injection in your schedule of jabs for yourself and members of your family. You should also warn children of the perils of cuddling strange animals which may harbour other diseases in addition to the rabies threat.

Check that you have all your documents to hand – up-to-date passport, visas, cheque book, permits, health certificates, letter of appointment. Take spare passport photos – it is probably best for husband and wife to have separate passports – and all your diplomas and references, even birth and marriage certificates. The appetite for documents is well-nigh insatiable in some countries!

Melancholy though it may sound, you should also make some provision for the unthinkable: instructions in the case of death, disablement or catastrophe while you are abroad. The Standard Life Assurance Company issues a useful (free) document called a Personal Estate Planning Questionnaire which is a kind of checklist of all your assets and their values. It also includes a personal financial inventory, which is a record of where and by whom your records are kept: invaluable to leave with your family or executor. The document referred to can be obtained from Standard Life or from Anderson Sinclair & Co, The Leatherhead Institute, High Street, Leatherhead, Surrey KT22 8AH.

If you have a reliable solicitor, you might also consider the possibility of giving him or her power of attorney. This is a simple legal transaction which essentially means that the person having that power can act in your stead. If you need a large sum of money to be sent out to you in a hurry, it is very useful to have a responsible person in the UK whom you can telex for it and who can raise the money from your bank. Likewise, if you have left your house in the hands of managing agents who are not doing their stuff, you need someone on the spot who can sort things out. Giving someone power of attorney obviously implies a high degree of trust, but there are occasions when it could save you the cost of a return fare home.

Settling in

You arrive, with or without your family, and may find you are not met at the airport. This is the first of many irritations which people going out to work for overseas governments may encounter. It does not usually happen with companies. You may have to stay in a hotel or hostel for a considerable time, so make sure in advance who is going to foot the bill. You will need money to meet such contingencies – and to pay for telephones and taxis to and from the airport.

Even if you are lucky enough to move into a house or apartment, you will find a bare larder. This is where any tins or packet foods you brought with you will come in useful. (In Jamaica, the Women's Corona Society branch will provide a loan of a 'basket' of essentials for people waiting for their baggage to be unloaded.)

One early need will be to fix up domestic help, if you want it. It is usually best to engage a house steward and/or any other servants on the personal recommendation of the previous occupant (you may inherit their staff) or a neighbour. Find out from the local labour office what the going rate is and negotiate accordingly, making it quite clear from the start what duties the staff will be expected to perform, eg in the kitchen, washing and housework. Living quarters are usually provided, but find out beforehand whether your steward plans to bring all his family and relatives to stay with him!

Both for insurance purposes and your own peace of mind, make proper security arrangements. Some people, either individually or in groups, employ nightwatchmen; others rely on dogs, or on special locks. The extent of pilfering and burglary in many African countries has grown alarmingly in recent years, so make sure your precautions are fully adequate.

At an early stage it is a good idea to see to all your requirements for banking and for obtaining work and residence permits; income tax coding and the driving licence and test requirements where necessary. Find out also about health products and medical facilities, contributions to provident funds and subscriptions to clubs. Many employers pay for these.

Finally, keep a close eye on the health of young children, particularly on persistent tummy upsets and fevers. It is advisable always to use water you have sterilised yourself, not bottled water of unknown provenance.

Briefing

There is also the question of preparation, other than physical, for your move. Do you know what the country you are going to is like? What facilities are there for shopping, leisure and entertainment? What is the climate like and what clothes will you need? Are there any pitfalls you should know about or any special behavioural dos and don'ts? Nowadays, overseas countries are very sensitive about foreigners understanding that their new patterns of government and economic development are not just pale imitations of the West.

The importance of getting properly briefed beforehand cannot be overestimated. This will not only save you from possible embarrassing situations – say, if you don't know the rules about short skirts and long hair

in Malawi – but will help you decide what you need to take with you and give you some idea of the atmosphere in which you will work and live.

Many commercial firms and recruitment agencies try to ensure that staff are briefed before they are posted overseas, but for some people it may be their first long stay abroad (apart from their annual holiday) and they will be starting from scratch. Others may be old hands who feel more at home in a foreign country than in the UK. But for everyone, wherever they go, getting up-to-date information about conditions will be time well spent. The Centre for International Briefing at Farnham Castle, Surrey, provides intensive residential courses on various countries throughout Africa, the Middle East, Latin America, the Caribbean, Asia, the Pacific and Europe (see page 168).

Another organisation which you will find helpful is the Women's Corona Society, Commonwealth House, 18 Northumberland Avenue, London WC2N 5BJ; tel: 071-839 7908. The Society's *Notes for Newcomers* series on over 100 countries contain all the practical and day-to-day information needed for the preparation for a move, what is available on arrival, medical services, education, recreation facilities and a great deal more (£3 per set). 'Living Overseas' one-day courses are held in London at set dates and also on special request (see page 168). The Society's overseas branches, affiliated societies and groups in 26 countries and personal contacts with members in many other locations provide a welcoming link for newcomers.

Employment Conditions Abroad Ltd is an organisation which has all the answers to your questions about living costs, working conditions, salaries, taxes etc. It does not, however, provide individuals with information or answer personal inquiries. ECA's services are confidential and exclusive to its 600 or so member companies (which include nearly all the major British companies and corporations which employ personnel overseas). These services include detailed reports on the cost of living in 170 countries and employment information with salary comparisons and personal tax for some 75 different countries, although its information base is virtually world wide. It also provides one-day 'cultural awareness' briefing courses which are run for individuals going abroad, and are given to non-members.

Going through diplomatic channels

Expatriates who work for British companies or those from other western countries in the developing or newly industrialised world can usually expect their employers to come to their aid in case of a political upheaval, or even if they get into personal difficulties – deserved or otherwise. Furthermore, they can expect their contracts of employment to be clear-cut and to conform to western norms. Neither of these things is necessarily true if you work for a local employer, as is increasingly the case. The money is often better, but the risk is also greater.

Some guidance on points to watch out for in taking up an appointment with a local employer in the Third World is given in the Employment Conditions Checklist on page 170. Ultimately, though, you have no protection other than your own vigilance and UK diplomatic channels in the country concerned. They are generally very much criticised by expatriates as being ineffectual or indifferent, but the Foreign Office claim this is because their role is not understood. For a start, they cannot intervene in contractual disputes, *unless* a British subject is being discriminated against in comparison with other employees. They can, however, recommend you to a local lawyer who may be able to help you and they maintain carefully vetted lists of reliable legal firms. Best of all, they say, is to write to the British Embassy or consulate nearest to your location before you leave the UK and ask them to put you in touch with someone who can give you a line on your prospective employer. Though UK diplomatic sources do keep track of known bad hats among employers, in the main they prefer such information to go through non-diplomatic channels, for obvious reasons.

The consular service of the Foreign Office are now very sensitive about the criticisms that have been made of them. If you fail to get an answer from the embassy or consulate you have contacted, you should write and complain to the Director of Consular Services at the Foreign Office.

Primarily, of course, the role of British diplomats is to protect British subjects from the consequences of political upheavals. For instance, they got them and their dependants out of Iran and Lebanon, though there seems to have been some, perhaps understandable, disarray in the advice given to expatriates in Kuwait following the Iraqi invasion in August 1990. They were less successful, also, in protecting expatriates from the reprisal arrests in Libya, but any expatriate who goes to a notoriously high-risk place like that must take into account the circumstances there before deciding to accept an appointment. They are also not able to protect you from the consequences if you break the law of the land you are in. At most they can visit you in prison, arrange for you to be properly represented legally and intercede discreetly for an amnesty for you. A UK or multinational company would, in such cases, arrange for you to be flown out on the first available plane, usually with the connivance of the authorities.

Whatever your feelings about the efficacy or otherwise of British diplomatic protection, you should register with the embassy or consulate as soon as possible after you arrive to work in any developing country. This means they can contact you if a sudden emergency arises, whether personal or political. It cannot do any harm; and if you wake up some morning to the sound of gunfire, as has happened to many an expatriate, you may be very glad that you took that precaution.

Personal security

There are overseas countries where crimes against persons, either for gain or to make political points, are a serious hazard. Lebanon is a notorious case in point, and for that reason hardly any expatriates or even visiting businessmen now go there. But there are other places, notably in Africa and Latin America, which qualify as high risk locations in terms of personal safety. There are also corporate or national connections which may be the target of terrorists:

- Anything to do with Israel or South Africa. It is advisable to carry separate passports if you have visas for these countries but also travel to those that are hostile to them.
- Employees of companies associated with pollution, nuclear waste and animal experiments.
- Nationals of countries which have recently been or are currently in serious dispute with countries in which an expatriate is living – or even its allies.

According to the international security consultants, Control Risks, resident expatriates tend to be more at risk in these circumstances than visiting businessmen and, in a recent interview with the author, they spelled out some security precautions that people living in exposed locations should take.

1. Avoid daily routines, like taking the same route to work every day at fixed times.
2. Remove bushes and thick vegetation around the entrance to your house or place of work – they could make a hiding place for criminals and people tend to be least vigilant as they approach familiar places.
3. If you think you are being followed, head immediately for a place where there are as many other people around as possible. Criminals prefer not to strike when there are witnesses about.
4. Report suspicious incidents to the police and encourage your family to be alert for them; for instance, 'students' coming to your door to make unlikely sounding surveys. If you get threatening telephone calls, report these to the police also and try to remember any peculiarities of voice or accent, or any background noise that might give a hint as to where the call was made from.
5. Watch out for abandoned cars in the vicinity. These are sometimes dumped by criminals to test police vigilance.
6. Avoid conspicuous displays of affluence.
7. Try to have a room in your house to which you and your family can retreat if serious danger threatens. It should have good doors with stout locks, and windows which can be secured from the inside but which do not bar escape routes. If possible get professional advice on how to prepare what is called a 'keep' in your house.
8. Using firearms as a form of self-defence is fraught with danger. You

will nearly always be faced with more than one assailant and you have to be prepared to shoot to kill. That in itself is much less easy than it is made to look in the movies; furthermore, in some countries foreigners are always in the wrong in such circumstances.

9. The best form of defence and survival is to rehearse a plan of action in your mind in case you are attacked or in danger – and to stick to it if you can. The thing to avoid above all is panic, because that way you lose control of the situation.

Reading matter

You may never have been much of a book buyer while living in the UK, but many expatriates report that not being able to get hold of books when they want them is an unexpected deprivation, especially in postings where other forms of entertainment, at any rate in English, are hard to come by.

Many places do, of course, have bookshops which stock some English titles, but the selection is often very limited (children's books are particularly hard to get) and prices are always much higher than the UK price shown tantalisingly on the jacket. You can, however, import your own books through the admirable Good Book Guide (91 Great Russell Street, London WC1B 3PS; tel: 071-580 8466). They are a mail order book service with a substantial trade among expatriates all over the world. You can choose your books from their bi-monthly guide, for which there is a modest annual subscription, but they can also get any book in print for you, including paperbacks. There is also a bumper annual edition which comes out around Christmas.

The choices in the guide are accompanied by brief, helpful notes written by outside experts (eg Patrick Moore for astronomy) and the selection of titles is broad, covering both high-brow literature and commercial best sellers. The subject areas are broad too, ranging through all kinds of interests and including children's books. However, the Good Book Guide is not a book club – there is no obligation to buy.

Payment is on a cash with order basis and clear instructions are given with each issue of the guide on how to pay from anywhere in the world.

Home comforts

Sending for goods through mail order catalogues can make up for deficiencies in local shops when working abroad. Although many companies who provide goods by mail order confine their activities to the UK and will not send goods abroad (no doubt because of potential payment problems), there is nothing to stop you making arrangements to get catalogues through UK friends or relatives and ordering through them. Expatriates with young children are reported to find the Mothercare catalogue very useful. Harrods and Fortnum & Mason will send goods

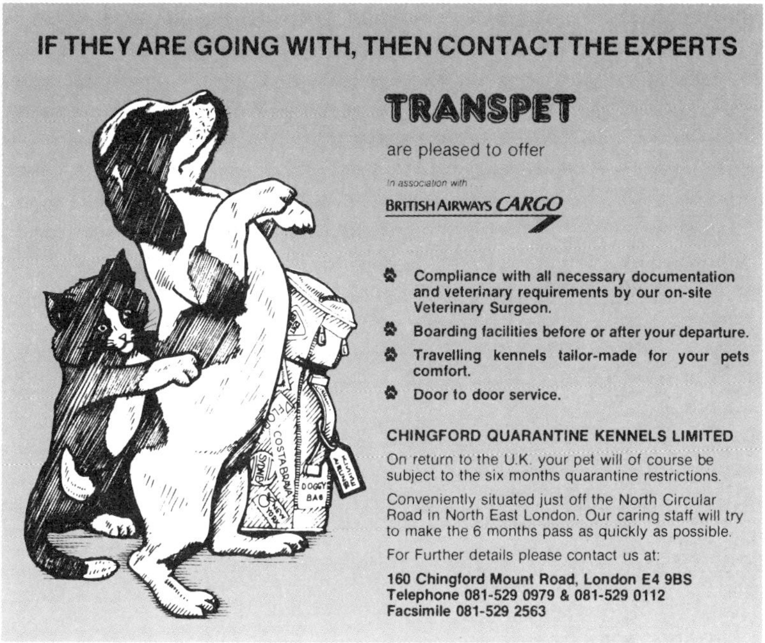

anywhere in the world and you can pay by credit card. Harrods also operate worldwide accounts.

Coming home

Coming back to live in the UK may seem straightforward compared with the complexities of moving out to a job abroad, but if you are to reap the full benefit of a spell as a non-UK resident, planning for your return also requires forethought and preparation.

Take the matter of bringing back personal possessions. Price differentials between countries are no longer as great as they used to be, but there are still quite a number of places where, even taking freight into account, it is worth buying things like electronic or audio-visual equipment – even cars – locally and shipping them back home. In countries which operate exchange controls this may also be a possible way of taking out assets in the form of goods. But beware of the catch: unless you can show that an article has been used and owned for six months, you are liable for import duty – and VAT on top of that. It is no use asking an obliging vendor to provide backdated invoices, because if you are unlucky enough to come under investigation, customs officials check serial numbers as well as documents.

Even with well-used goods, you can be in for unforeseen costs unless you get your timing right. The problem is that possessions shipped back to the UK will not be released until their owner arrives home. You can get a relative to clear them on your behalf, but that person would be liable for provisional duty on their value which is only repaid when you yourself get back. It takes about a fortnight to clear goods through customs anyway, so you will need expert advice at the other end if you are to steer the difficult course between paying warehouse charges in the UK because the goods have arrived too soon, or finding yourself without the basic necessities of life because you have sent them off too late.

The most important thing, though, is that they should actually arrive. The cheapest form of shipping may not be the best. The right course of action is to find a local firm that has a reputable agent in the UK, and to make sure you get door-to-door insurance cover.

You should also notify the letting agents who are looking after your UK property at least three months before your return, so that they can give due notice to tenants.

However, unless you have been sent out by a UK employer, the biggest problem in returning home can be in finding another job. Well before that point you should be sending your CV round to headhunters who are always on the lookout for those with specialist qualifications. If you feel that you may have difficulty placing yourself on the job market on grounds of age or lack of specific skills, it may be worth consulting a career counsellor. They cannot 'find' you a job and you should be wary of those who imply otherwise, but their advice, though not cheap, has been found to be a good investment by many mid-career job seekers.

Chapter 9

Your Children's Education

Corinne Julius
Adviser on Expatriate Concerns

A major consideration for many prospective expatriates is what to do about their children's schooling if they accept a job abroad. Dissatisfaction with the available options often leads to the rejection of overseas job opportunities and is also an underlying factor in the decisions of many expatriates to terminate their contracts early, and when the educational solution proves unsatisfactory it creates an unhappy family atmosphere which has an adverse effect on an employee's work. It is in the interests of the employer to ensure that no serious educational problem arises. Certainly the full implications of an expatriate posting for family life, particularly with regard to education, need to be thought through in some detail. Most options have their disadvantages and most parents experience a degree of anxiety about the correctness of their choice. For example, some children left in boarding school in the UK may have difficulty in adjusting (as may their parents) and some children taken abroad may suffer educationally.

The final choice will be dictated by the age, level of schooling, ability and character of your child, as well as by the kind of education available abroad and the likely duration of your contract. Among the possibilities to be considered are:

1. A boarding school in the UK.
2. A day school in the UK.
3. An expatriate school abroad.
4. A local school abroad.
5. A company school abroad.
6. Home teaching abroad.

Corinne Julius is an adviser on expatriate concerns. She trained as an environmental social psychologist and has worked in Europe, Africa and Latin America. She is an adviser to a wide range of companies and organisations. She worked at the Industrial Society where, in conjunction with the Centre for International Briefing, she originated and ran courses on working and living abroad. She now prepares company briefing material and courses, and writes, lectures and broadcasts on the family aspects of expatriate life.

The decision will be based not only on what you feel is best for your child but also on what you can afford and on the educational policy of your prospective employer.

Most major British and multinational companies provide an educational allowance by paying either all or a major part of the school fees either for a UK boarding school or locally. Some companies in some parts of the world may be more willing to pay towards the cost of boarding school in the UK, particularly for children over 11, but for continental Europe most companies which provide assistance with fees do so by giving a choice between a locally situated fee-paying school and a UK boarding school.

In the Third World, few locally owned companies include an educational allowance in their benefits package; others, including some British companies, state that the salary they offer includes an unspecified sum towards the cost of schooling. Few companies give any help with boarding school fees once the tour abroad has been completed, and it may come as a shock to newly returned expatriates to have to finance school fees from a lower, or more heavily taxed, income.

While a child is in full-time education in the UK (usually up to 18 or 19 years) most companies will pay two return sets of air fares and ancillary travelling expenses per child per annum, or in some instances will pay for one return air fare for the mother and one per child per annum.

Although these financial constraints are important, the major consideration must be the individual child, his or her age, abilities and potential. You will want to select a form of schooling that will help your child to develop in an atmosphere suited to his or her psychological make-up. Although your job abroad may only be for two, three or four years, the effect on your child's education can have long-term implications: for example, transferring your child from one school to another once a GCSE or A level course has begun can spoil your child's chances of getting good results; or, if you choose a school abroad with a curriculum unrelated to that which your child will follow on returning to the UK, your child may find it very hard to make up lost ground.

Schools in the UK

Within the UK there is a considerable choice of schools: private or state, boarding or day, single sex or co-educational.

Boarding schools

Some parents opt for a job abroad largely to finance their children's education in a public school. The costs of boarding school education vary, but you should expect to pay between £1100 and £2150 per term for a preparatory school, somewhere between £1400 and £2900 per term for a senior boys' boarding school, and in the range of £1600–£2600 for a senior

girls' boarding school. These figures do not allow for the cost of uniform, special classes and other incidental extras. Your child may find it relatively easy to make the changeover from state to private school, but you should consider whether at the end of your tour abroad you will be able to afford to keep your child at private school, as adapting back to life in the state system can be difficult for the ex-public school pupil. Allow your child time to adjust to boarding school. If possible, one parent should remain behind to help to settle the child in, and perhaps see the child through to the first half-term break. Most children cope quite well, and it is usually the mothers who are distressed by the separation. Try to make arrangements in advance to cope with any likely emergencies and with half-term holidays. Make it clear to the school how you may be contacted, particularly as communications with developing countries are sometimes rather unreliable.

You should select a school well in advance of moving abroad, as competition for certain schools is intense, but whereas all schools in continental Europe and some elsewhere are geared to accept a pupil at any time of the school year, term, month or even week, there are schools which find it difficult to do so. Choosing a school appropriate to your child's needs (eg catering for your son's musical talents or your daughter's scientific aptitude or near enough for grandparents to get to on visiting days) can be a complicated business, but several organisations exist to help you make your choice.

The Independent Schools Information Service (ISIS) publishes several useful leaflets and booklets and an annual paperback guide, *Choosing Your Independent School*. They are available from: the Independent Schools Information Service, 56 Buckingham Gate, London SW1E 6AG; tel: 071-630 8793/4. ISIS International, at the same address, provides placement and consultancy services for a fee. For a nominal handling charge it also provides a list of six suitable schools prepared to offer places under its clearing house system. They can be consulted by telephone on 071-630 8790 or by telex 28905 MON 2246 G and fax 071-630 5013. Advice can also be sought free of charge from the Gabbitas, Truman & Thring Education Trust, Broughton House, 6, 7 and 8 Sackville Street, London W1X 2BR; tel: 071-734 0161, telex 28707. The Trust will help parents by suggesting two or three suitable schools.

When, with or without the help of these organisations, you have shortlisted several schools, you would be well advised to read each school prospectus carefully and to compose a list of queries before making an appointment to visit each school with your child, preferably during term. While you should inspect the physical facilities of each school, ultimately these are less important than the curriculum followed and the relationship between staff and pupils. Nevertheless, there is no excuse nowadays for lack of hot water, unheated or dirty rooms and classrooms, and inadequate food. A boarding school is a child's 'home' for a major part of the year and it is wrong to attach too little importance to the physical facilities,

especially if they have not changed since the father was at the same school!

You should ask the headteacher about the curriculum, checking whether it is broad-based and includes practical as well as academic subjects. You should ascertain what subjects are taught at GCSE and A level and whether your child will be able to pursue the subjects for which he or she shows an inclination, or which will be necessary for a particular career. Some schools seem to achieve good examination results by concentrating on a narrow syllabus and by early specialisation – not a sound basis for a good education. The staff/student ratio is another important factor and, while your child will benefit from smaller classes at A level standard, there are occasions on which classes can be too small to be stimulating.

Check up on the qualifications and experience of the staff. Ask about exam results obtained and what kind of schools, colleges or careers former pupils have gone on to. Try not to make your list of questions into an interrogation, as some headteachers can be a little touchy, but at the same time you should show that you are concerned about your child's education. Ask to see some classes in progress and try to assess the relationship between staff and pupils. Absolute silence is no indication of a stimulating education. Try to assess whether the children's attention is being held and look for a lively response to questions. In addition you should try to assess the range of non-academic activities offered for children out of study hours. Ultimately the choice must rest with what school is best suited to your child's abilities and interests.

Some parents may not be happy about sending their child to an independent school, or may simply not be able to afford the fees. Some local authorities (mainly in rural areas) run their own boarding schools or have boarding facilities attached to day schools. These schools are normally of a good educational standard, and many of the pupils are likely to have parents in the armed forces and other government agencies employing staff abroad. Children from any education authority are eligible for a place at such a school, but priority is normally given to children from the local area and parents may be asked to pay fees on a scale proportional to their income. Details of schools in a particular area are available from the local education authority.

Parents with children at boarding school are normally anxious about travelling arrangements for their children on visits abroad. A children's escort service (airport to school and vice versa) is available to members of the Women's Corona Society, Commonwealth House, 18 Northumberland Avenue, London WC2N 5BJ; tel: 071-839 7908. Overnight accommodation is provided where necessary. Children's escort services on a commercial basis are also run by Universal Aunts Ltd, PO Box 304, London SW4 0NN (tel: 071-371 9766) who can also arrange short- or long-term accommodation, and Education and Guardian Advisory Services Ltd (EGAS), 11 Seaton Avenue, Mutley, Plymouth PL4 6QJ; tel: 0752 261229.

These organisations will collect your child from school, accompany your child to the airport, and in the event of a delay will look after him or her and provide food and accommodation. They conduct the same service in reverse at the end of the holiday.

What to do with your youngster during half term, weekend leaves and other short holidays can be a worry for the parents of expatriate children. Most boarding schools now require parents to appoint a local guardian and several organisations offer a guardianship scheme. A complete guardian service will include an escort service and arrangements to accommodate your children during exeats, half terms and holidays when your children are unable to join you abroad in a family, where possible with children of similar ages to your own. Guardians may also be responsible for pocket money, the purchase of uniforms, organising treats and liaising with the school on educational matters such as choice of subjects. EGAS, Universal Aunts and Gabbitas, Truman & Thring all offer some form of guardianship arrangement.

Boarding school is suited to the needs of many expatriate children, but to be admitted to the school of your choice your child will normally have to demonstrate his or her ability by sitting the common entrance examination, usually at 13 for boys and at 11, 12 or 13 plus for girls. Each school sets its own entry standard based on common entrance results and is responsible for marking the papers of its own applicants. Some of the more 'academic' schools set their own independent examinations in addition, or as an alternative, to the common entrance.

The common entrance examination for boys has seven compulsory papers: three (English, French and mathematics) are essential qualifying papers, and the others (history, geography, science and religious knowledge) are supporting papers. In addition there are three optional papers: Latin, Greek and additional mathematics. The system for girls is slightly different, and many girls' schools set their own entrance examinations. Clearly, however, the child who has been to a private preparatory school which prepares its pupils for the common entrance is at an advantage.

Selection is supposed to be on the basis of academic ability and a child educated in a more formal school will find it easier than a child who has been taught by less traditional methods. Children entering from abroad or from state schools often experience difficulty with French and mathematics, unless they have had some special tuition. Thus getting your child admitted to the school of your choice will to a large extent depend on the educational choices you have made in the past.

Many secondary age children thoroughly enjoy boarding, particularly as they have ample opportunity to be involved in extra-mural activities ranging from drama to computer studies. While the child of secondary school age is well catered for at boarding school, this type of school is less suitable for a younger child. Few schools now provide boarding facilities for children under eight, as it is recognised that young children separated from their parents may experience emotional deprivation. Boarding

education is not recommended for young children and few parents are willing to be separated from their young ones. Large numbers of current expatriates were educated in the state system, with no tradition of separation from their parents, and fewer and fewer of them wish to be parted from their children, particularly those under 11.

A recent study in Belgium, France, Germany, Holland and Italy of the educational requirements of British expatriate families (undertaken by a consultant for COBISEC) showed that 77.39 per cent of the families consulted preferred not to send their children to a boarding school; when asked about the importance to them of keeping the family together, 84.35 per cent felt strongly that they wanted the children with them, while 8.89 per cent were fairly neutral, and only 8.76 per cent were of a different opinion. The attitude towards boarding was influenced considerably by the age of the father, the majority against boarding being 20 to 1 if the father was younger than 30, 7 to 1 if he was between 30 and 39, 5 to 1 for ages 40 to 49 and 3 to 1 for fathers over 50.

On the other hand, there is no doubt that an uninterrupted education is much more desirable if the family expects to move from one foreign country to another over a period of time; for them the UK boarding school offers the best solution. Indeed, the percentages mentioned above will have been influenced by such families, as some of them are diplomatic families.

A final word of advice: it is essential to choose a boarding school suitable to your child's academic abilities. Some public schools are highly academic and progress at speed through the curriculum, but if your child is unable to stand the pace the result can be catastrophic. A highly academic school cannot guarantee to produce sensational results and it can be a wrong choice. Parents with little experience of public schools need to be warned of this problem.

Day schools

If boarding school is not the answer for your child, you may be able to arrange for your child to attend a day school and to be cared for by family or friends. This is often the best solution for older children who are happy at their present school or who are at a stage in their education – for example, in the run-up to GCSEs – when it would be very disruptive to move schools. Teenagers find it much harder than younger children to adapt to life overseas, not only because of disruption to their education but also because of their friends and interests.

You may find that a sixth-form college provides the education best suited to the talents and potential of 16- to 18-year olds, and this has the added advantage of being available at no cost.

Few employers have developed a realistic policy to cope with the child in day school. Some employers will make a token contribution to the board and lodging costs of your child, but, although this option is much more economic for the company than paying boarding school fees, the allowance is normally rather low. In some instances, where there are no relatives or friends to call on, the mother may have to stay behind to see a youngster through school. Although this has advantages for the child it is likely to have repercussions on the marital relationship and on the financial benefits of the posting.

Education abroad

The availability of suitable schools abroad varies considerably according to the area. Good, and indeed excellent, schools can be found in many continental European cities and, while they are rare in Third World countries, educational solutions are possible in a great many countries world wide.

Apart from British and 'International' Schools abroad, the local national schools (except in France and Germany, for example, where the local education is excellent) may be of a lower standard and more restricted than schooling in the UK. However, there is no doubt that for some children the experience of another system, including another language and a view of another culture, can be valuable. Apart from the importance nowadays of learning a foreign language, children profit from the experience of living abroad and benefit enormously from mixing with children of other nationalities. Nevertheless, there is no doubt that an interrupted education will have an adverse effect on those due shortly to sit for GCSE or A level examinations.

Pre-school

There is rarely any problem in educating children under five. However, in most countries formal education starts at six or seven and this is a handicap for children who will be returning to the UK at the primary level. Nursery schools in Third World countries are few and far between, but there are many kindergartens and playschool groups run by local expatriate wives.

Many expatriate parents of young children are concerned that their children are missing out on a range of educational experiences. The Worldwide Education Service of the PNEU, 10 Barley Mow Passage, Chiswick, London W4 4PH; tel: 081-994 3622 can provide a comprehensive nursery package, 'Learning to Learn'. Consultation with a tutor is included in the price of £350 for a two-year course. The materials may also be used as a basis for group activity. A series of helpful leaflets giving practical advice on the development of the pre-school child can be purchased from the Pre-School Playgroups Association, 61–63 Kings Cross Road, London WC1X 9LL; tel: 071-833 0991. Books for this age group are in short supply overseas. Information and books for pre-school and older children can be obtained from the Good Book Guide, 91 Great Russell Street, London WC1B 3PS; tel: 071-580 8466.

Expatriate schools

Whereas the French spend £130 million annually, the Germans £90 million, the Japanese £65 million and the Swiss £7 million on their schools abroad, Britain provides no financial assistance or encouragement in the creation and running of schools for British expatriates. This means that as expatriate schools have been created entirely without British government support their fees have to be very high, making it impossible for a great many British expatriate families to use them unless the employer pays all or a major part of the fees. Before accepting a job abroad it is essential to ascertain company policy on the payment of school fees.

Because of these financial restrictions expatriate schools vary in quality from the excellent to the poor. British and non-British pupils attend them and this has the advantage of giving a useful experience of different languages and cultures, from which the schools certainly profit.

In the EC, schools which are members of COBISEC (Council of British Independent Schools in the European Communities) follow a British system of education and use English as the language of instruction. Member schools are regularly inspected by HM Inspectors of Schools. Further details are available from the COBISEC Secretariat, c/o The British School of Brussels, Chaussée de Louvain, Tervuren B3080, Belgium; tel: Brussels 767 47 00.

THE BRITISH SCHOOL OF BRUSSELS

A FIVE STAR EDUCATION

* The best of British education in the heart of Europe.
* Traditional values of courtesy, industry and self-discipline developed within a caring atmosphere.
* Small teaching groups from Kindergarten to Sixth Form.
* Excellent facilities and resources - academic, technological, cultural and sporting - plus Learning Support Department.
* Outstanding academic record - choice of 21 'GCSE' and 16 'A' level subjects - 82 % pass rate at 'GCSE' level and 88 % at 'A' level leading to University (including Oxbridge) and Higher Education.

BOARDING

* Arranged with English, French or Dutch speaking families.
* Day to day care in a family atmosphere.
* Private study bedrooms.
* Close to the school.
* Wide range of evening and weekend activities.

FOR TOMORROW'S EUROPEAN

Leuvensesteenweg 19 · 3080 Tervuren · Belgium
Telephone : Brussels 767 47 00

BRITISH INTERNATIONAL SCHOOL
OSLO NORWAY

SCIENTIAE ET VITAE

- Founded 1963
- Independent Co-educational
- British System to 16 years
- University of London G.C.S.E. Examination
- International Baccalaureate 16-18 years
- Situated Junior and Secondary Departments Central Oslo
- Infant Department in country 20 min West
- Well-Equipped Laboratory, Library, Art, Music and Computer Rooms
- Ski-lessons in winter 5-11 years
- Winter Camp One week 11-14 years

For further details contact:-

Headmistress
P.O. Box 7531
Skillebekk
0205 Oslo 2
Tel: 47/2/444916

However, other 'British schools' abroad are not in any way government-approved, but will have a curriculum more or less similar to schools in Britain and, in theory, should equip your child to fit back into a school in the UK. In practice, however, much will depend on the staff, and in particular the headteacher and the strength of the local British community. Unfortunately there are many areas where no British school exists. However, a satisfactory solution can sometimes be found at a so-called 'International' School. These are usually American-type schools with a high percentage of American children. Naturally their main aim is to offer an American curriculum, but many also offer a good British curriculum up to GCSE level. American schools do perhaps present two problems: they do not normally admit children until the age of six (ie a year later than UK schools) and the educational approach and the content of the syllabus are quite different. This is a disadvantage for a child who will ultimately be returning to the UK, particularly at either the lower or upper end of the school. International Schools are independent of any state system and are 'international' in that they offer a curriculum typical of a country other than that in which the school is situated; in practice, it is often largely American in flavour. The pupils at International Schools tend to be drawn from a variety of nationalities and races, usually with a high proportion of American children. Most International Schools in Europe – and increasingly elsewhere – prepare children for the International Baccalauréat which is accepted by most British universities.

Information on schools can be found in *The International Schools Directory*, price £17, available from the European Council of International Schools (ECIS), 21B Lavant Street, Petersfield, Hampshire GU32 2EL; tel: 0730 68244. The directory lists the name, address, telephone number, name of head, enrolment, curriculum and range of fees of all International Schools (arranged geographically) known to it. It is not, however, a guide to academic standards.

Advice from other expatriates with experience of schools in the area to which you are to be posted is also useful, but bear in mind that other people may have standards somewhat different from your own. If you decide to wait to see what is available locally, remember that the schooling may be unsuitable or that the waiting time for admission can in some instances be a full academic year. Either way your child will lose out. However, a great many schools do have space available and they are geared to accept a pupil at virtually any time because of the extreme mobility of families. In many parts of the world, other than continental Europe, the choice of an expatriate secondary school is more limited than for the primary age group.

When trying to establish whether a school will provide a good education for your child, it may be helpful to consider some of the advice given earlier on selecting a boarding school. However, there are several other factors to consider when assessing expatriate schools. First, what is the turnover in staff and students? Might your child be taught in any subject by a

succession of different teachers in one year? Second, does the headteacher have an overall plan for the curriculum? This is particularly important as a child may otherwise be taught the same things over and over again by successive teachers, or one part of the syllabus may bear no relation to another. Ask about the nature of the curriculum and what it covers. Third, what is the proportion of pupils and staff for whom English is not a first language to native English speakers? What kind of English is used – American, British or Nigerian English? Are there special classes for non-English speakers? If not, will non-English speakers hold back your child's progress? What kind of report and record-keeping system is in operation in the school? What help will you be given in helping your child transfer to the next school?

Having completed your inquiries you may find that in some areas the competition for school places is so fierce that unless your employer has influence on the school board, or you have applied for admission well in advance, your child may be on the waiting list for admission to the school for some months. The choice of expatriate secondary school is considerably more limited than for the primary age group. There are far fewer British secondary schools offering GCSE and A levels. Many of the International Schools offer GCSE courses alongside the Baccalauréat and other European examinations. American schools usually cater for their own high school graduation exams.

British schools aim to make it easy for a child to leave a UK school and enter one abroad with a similar curriculum so that it is possible to re-enter the UK system after a few years abroad with the minimum of trouble. Naturally, there are big differences world wide between the quality and organisation of schools abroad and much will depend on the headteacher, the staff and even the strength of the local British community. Many of these schools, especially those in continental Europe, are run as non-profit making foundations controlled by boards composed of leading businessmen, frequently with an important parent input. In many cases senior staff of the companies whose families use the school are on the board, thus ensuring that the facilities made available to their employees are good.

In many schools the turnover of pupils is high owing to the constant movement of personnel by companies. This should not be the case with more than a small percentage of the staff, or there is a risk that there will be a lack of continuity in the curriculum. Schools vary according to the beliefs and practices of their staff, which are reflected in the levels of academic attainment.

Most British schools are not monitored regularly from an inspection point of view by an outside agency but all the member schools of COBISEC are inspected every few years by Her Majesty's Inspectors, following an exclusive arrangement with the Department of Education and Science in London. These inspectors are required by law to inspect state schools in the UK. Their work is of great value to the schools abroad, and is a useful guarantee for parents, especially since schools abroad can

become out of touch with educational developments in the UK, and often it is difficult for teachers to attend training courses and maintain professional contact with Britain.

Many employers allow a family to visit the country before moving there, especially for countries near Britain, and every advantage should be taken of this opportunity. Where it is not suggested a request should be made. Several schools can be visited (it is useful to obtain prospectuses in advance) and meetings can be arranged with other families. This can be done either through the employer or with the help of schools. Most have highly organised parents' groups which are anxious to give advice to families on a wide variety of aspects of the projected move.

It is desirable to link home hunting with the choice of a school so that long bus or car journeys to and from school are avoided, especially for young children. In many countries the British school becomes a sort of community centre and families who have not previously been abroad can find this a great advantage.

ECIS reports that the minimum annual cost for a child beginning half-day kindergarten in Brussels is 80,000 Belgian francs. Full day fees at one school vary from BFr 148,000 in reception class to BFr 446,000 in the final year of secondary school. In New York a typical range is US$6300 (primary) to US$9100 (high school). In Indonesia you would be faced with fees of around US$5700 for an eight-year-old, and in Jeddah annual fees for a 10-year-old would be about 15,450 riyals. In addition to these fees, some schools may require you to buy a bond or share when your child is admitted.

Local national schools

In Europe it is often possible for your child to attend a local national school, though a certain competence in the local language is normally required of older children. Schooling in Europe starts at six, and in France and Germany the approach to education is more formal than in the UK. While the education offered may be excellent, fitting back into a UK school can be difficult.

In other parts of the English-speaking world the transfer to and from systems can also pose problems. For example, in Australia formal schooling starts at six and secondary education at 12 years, effectively a year later than in the UK. The Australian examination system is the matriculation, roughly equivalent in standard to halfway between GCSE and A level. Only students graduating at the very top of the system in each Australian state would be accepted by a British university. Young people educated in the South African system face similar problems, but their difficulties are compounded by the requirement to learn Afrikaans in state schools and by a curriculum shaped by religious and political beliefs.

In the Third World a local school is unlikely to be suitable for your child as the curriculum is usually geared to local needs. Even in countries where

STATE BOARDING SCHOOLS

For whatever reasons, state boarding schools appear to be one of the best kept secrets in boarding education. This is surprising because many of these establishments more than stand comparison with independent schools in academic successes, extra-curricular activity, and a supportive boarding environment. The fact that they are able to offer these features at a fraction of the cost makes state boarding a very attractive financial option.

Simply put, the education element is funded by the state, and parents pay only for the boarding element. While over 50 state schools offer boarding facilities to some extent, there are five or six that are primarily boarding establishments.

Children of parents based overseas are generally eligible if they are nationals and have strong links with the UK – for example a family home in UK or having close relatives living there. Applications can be made directly to the school concerned, which need not be located near to the family home or relatives.

The state education field is changing rapidly with more schools opting out of local authority control by becoming grant-maintained.

The advantage of this is that such schools now have a far greater decision-making role and capability. They are able to be more responsive to the demands for services made upon them by pupils and parents. This means that the day of the Grant-maintained Boarding School has now arrived, offering the advantages of both a state-funded education and a dedicated and well-run organisation.

VALUE AND VALUES FROM THE STATE

When considering boarding schools, it is usual to think only in terms of a private education. But not everyone may agree with the associated elitism, nor be able to afford the normally high fees involved.

There is an alternative however – State Boarding Schools.

Many parents may never have heard of such establishments before, but they have been around for many years and there are now over 50 of them around the country offering boarding in addition to normal day-attendance education.

They work out considerably cheaper than their private counterparts, due primarily to the fact that parents only pay boarding fees – while the State pays for the educational element.

Normally domicile in the UK but working abroad, is sufficient qualification for parents to be able to send their child to a State Boarding School.

One such establishment is The Woodroffe School. Perched high above the pretty Dorset seaside town of Lyme Regis, this day and boarding comprehensive accepts boys and girls between 11-18 years of age.

''In *loco parentis* we seek to provide a well-balanced, secure and caring atmosphere in our three boarding houses,'' said headteacher Paul Vittle. ''Houseparents and their assistants are all experienced and committed staff who fully understand the special needs of young people living away from their parents.''

Boarding fees at The Woodroffe School are £1,250 per term, and consideration is given to all applicants without regard to academic ability – as long as the parents are working abroad or there is a genuine boarding need.

''We insist that a UK-based guardian is appointed as a point of contact,'' continued Paul Vittle, ''and we are always happy to escort and pick up younger children from Heathrow as necessary. At present we have 125 boarders living in three boarding houses set in their own idyllic grounds.''

Further information may be obtained from: Headteacher's Secretary,
The Woodroffe School, Lyme Regis, Dorset DT7 3LS. Telephone: 0297 442232.

English is the common language, teaching at primary level will be carried out in the local language. At secondary level, even where English is the medium of instruction, for many of the pupils and staff it will be a second or even third language. Teaching methods in local Third World schools are normally very traditional and heavily dependent on rote learning. The curriculum is likely to be very restricted and schools are usually poorly equipped. Discipline tends to be harsh by UK standards.

In most developing nations education is highly prized, the pressure for places is intense and expatriates will not be encouraged to consume the scarce educational resources available. If you decide to send your child to a local school it is advisable to supplement the work done at school with extra teaching at home, particularly in the basic subjects.

Perhaps more words of warning are necessary about local schools. Experience shows that parents, especially those who do not speak a foreign language, tend to believe that local education will have many advantages. In many cases this belief is correct, but it will depend enormously on the age and ability of the child to adapt successfully as well as the amount of time to be spent abroad. Learning all subjects in a language to which one is not accustomed can be very frustrating. It should be remembered that parents who do not speak that language will be unable to give encouragement and advice, comment on school work, and help with homework. Certainly for an older child, and especially one working or shortly to work for GCSE examinations, the experience can be undesirable. Links with other families using the school will also prove difficult. However, many families are forced for financial reasons to adopt this solution.

Site schools

The children of expatriates employed on large-scale projects are often catered for in site-based schools set up by one or more companies operating on that site. The quality of the education in such schools will again depend largely on the teaching staff, often the wives of other on-site employees. Many of these schools are very small – rather like the traditional village school with perhaps five to 20 children of different ages and ability taught in one class by one teacher. The curriculum can be limited and, without external monitoring, such schools may offer a rather limited education. Some company schools are assessed by an outside source. This ensures that schools in isolated locations are kept in touch with educational developments and that their standards are satisfactory.

Some companies set up the schools through their personnel departments but others use bodies such as the World-wide Education Service (WES). This organisation provides a complete service: recruiting teachers, providing a core curriculum, specifying all the books and materials, assessing school standards and paying regular advisory visits to the site.

Home teaching

If your inquiries prior to accepting a post reveal that there are no schools, or at least no suitable schools, in the area, you may feel that it will be almost impossible to take your child abroad with you and you may even turn down the job. It is possible, however, to teach your child yourself, although it is a demanding and time-consuming activity.

Some parents are not dismayed by the absence of suitable schools and make the assumption that their children can cope adequately for a year or so without formal schooling. Even if children are learning in an informal way in the new environment it will be very difficult for a child to catch up on the work he or she has missed.

Faced with this situation you may consult the school that your child is currently attending. However, some teachers take a rather dim view of your removing your child from school and going abroad, and your request is likely to incur their disapproval. This is rather short-sighted and, fortunately, many teachers now have a more positive attitude. Your child's teacher may be able to provide you with a list of books that will be in use during the academic year and may offer to have your child back in the classroom if your leave period coincides with the school term. This can be helpful, but it can be very daunting to try to teach your child solely from a list of books and without regular help on teaching problems as they arise.

A more satisfactory method is to teach your child with the help of the World-wide Education Service (WES) of the Parents' National Education Union (PNEU), an educational charity that for over 90 years has been helping expatriates around the world to educate their children.

WES runs a 'home school service' in which a parent, normally the mother, teaches the child under the guidance of WES. If you enrol your child with WES you receive a year's programme of work geared to the age and ability of your child. This also contains detailed advice on when, what and how to teach your child. This printed advice is backed up by the support of a London-based WES tutor who you can contact at any time for help and guidance.

Once a term you are asked to submit to the tutor an assessment of your child's progress and your own as teacher, and to send in a selection of your child's work to be assessed by your tutor. On home leave it is normal for families to call in to see their tutor.

The home school is not a correspondence course, as young children need to be taught how to learn. WES provides all the books and equipment you will need for the year and courses cater for children between the ages of 3 and 11. WES also offers single subject courses for children who attend local expatriate or national schools where a subject is inadequately covered or is not taught at all.

Although children educated through home school can be isolated socially from their peers and miss out on the competitive element of traditional schools, WES claims that children taught by this method are usually in advance of their contemporaries at schools in Britain and, unlike many other expatriate children at school abroad, follow a broadly based curriculum, endorsed by the Department of Education and Science.

Distance learning courses are also available from Mercers College, Ware, Hertfordshire SG12 9BU; tel: 0920 465926. Mercers provide part-time and full-time courses leading to GCSE or O level (overseas) and A level for children of school age, which require relatively little parental guidance. They also offer a reading and numeracy scheme for the younger child.

However, the advantage of home teaching for younger children is that your child's education can be arranged to take account of when your contract starts and of your leave arrangements, whereas children in traditional schools may have to start school halfway through a term and miss weeks of teaching when your leave falls during term. The flexibility of home teaching also allows the course to be studied anywhere in the world, providing the continuity in education lacking for many expatriate children. A fringe benefit of teaching your child is that the whole family enjoys learning together, and mothers who in many parts of the world are prevented by law from taking up paid employment have a worthwhile, absorbing and rewarding occupation.

The problems of home teaching are greater for older children. GCSE and A level correspondence courses are available from the National

Extension College, 18 Brooklands Avenue, Cambridge CB2 2HN; tel: 0223 63465. It is, however, difficult for a teenager to study completely alone, and you are unlikely to have all the knowledge necessary to teach older children specific academic subjects. An additional difficulty with correspondence courses is that they rely on an efficient postal system – a rare commodity in the Third World. Social isolation is another problem, particularly as teenagers find it more upsetting than younger children to pull up their roots, leave their friends and settle in a location where there may be few other young people of their own age and out-of-school activities are somewhat restricted. Relatively few parents keep their older children with them abroad unless there are special medical or psychological reasons.

Special educational problems

If your child suffers from a learning disability you will find the education problem more difficult to solve than the parent of the 'average' child. Few boarding schools in the UK can cope with the special needs of remedial children and even fewer expatriate schools are equipped to help them, although you may get some help from the World-wide Education Service in evolving a special course for your child.

However, a number of schools in continental Europe possess special departments equipped to look after children who are educationally backward owing to the fact that they have moved to several countries in a short space of time.

Further education: universities and polytechnics

A great many parents do not realise the serious implications for the future higher education of their children when the family has lived abroad. A UK resident obtains a free or virtually free higher education as a 'home student' but expatriates working outside the EC run a serious risk of being classified as 'foreign students' for whom the university fees are very high and for whom no financial assistance is available in the UK. This means that many families realise too late that their time spent overseas will make it prohibitively expensive for their children to attend a university or polytechnic.

Students from EC countries are able to have their course fees reimbursed by the UK government, provided they satisfy conditions broadly similar to those which apply to students living in the UK. Families living outside the EC, however, will have to satisfy the authorities that they are 'temporarily' living abroad.

Further details are given in the DES publications, *Grants to Students – A Brief Guide* and *Supplementary Fact Sheet – Awards for Families of UK Citizens Working Overseas*, available from the DES Publications Despatch Centre, Honeypot Lane, Canons Park, Stanmore, Middlesex HA7 1AZ.

Advice is also available from international schools and from the COBISEC Secretariat, c/o The British School of Brussels, Chaussée de Louvain 19, Tervuren, Belgium B3080; tel: Brussels 767 47 00.

Conclusion

Whatever your child's abilities you should make plans as far in advance as possible, especially if you want a place for your child at an expatriate school. Try to consult the personnel officer or recruitment agent dealing with the job offer about schools locally, but bear in mind that they may have a vested interest in reassuring you about the educational facilities available.

If the foreign country is near the UK, ask your employer to give you and your wife a free trip of two or three days to enable you to be better placed to take the necessary decisions on education and housing and to get some idea of local living conditions and costs. In addition, do not forget the problems which might be in store for later higher education.

The major problem for the children of expatriates is the lack of continuity in their education. This is particularly true for children of the career expatriate, transferred from country to country every few years. If this is likely to be your career pattern your child may experience a new school, new teachers, new friends, new books and a new syllabus every two years – hardly the way to ensure a satisfactory education. Try to provide your child with some educational stability, either by arranging suitable boarding school education or an effectively monitored home education course, so that the curriculum and teachers your child encounters will offer continuity, no matter where in the world you are employed.

Whichever form of schooling you choose for your child it will be helpful to provide the school with reports of your child's progress to date and, if possible, the titles of the books he or she has been using and what level he or she has reached. Armed with this information it will be easier for a teacher to help your child to settle down satisfactorily to life in a new school.

Chapter 10

Adjusting to Living and Working Abroad

Corinne Julius
Adviser on Expatriate Concerns

Living and working overseas can be extremely rewarding in personal, financial and career terms. It is also likely to herald a dramatic change of lifestyle. All expatriates, no matter to which country they are posted, have to make some adjustment to life overseas, and all members of an expatriate's family will be affected by the move, whether or not they venture abroad. If, as a married person, you go abroad 'on unaccompanied status', you and your family will have to make a number of adjustments to living separately. There is much to be gained in going abroad as a married couple, but in so doing you may be asking your spouse to give up a job and possible future chances of employment, disrupting your children's education, and removing your family from their normal sources of comfort and support.

Much of the burden of adjustment falls on the expatriate wife, who is required to establish a home in a new country where, in spite of not speaking the language, she has to cope with shortages, difficulties of communication and, above all, different ways of doing things. If your wife and family fail to adjust to the tensions between home and work, it will make it harder for you to concentrate on the job you are there to do. Should you or your family fail to adapt, you may decide to terminate your contract early. Such unscheduled returns to the UK tend to cause considerable disturbance and hardship to all concerned. There is a high turnover rate among expatriates, so before you commit yourself and your family to working abroad it is important to discuss the likely consequences of the move with other members of your family.

In contemplating a move overseas you have probably tried to imagine what it will be like. Most people think about the physical differences; the heat, the humidity, the dirt etc, although they are rarely able to assess how these differences will affect their daily lives. How will working in 90 per cent humidity impair your effectiveness? Could you negotiate an important contract in an atmosphere more suited to the tropical house of your nearest botanical gardens? It is difficult to appreciate how much of the background to daily life is taken for granted; for example, drinking water from a tap, flicking a switch for light, pushing a button for instant entertainment. In the Third World many of these basics of everyday life either do not exist or function irregularly. While it is easy to imagine that things will be different, it is hard to envisage how this affects the quality of daily life and your sense of well being.

But the differences that prove the greatest barrier to adjustment are the ones which cannot be seen and which are not normally even thought about. Despite regional differences in the UK most people have grown up with common experiences and expectations of how the world works. In any given situation, most people have a fairly clear idea of what is expected of them and what they expect of others. However, different nationalities do not necessarily share the same assumptions and expectations about life, or about how other people should behave. In Britain we share a common culture and, on the whole, common beliefs about what is right and proper. Other cultures, though, have quite different underlying values and beliefs, different expectations and concepts of 'normal behaviour'.

Britain is nominally a Christian country, yet although much legislation and ordinary behaviour have their origins in Christian teaching, a relatively small proportion of the population would see Christianity as the driving force of British society. By contrast, in Saudi Arabia, Islam underlies everything. It regulates the legal and political system and the conduct of all aspects of everyday life and is so perceived by its own nationals. It can be difficult to understand how other people operate; it is easy to assume that the motivations of others are understood, while misunderstanding them utterly. In Britain the ground rules of human behaviour can be taken for granted, but overseas they must be questioned and come to terms with. For example, in Malaysia it is not uncommon for expatriates to feel that their local subordinates are disloyal when, instead of discussing some decision with which they disagree, they simply choose to ignore it. Yet to the Malaysian it would be unpardonable to cause a superior to lose face by questioning him in public; far more polite simply to ignore what is considered to be a poor suggestion.

Even unconscious behaviour is open to misinterpretation. For example, in the UK an individual who avoids eye contact would usually be categorised (unconsciously) as shifty or guilty. In Nigeria the same individual would be seen as respectful, because to avoid eye contact with an older person is a mark of respect. The classic example of how the smallest physical cues are subject to different interpretations is one of distance. The British tend to feel comfortable standing two to three feet apart when chatting; the Saudis prefer to stand closer together. A Saudi and a Briton talking to each other will each unconsciously try to establish the distance at which each feels comfortable. The Briton will feel threatened when the Saudi edges nearer and the Saudi will feel rebuffed as the Briton sidles backwards. Neither will appreciate the impact of his unconscious behaviour on the other. This kind of disorientation is experienced constantly by the fledgling expatriate, causing many expatriates to respond aggressively when no hostility was intended.

The expatriate experiences considerable anxiety when faced unknowingly with the loss of minor cues: the familiar signs and symbols which are taken for granted in the UK but are open to different interpretations in the host country. This constant disorientation is unnerving and can cause considerable stress. The syndrome is so common that it has been given a name – culture shock. Doctors have long recognised that changes in normal lifestyle can result in stress, and ultimately physical and mental illness. Change of home, change of friends, change of job, change of lifestyle, loss of or separation from the marital partner may all be experienced by the expatriate, who may be deprived of his traditional means of support and solace. A new job is always stressful, but when the job is in a new (and seemingly hostile) environment, the tensions are even greater. Most expatriates eventually settle down, more or less successfully, but there is a predictable cycle to the adjustment and three main stereotyped responses to adaptation.

First, there is the chauvinistic expatriate, whose response to his or her predicament is to try to create a mini encapsulated UK or 'Little England'. This expatriate's attempts to understand the local way of doing things, or local colleagues, are minimal. Faced with the difficulties of this new environment he retreats from what is perceived as a hostile host country and people. The blame for misunderstandings is never anything to do with him, but is always the fault of the 'stupid' locals. This expatriate falls into a trap of denigrating everything local and idealising everything from home, ultimately provoking real hostility from local counterparts and making a reality of his view of himself alone against the world. Local expatriate clubs are full of this kind of expatriate, who indulges his aggression over more drinks than are good for him.

The chauvinistic expatriate is experiencing culture shock. He is disorientated by his environment and feels constantly at sea. The symptoms of this state are incessant complaining, glorification of the UK, alcoholic over-indulgence, marital difficulties and general aggression. At this stage the expatriate will find it hard to work with local colleagues or clients and will be permanently miserable. It is at this stage also that expatriates tend to terminate their contracts, prior to completion, with major repercussions for their families and their own careers. Fortunately for most expatriates, this is a passing stage and after their first home leave, when the realities of life in Britain are forced upon them, they manage to adapt successfully.

The second, much rarer, response is to 'go bush'. This expatriate eshews the company of his fellow expatriates, and tends to over-idealise all things local. He identifies totally with the host culture, which many of his local colleagues find both patronising and suspect.

The third and probably most appropriate response, but the most difficult to achieve, is that of the 'open-minded expatriate' who, without abandoning his own values, is able to accept the new culture and attempt to understand it. This involves understanding how the host society's values are reflected in everyday behaviour. Decisions are made without the necessity for qualitative judgement. While differences are acknowledged, they are not categorised as better or worse.

If, prior to arriving abroad, you can come to terms with the idea that there are real cultural differences which need to be understood, you will find it much easier to adjust. These cultural differences affect work and home life. Often at work the differences are hidden because on the surface the work to be done is the same as at home, but local colleagues may have different ways of doing business and different attitudes to time and concepts of loyalty. Management styles may differ and motivation and discipline have quite different connotations. For example, many other nationalities find Western haste in business negotiations unpalatable; it is good manners and a useful way of assessing a business associate to chat seemingly inconsequentially before getting down to real negotiations. The Westerner considers it a waste of time, even insulting. In many parts of the world ethnic loyalty is a salient feature of everyday life, and a member of one tribe may be under an obligation to find jobs not only for his extended family, ie sons and daughters of aunts, uncles, cousins, and children of his father's other wives, but also for members of his own ethnic group. Outside the West, age is still considered to bestow authority and seniority, even at work. Social adjustment can also be difficult. Business is often conducted at social events; business entertaining at home may be the norm. Social life can be restricted, as in many areas expatriates make little attempt to get to know local people and mix almost entirely in expatriate circles. This can cause considerable pressure, as any minor upset at work or at home is common knowledge and long remembered.

The married expatriate living alone abroad often has the most difficulty in adjusting, both when he is working and when he is on leave. Single people often feel excluded from much social activity which revolves around the family. Single women suffer especially, as other expatriate women may resent or even fear them, and friendship with local colleagues can be misinterpreted. However, it is often the wives who bear the brunt of culture shock and have the greatest difficulty in adapting. At home most expatriate wives have had their own careers, or run their own homes. Abroad the opportunity of working is usually denied them. Neither do they have sole charge of their homes. While domestic help can be one of the boons of life abroad, dealing with domestic staff can be difficult, especially as many women find their staff taking control and fulfilling their own home-making role. Deprived of work, home role and often identified only by their husband or his job, many women experience a loss of confidence and self-identity, which makes dealing with the everyday difficulties of getting things done in a foreign country, in a foreign language, with none of the usual means of support, even more difficult. Many women go through a cycle of depression or 'boredom syndrome', made worse by the fact that they feel they ought to be enjoying themselves. Thinking the problem through in advance can do much to reduce its potency, especially if a determined attempt is made to try out new interests and activities.

So how can you, as a prospective expatriate, prepare yourself and your family to make the appropriate adjustments? First, you and your family should try to find out as much as possible about the country before you accept the assignment, and preferably before you go to the job interview. Once you have accepted a job offer, some employers will give you a briefing of some description. Relatively few employers seem to appreciate that the cost of staff turnover, in money, time, effort and damage to relationships with their clients, merits an outlay on briefing expatriates and their families prior to their departure.

You will need to know something about your employer, the nature and responsibilities of your job, the terms and conditions of your contract and whether the benefits offered match the prevailing conditions in the country. You will want to learn about the country, its history, geography, climate, politics, economics, form of government, people and religion etc. Much of this basic or factual information will be available in standard publications from the national embassies and tourist offices (although most countries nationally like to present a favourable picture of themselves). There are a number of specialised directories available in public reference libraries containing this information and banks such as the Hong Kong and Shanghai produce factual booklets. A useful series, *Hints for Exporters*, on many countries is available from the Department of Trade and Industry, 1–19 Victoria St, London SW1H 0ET; tel: 071-215 5000. The Women's Corona Society (see page 130) produces its own *Notes for Newcomers*, price £3.50 including postage, which contain background on each country with advice on setting up home.

The financial problems of expatriate life such as personal taxation, insurance etc and other aspects of interest to expatriates are covered in several magazines catering specifically for their needs, available on subscription: the *Expatriate*, published by FMI, 56A Rochester Row, London SW1P 1JU (tel: 071-834 9192); *Expatxtra*, PO Box 300, Jersey, Channel Islands (tel: 0534 36241). (*Expatxtra* is distributed free to employees by some companies.) *Home and Away* is published by Expats International, 29 Lacon Road, East Dulwich, London SE22 9HE (tel: 081-299 4986); *Nexus* is published by Expats Network Ltd, 3rd Floor, Caroline

House, Dingwell Road, Croydon, Surrey CR0 9XF (tel: 081-766 6336); and *Resident Abroad* is available from 102–108 Clerkenwell Road, London EC1M 5SA (tel: 071-251 9321). All these magazines provide some kind of readers' answering service.

However, the most effective way of gaining information is a briefing course. Some companies run their own, others use outside organisations. If your employer will not pay for you to attend a course, it would be worth while paying out of your own pocket. Ideally, husband and wife should both attend, and children can also benefit.

The Women's Corona Society runs one-day 'living overseas' briefing sessions for men and women (price £80 for one, £100 for a couple) and afternoon briefings (£60 for one, £70 for a couple), providing information and advice on living abroad and a one-to-one briefing on the country of your posting. Special briefing courses are also organised – fees for these can be obtained on request.

The Centre for International Briefing at Farnham, founded in 1953, provides intensive residential courses covering practical, up-to-date information on the commercial background, business ethics and techniques, the people and characteristics of more than 135 countries throughout the Middle East, Africa, Asia and the Pacific, Latin America and the Caribbean, and Europe. It is the only full-time residential briefing centre of this type in the United Kingdom. The courses, costing £880 (£840 for accompanying partner) for a four-day regional briefing, are also suitable for home-based managers responsible for their company's international activities. There are also regular courses for North America, and for those returning to the UK.

Special courses can be designed to meet specific requirements of individual companies. Information can be obtained from the Registrar, Farnham Castle, Farnham, Surrey GU9 0AG; tel: 0252 721194, fax 0252 711283.

For expatriates going to Japan or South Korea individually prepared briefing sessions are available from Japan Business Services, The University of Sheffield, Sheffield S10 2TN; tel: 0742 768555. Similarly, individually tailored courses on oriental and African countries can be organised by the External Services Division, School of Oriental and African Studies, Malet Street, London WC1E 7HP; tel: 071-637 2388.

These courses, and some employers, arrange for you to meet recently returned expatriates, and this is particularly useful if you can work out in advance, preferably in the form of a checklist, what you and your family really need to know. Such a checklist can also be useful if you are offered, as occasionally happens for very senior positions, the possibility of a 'look-see' visit to the location in question.

Some expatriates have reported that the British Council are often helpful in terms of overcoming entry shock and giving advice and information about local amenities and activities.

A further aspect of learning about the host country is to master a few basic greetings in the local language. Even when it is not strictly necessary, familiarity with the sound of a language makes everything seem less strange and it is appreciated locally.

Once you arrive overseas you should take it easy, adjusting to climatic changes, as they will affect your physical and subsequently your mental state. Coping with so many new stimuli all at once is overpowering and you will need time to find your bearings. Tiredness and depression make it hard to react positively to your new situation. It is part of the adjustment cycle to feel frustrated and depressed, but if you can make the effort to understand the underlying cultural reasons for your frustration, you will be well on your way to adjusting successfully and enjoying your life abroad. After that you just have to cope with the culture shock of returning to the UK at the end of your tour.

Chapter 11

An Employment Conditions Checklist

Salaries for jobs abroad nearly always sound like the proverbial offer you cannot refuse. Bear in mind, though, that you will incur a whole range of expenses which would not arise if you were employed here. It is vital to consider these expenses and to check whether your remuneration package covers them, either directly or in the form of fringe benefits.

If you are going to work for a reputable international company, it will probably know what the score should be. But if your employer is new to, or inexperienced in, the game of sending people to work abroad (especially if he is a native of the country to which you are going and therefore possibly not aware of expatriates' standards in such matters as housing) here are some of the factors you should look at in assessing how good the offer really is.

To help you arrive at realistic, up-to-date answers, it is worth trying to talk to someone who has recently worked in the country to which you are thinking of going, as well as reading the relevant sections in this book.

1. Is your employer going to meet the cost of travel out from the UK for your family as well as yourself?
2. Is he going to provide accommodation?
   (a) Of what standard?
   (b) How soon will it be available after you arrive?
   (c) Furnished or unfurnished? If furnished, what will be provided in the way of furniture?
3. If accommodation is not free, but there is a subsidy, how is this assessed?
   (a) As an absolute sum? In this case, is it realistic in the light of current prices? If not, is there any provision to adjust it?
   (b) As a proportion of what you will actually have to pay?
4. Who is going to pay for utilities (gas, water, electricity, telephone)?
5. If there is no subsidy and accommodation is not free, are you sure your salary, however grand it sounds, is adequate? Do not accept the job unless you are sure about this.
6. Will the employer subsidise or pay for your and your family's hotel bills for a reasonable period until you find somewhere to live? Is the figure realistic in the light of local hotel prices?

7. Will you be paid a disturbance allowance?
   (a) Is it adequate to cover the cost of shipping (and, possibly, duty at the other end) for as many household and personal effects as you need?
   (b) Will your eventual return to the UK as well as your departure be taken care of?
8. What arrangements will be made
   (a) To cover legal and other fees if you have to sell your UK home?
   (b) To cover the difference, if you have to let your UK home while you are away, between the rental income and such outgoings as insurance, mortgage interest and agent's management fees (see Chapter 6)? Will you be compensated for any legal expenses you incur, eg to get rid of an unsatisfactory tenant?
   (c) To cover the cost of storing household effects?
9. Will you be paid a clothing allowance, bearing in mind that you will need a whole new wardrobe if you are going to a hot country? Will it cover just your clothes, or those of your family as well?
10. Will your employer pay for or subsidise household items (eg air conditioning) that you will need in a hot climate and that are not included in an accommodation package?
11. Will your employer provide/subsidise the cost of domestic servants? If not, is your salary adequate to pay for them yourself, if they are necessary and customary in the country and at the level at which you are being employed?
12. Is a car going to be provided with the job – with or without driver?
13. Will the employer pay for or subsidise club membership and/or entrance fees?
14. Will you be paid an allowance for entertaining?
15. If your children attend UK boarding schools, what arrangements are there for them to join you in the holidays? Will the employer pay for their air fares and if so will this be for every holiday or only some of them? If the latter, can you arrange for them to be looked after at Christmas or Easter?
16. What arrangements are there for your own leaves? Does the employer provide return air fares to the UK or another country of your choice? Will these cover your family? And for how many holidays?
17. Will the employer pay for/subsidise all or any additional insurance premiums you may incur? In some countries (eg Saudi Arabia) it is advisable to insure your servants; or costs of motor vehicle insurance may be inordinately high because of poor roads and low driving standards.
18. If social security payments are higher than in the UK (eg some EC countries) will your employer make up the difference?
19. Will he contribute to your medical expenses if free medical attention is not available or inadequate?

20. If your salary is expressed in sterling would you be protected against loss of local buying power in case of devaluation? Equally, if your salary is in local currency, would it be adjusted for a rise in sterling against that currency?
21. Is your salary in any way index-linked to the cost of living? How often are the effects of inflation taken into account in assessing and adjusting your current level of remuneration?
22. If there are any restrictions on remittances, is your employer prepared to pay a proportion of your salary into a UK bank or that of some other country with a freely negotiable currency? This would not attract UK tax if you are away for more than 12 months.
23. Does your employer contribute towards language teaching for you and/or your wife?
24. Is the legal status of your appointment clear? If you are held to be your employer's sole or principal representative you may be personally liable in some countries for any obligations he incurs, eg the payment of corporate taxes or social security contributions.
25. Have all the terms of the job and the provisions of the renumeration package been confirmed in writing?
26. Are the contract and conditions of employment subject to English law and, if not, do you or your advisers clearly understand how they should be interpreted should a dispute arise?
27. If the job is with a foreign company, particularly a locally based one rather than a multinational, there are a number of points that need special attention.
    (a) Are the duties of the job clearly spelled out in writing in a contract of employment?
    (b) Are the normal working hours laid down? How long will your journey to work be?
    (c) Are all matters affecting pay, including when it is due and whether you will be paid for overtime, clear and in writing?
    (d) If there is a bonus, are the conditions under which it is due unambiguous?
    (e) Are there satisfactory arrangements for sick pay?
    (f) Would there be any restriction on your changing jobs if you got a better offer from another employer or decided to leave? (This one obviously has to be handled with particular tact!)
    (g) Do leave conditions clearly specify whether the leave is home or local? For the former, has the employer unambiguously declared his intention of paying your return air fare and that of your wife/family, if you are married?
    (h) Will legitimate expenses be paid in addition to salary?
    (i) Have you taken any steps to check the bona fides of the prospective employer, eg through a Chamber of Commerce (the local/British Chambers of Commerce to be found in many main centres are much more obliging and better informed than

commercial sections of British embassies), bank, trade association, or Dun & Bradstreet's Business Information Services?

28. Is there a legal obligation on the employer in a high-risk country to continue to pay your salary if you are taken hostage?
29. Will the employer offer you a special training course to cope with the risks involved in living in a very high-risk country?

Part 2
Country Surveys

Some International Comparisons

Table 1 *Living costs in principal expatriate locations*

Taking the cost of living in the UK as 100, the following table illustrates the differences in the cost of living between a number of major expatriate locations. The statistics exclude housing costs.

Japan – Tokyo	134.4
Norway – Oslo	119.2
Finland – Helsinki	112.0
Switzerland – Zurich	108.8
France – Paris	105.6
Austria – Vienna	102.4
UK – London	100.0
Denmark – Copenhagen	97.6
Italy – Milan	97.6
Spain – Madrid	91.2
Germany – Frankfurt	89.6
Belgium – Brussels	85.6
Ireland – Dublin	84.8
Netherlands – Amsterdam	81.6
USA – New York	80.0
Australia – Sydney	78.4
Greece – Athens	69.6
Portugal – Lisbon	64.8
South Africa – Johannesburg	51.2

Source: Business International Ltd

Table 2 *Extracts from ECA's inter-country executive remuneration comparisons 1990*

Country	*Gross pay* £	*Net after tax** £	*What that buys* £	*Gross pay* £	*Net after tax** £	*What that buys* £	*Gross pay* £	*Net after tax** £	*What that buys* £
UK	22,915	17,967	17,967	31,619	23,566	23,566	44,170	31,096	31,096
Australia	23,731	16,432	16,975	31,329	19,942	20,601	41,883	25,404	26,243
Belgium	33,858	23,915	24,578	47,286	30,535	31,382	68,780	38,887	39,966
Canada	27,052	19,060	21,882	36,224	24,009	27,564	49,960	31,179	35,796
Denmark	32,558	17,549	13,625	44,501	21,264	16,509	61,976	26,699	20,729
France	29,317	23,389	22,840	40,650	30,763	30,041	58,127	42,044	41,058
Germany (W)	37,007	26,438	26,544	52,505	36,626	36,773	75,383	49,729	49,928
Greece	15,265	11,033	12,904	22,121	15,084	17,642	30,242	19,730	23,076
Irish Republic	24,427	16,051	16,115	32,018	19,543	19,621	42,871	24,535	24,633
Italy	30,032	20,838	19,998	43,973	28,716	27,558	63,350	39,509	37,916
Netherlands	28,805	18,853	21,351	40,575	23,561	26,682	55,812	29,655	33,584
Norway	24,722	19,058	15,137	32,550	22,749	18,069	43,073	27,710	22,009
South Africa	14,611	10,600	16,307	20,554	13,950	21,461	28,516	18,408	28,320
Spain	29,065	21,307	21,264	40,602	28,004	27,948	58,818	36,642	36,568
Sweden	27,329	15,637	12,661	36,521	18,674	15,120	48,519	22,640	18,331
Switzerland	47,015	37,795	29,853	64,489	48,540	38,341	89,337	63,063	49,812
USA	32,072	23,038	29,347	44,406	30,602	38,983	61,148	40,864	52,056

* After employee social security contributions and tax at the rates prevailing in September 1990.

The table below is an approximate guide to salary weightings in various expatriate posts to compensate for hardship factors. These include political and security risks, climate, health, cultural facilities, the availability of housing and education and the extent to which goods and services (including alcohol) can readily be obtained.

Table 3 *Classification of countries according to their relative hardship*

A (0–50 points)	B (55–85 points)	C (90–125 points)	D (130–165 points)	E (170–205 points)	F (210+ points)
Australia/Melbourne, Sydney	Bahamas/Nassau	Argentina/Buenos Aires	Algeria/Algiers	Bangladesh/Dhaka	
Austria/Vienna	Bahrain/Manama	Botswana/Gaborone	Cameroon/Douala	China/Beijing	
Barbados/Bridgetown	Brunei/Bandar SB	Brazil/Rio, Sao Paulo	Colombia/Bogota	Ethiopia/Addis Ababa	
Belgium/Brussels	Germany (E)/(E) Berlin	Bulgaria/Sofia	Cuba/Havana	Ghana/Accra	
Bermuda/Hamilton	Hong Kong	Chile/Santiago	Egypt/Cairo	Iraq/Baghdad	
Canada/Montreal, Toronto	Israel/Tel Aviv	Costa Rica/San Jose	Guatemala/G City	Libya/Tripoli	
Cyprus/Nicosia	Japan/Tokyo	Czechoslovakia/Prague	India/N Delhi, Bombay	Mozambique/Maputo	
Denmark/Copenhagen	Morocco/Rabat	Ecuador/Quito	Indonesia/Jakarta	Nepal/Kathmandu	
Finland/Helsinki	Neth Antilles/Willemstad	Fiji/Suva	Ivory Coast/Abidjan	Nigeria/Lagos	
France/Paris	Oman/Muscat	Hungary/Budapest	Korea Rep/Seoul	Pakistan/Karachi	
Germany (W)/Dusseldorf, Frankfurt	Puerto Rico/San Juan	Jamaica/Kingston	Madagascar/Antananarivo	Sierra Leone/Freetown	
Greece/Athens	St Lucia/Castries	Jordan/Amman	Nicaragua/Managua	Sudan/Khartoum	
Irish Republic/Dublin	Singapore	Kenya/Nairobi	PNG/Port Moresby	Tanzania/Dar es Salaam	
Italy/Rome, Milan	S Africa/Johannesburg	Kuwait/Kuwait City	Peru/Lima	Uganda/Kampala	
Luxembourg/L City	UAE/Dubai	Lesotho/Maseru	Poland/Warsaw	Yemen AR/Sana'a	
Netherlands/Amsterdam		Malawi/Blantyre, Lilongwe	Romania/Bucharest		
New Zealand/Wellington, Auckland		Malaysia/Kuala Lumpur	Saudi Arabia/Jeddah, Riyadh		
Norway/Oslo		Mexico/Mexico City	Senegal/Dakar		
Portugal/Lisbon		Panama/Panama City	Sri Lanka/Colombo		
Spain/Madrid		Philippines/Manila	Surinam/Paramaribo		
Sweden/Stockholm		Qatar/Doha	USSR/Moscow		
Switzerland/Geneva, Zurich		Swaziland/Mbabane	Zambia/Lusaka		
USA/New York		Taiwan/Taipei			
		Thailand/Bangkok			
		Trinidad/Port of Spain			
		Tunisia/Tunis			
		Turkey/Ankara, Istanbul			
		UAE/Abu Dhabi			
		Uruguay/Montevideo			
		Venezuela/Caracas			
		Yugoslavia/Belgrade			
		Zimbabwe/Harare			

Table 4 *World value of the pound (at 30 April 1991)**

	Local unit of currency	*Value of £ sterling*
Australia	Australian $	2.14
Bahrain	Dinar	0.62
Belgium	Belgian franc	61.10
Brunei	Brunei $	2.97
Canada	Canadian $	1.93
China	Yuan	8.93
Denmark	Danish kroner	11.35
Egypt	Egyptian £	5.54
France	French franc	10.00
Germany	Deutschmark	2.96
Greece	Drachma	319.80
Hong Kong	Hong Kong $	13.04
Italy	Lira	2190.25
Japan	Yen	230.75
Kenya	Kenya shilling	46.32
Kuwait	Kuwait dinar	unavailable
Libya	Libyan dinar	0.49
Luxembourg	Lux franc	61.10
Malaysia	Ringgit	4.62
Mexico	Mexican peso	5004.05
Netherlands	Guilder	3.34
New Zealand	NZ $	2.86
Nigeria	Naira	15.83
Norway	Norwegian krone	11.56
Oman	Rial Omani	0.64
Papua New Guinea	Kina	1.59
Portugal	Escudo	256.10
Qatar	Qatar riyal	6.07
Saudi Arabia	Riyal	6.25
Singapore	Singapore $	2.97
South Africa	Rand (financial rate)	4.70
Spain	Peseta	182.35
Sweden	Swedish krona	10.55
Switzerland	Swiss franc	2.48
United Arab Emirates	UAE dirham	6.12
United States of America	US $	1.67
Zambia	Kwacha	93.40
Zimbabwe	Zimbabwe $	5.03

* Exchange rates are determined largely by interest rates. Fluctuations in exchange rates – both of sterling and of other currencies (if you are paid in a foreign currency) – are crucial to your *real* earning power, so keep in touch with changes. Your bank manager or financial adviser will be able to offer assistance in this area.

Europe

The following section gives information about EC member states – Belgium, Denmark, France, West Germany, Greece, Italy, Luxembourg, The Netherlands, Portugal and Spain. It does not cover the UK or the Republic of Ireland. There are also sections on Switzerland and the Scandinavian countries, which are not EC members but have considerable influence on the European scene.

The European Community

Although 1992 has been publicised as the date for completion of the single market, its actual deadline is 1 January 1993. By then, all obstacles to the free movement of goods, services, people and capital within the EC will have been removed.

Debates continue between Britain and its partners about further steps towards integration – in particular, about the adoption of a single currency and setting up a European Central Bank. But whatever the pace of change, it seems almost certain that the EC will eventually adopt a common currency and that progress towards greater economic and political integration will continue.

In terms of employment, 1991 sees a very important change – the right of any professional from one EC state to become a member of an equivalent profession in another state without having to requalify (subject to a few safeguards). The rule applies to all professions to which access is in some way restricted by the state (or by Royal Charter in the UK) and which require at least three years' university-level education and appropriate job-based training. This should create many more opportunities for a whole range of professionals to work, set up businesses and offer services in other parts of the Community. Further details are given in the Department of Trade and Industry booklet, 'Europe – Open for Professions', available from DTI 1992 Hotline (tel 081-200 1992)

Other points that are worth noting are:

Passports and permits. A British citizen can work in EC countries without a work permit; all he or she needs is a valid passport showing that the holder is a British citizen. A visitor's permit is not enough and the applicant needs a residence permit, which should be obtained as soon as possible from the local authorities. This normally requires an employment certificate or letter from the employer, as well as production of a valid British passport.

Job opportunities. For details of job prospects and conditions, see the following sections on various European countries. In general, skilled or highly skilled workers and those with professional qualifications or particular technical expertise will be able to find employment, but priority will usually be given to qualified nationals. The best opportunities are with multinationals or with British firms operating in other European countries (lists can usually be obtained from the British embassy in that country, although embassies *cannot* help people to find jobs). Details of job opportunities can be obtained from the local Jobcentre or Department of Employment office, which keep in touch with the employment centres of EC countries about vacancies. Before you accept a job, it is important to know exactly what to expect in the way of terms and conditions. A useful leaflet entitled *Working Abroad* is available from Jobcentres and this leaflet provides a helpful checklist.

Unemployment benefit. If you are unemployed in the UK, you can draw unemployment benefit from the UK for up the three months while looking for a job in the EC. However, in view of the fact that this is nowhere near enough to live on while job-hunting, people who decide to prospect should make sure they have enough money to keep themselves during this period, or to get home at the end.

Driving licences. Since January 1983 anyone moving from one EC country to live in another has been able to exchange his or her driving licence for that of the new country of residence without having to take another driving test. Newly qualified drivers are now issued with a rose-coloured Community driving licence.

Belgium

Background

Belgium has about 10 million inhabitants, who live in an area of 12,000 square miles – one of the world's highest densities of population. Most of the country is flat, highly cultivated and built over. In the south, towards Luxembourg, are the rolling hills and forests of the Ardennes.

The country is divided into French-speaking Wallonia and Flemish-speaking Flanders. These are basically separate peoples with different languages and cultures. Belgian society has long been divided by clashes between these groups. However, in recent years constitutional reforms, introducing a high level of regional autonomy, have given the Flemish-speaking population a greater degree of control over its own affairs and have taken much of the heat out of the Francophone-Flemish debate.

Brussels has nearly a million inhabitants, and other important cities are Antwerp (490,000), Ghent, Liège and Charleroi; these five cities account for one-fifth of the total population. The majority are Roman Catholic.

Belgium is a constitutional monarchy, with a two-chamber Parliament. Since the second world war its governments have been coalitions.

Exchange rate: Belgian franc (financial rate) 61.10 = £1.

The economy

During the later part of the 1980s Belgium attracted wealth and investment out of all proportion to its size. At the crossroads of Europe, and host to the main EC institutions, Belgium has been well placed to attract investors. One of the most obvious signs of this has been extensive commercial and residential property development in Brussels.

Old industries have been restructured and small, hi-tech firms have been encouraged. The service sector now accounts for around 70 per cent of national income, with financial services making a major contribution.

The economy is now buoyant, although some long-standing problems – such as the burden of public debt left over from the 70s and early 80s – remain. However, inflation is under control and Belgium has succeeded in reducing unemployment more rapidly than any other EC member state. Most of the leading economic indicators look good, and by 1992 Belgium will be well placed to exploit its central position as the 'capital' of Europe.

Personal finance

The level of managerial and executive salaries is higher than in the UK. An upper-middle ranked executive could expect to earn at least £50,000 a year. Increasingly, a company car would be provided in addition to the basic salary.

Taxation

Income tax is levied at a progressive rate on all annual incomes. The rate is graduated and is considerably higher than in the UK. For instance, on a salary of BFr3m, a married man with two children, contributing to the Belgian Social Security Fund, would receive net take-home pay of just over BFr1.5m. Tax reliefs are given in the form of reductions for dependants and allowances for business expenses. However, there are very substantial tax concessions available to expatriates who are not permanently resident in Belgium.

Working conditions

EC nationals with valid passports are free to come and go, but they must register at the local town hall within one week of arrival. A temporary identity card, valid for three months, will be issued and can be extended for another three months if you have a job. After this initial period of six months, a regular identity card can be obtained.

If you are looking for work in Brussels, a knowledge of French is essential and of Dutch an advantage. You can advertise in the Belgian papers or seek out the local offices of *Office National de l'Emploi* (38 rue de l'Escalier, 1000 Brussels). Belgium is so near that visits from the UK to hunt for a job are easily made. There may be opportunities with international organisations, such as EC, NATO and SHAPE which have headquarters in Brussels. But the best hope is probably with Belgian-based British firms in areas such as insurance, banking, management consultancy, public relations and construction. The Belgian Embassy, 103 Eaton Square, London SW1W 9AB, issues a useful leaflet called *Memorandum for British Subjects Wishing to Settle in Brussels*, but offers no help in finding a job.

Living conditions

The enlargement of the EC has inevitably increased the cost of living in Brussels, though in most respects it is cheaper than Paris or Bonn. Food is somewhat dearer than in Britain: here are some examples:

	BFr
Bread (loaf 1 kg)	62
Tea bags (250 gm)	167
Steak (1 kg)	527
Chicken (1 kg)	147
Eggs (12)	69
Butter (250 gm)	52
Sugar (1 kg)	38
Milk (1 litre)	32
Potatoes (1 kg)	20
Instant coffee (250 gm)	332

Beer (the Belgians are great beer drinkers) is reasonably cheap and a 75 cl bottle of wine can be bought for BFr160–220. A bottle of Scotch costs upwards of BFr450, and a packet of cigarettes about BFr70.

Cars of all makes can be bought easily and are a good deal cheaper than in the UK. A 1600 cc car would cost about BFr45,000. Petrol costs about the same as in the UK.

Though the influx of diplomats and businessmen has tended to push prices up in Brussels, there is no serious shortage of accommodation. Most people find houses or flats through agents or press advertisements. Rents are reasonable in comparison with London. A deposit against which dilapidations will be set is usually demanded by the landlord. There is relief of customs duty on 'removal' goods provided they have been used and are for personal use.

Household goods are a little more expensive than in the UK. Electric current is AC, 220V, 50 cycles (in a few localities, 110V). Clothes are dearer than in the UK, so it is as well to shop at home.

Distances are so short that most travel is done by train or car. Rail services are efficient and there is a good network of roads and autoroutes, with ring roads round the large towns. Urban transport in Brussels is adequate, but buses and trams get very crowded.

The health services are part of the general social security system, which is a very comprehensive one. Everyone has to belong to a *mutualité* (sickness insurance fund). You have to pay for a visit to a doctor and for prescriptions but 70 to 80 per cent of the cost may be reimbursed by the *mutualité*. Many hospitals and clinics are run by different denominational groups. People who are currently insured under the UK social security scheme should obtain the necessary forms for reciprocal treatment from the DSS before leaving the UK.

Education, both primary and secondary, is free and compulsory for all Belgian children between 6 and 16. As well as the state schools there are many Catholic and independent schools in Brussels and elsewhere. There are a number of International Schools. The International School of Brussels takes in children from 3 to 18 in kindergarten, elementary and secondary schools and has over 1000 boys and girls, the majority being from the USA. There is a smaller International School at Antwerp. The British School of Brussels, which follows a UK curriculum, has over 1000 students aged 3 to 18. The majority of pupils transfer from British schools (or vice-versa), but the school is genuinely international, with pupils from many other nations. There is also a school in Antwerp offering a British curriculum. The small English Primary School in Brussels caters for children from 3 to 12. The St John's English-speaking school at Waterloo, near Brussels, caters for children between 3 and 19 and takes in boarders.

There are French and Dutch speaking 'free' universities at Leuven and Louvain-la-Neuve, state universities at Ghent and Liège and university centres at Antwerp, Mons and Diepenbeek. Education is free and standards are high.

The Belgians are a reserved and cautious people. A knowledge of French is essential in Brussels and Wallonia, but in Flanders many people speak English (or German). The business community tends to be formal and punctilious.

There are plenty of cinemas, theatres, and places of entertainment in Brussels, though there is no night life on the scale of, say, Paris. Coastal resorts like Blankenburg offer golf, sailing and tennis, as well as casinos and night clubs. The country round Brussels itself is dull, but attractive towns like Bruges and Ghent are within easy reach and the Ardennes is a good place for holidays.

Shopping and business hours are usually 8.00 or 9.00 am to midday and 2.00 pm to 5.00 or 6.00 pm. Most establishments take a fairly long break for lunch.

There is a sizeable British community in Brussels, including staff of the EC, NATO and many international organisations which employ English-speaking personnel. There are a number of British shops (eg Marks and Spencer and W H Smith) and some British pubs.

The closeness to the UK and cosmopolitan atmosphere make Brussels an attractive city to most British people. Despite its central role in the administration of the EC, which has produced a great influx of administrators, diplomats, translators and their ancillary staff, prices have not rocketed, accommodation is still available and reasonably priced, and Brussels is still less expensive than, for example, Paris, Dusseldorf and Geneva.

Denmark

Background

Denmark is an archipelago, with numerous islands linked by road, rail and ferry. The capital, Copenhagen, is situated on Zeeland, the largest island, and contains about one-fifth of the total population of just over 5 million. Greenland and the Faroe islands are semi-autonomous.

The Danes have a well-earned reputation as a hardy, industrious, democratic and liberty-loving people. They pay high taxes, but welfare benefits are generous and public services efficient. Denmark was the first country to appoint an Ombudsman. It is the only one of the Scandinavian countries to belong to the EC. It also belongs to NATO.

Denmark is a constitutional monarchy but the monarch has no political power. The single chamber Parliament (*Folketing*) of 179 seats is elected on the basis of proportional representation. The government is a conservative/liberal coalition.

Exchange rate: Danish Kroner 11.35 = £1.

The economy

Demark is traditionally an agricultural country and nearly three-quarters of its land is still used for farming and horticulture. Though reduced in area since the end of the war, agriculture is highly efficient and food and dairy produce account for about one-fifth of total exports. The UK is a long-established market: Danish bacon and butter are found on many British breakfast tables. There has been a marked shift of resources towards manufacturing, the most important industries being food processing, metal and electrical engineering, transport equipment, textiles and clothing, paper, furniture, glass and brewing. Firms are small scale; about two out of three manufacturers employ fewer than 50 workers. Standards of design, styling and craftsmanship are high.

Personal finance

The level of management salaries is appreciably higher than in the UK but deductions for tax and social security are higher too. On a salary of Kr 350,000, for example, almost half would be deducted in taxes and social security contributions.

Income tax is payable both to central and local government. It is levied on a PAYE basis and imposed at a percentage rate. Local councils fix their own rate of tax which is assessed on the same taxable income as for central government tax. There is a dividend tax, a capital or wealth tax on assets over DKr1,424,500 and a small church tax. Income tax is subject to the usual range of deductions. Expatriate workers are allowed a special tax concession provided they are not working in Denmark for more than three years and are paid by a foreign employer.

Working conditions

It is not easy for foreigners to find work in Denmark, despite the free movement of labour provisions of the EC. Most Danes speak English. Rented housing is scarce and people are advised to try to arrange accommodation beforehand. Foreigners must apply for a *residence permit* to stay in Denmark for more than three months. Applications for residence permits should be made to the Danish Embassy in London. If you are in Denmark and have a visa or a residence permit which has expired, you may have the permit renewed in Denmark. You should apply to the local police (in Copenhagen to the Aliens' Division of the Police, Anker Heegaardsgade 5). EC nationals do not require work permits, but it is difficult to find employment unless you have a good knowledge of Danish.

The Danes have a good record of stable labour relations and cooperation between employers and unions. They have one of the lowest strike records in Europe.

Many firms provide medical services. The system of social security provides full cover against sickness, accident, retirement and other contingencies.

Living conditions

Denmark's per capita income and standard of living are among the highest in the EC, but living costs are also high. The cost of living is particularly high in Copenhagen and the table below gives a selection of food prices there in 1990.

	DKr
Steak (1 kg)	173
Chicken (1 kg)	34
Eggs (12)	19
Butter (1 kg)	43
Sugar (1 kg)	11
Milk (1 litre)	6
Potatoes (1 kg)	9
Instant coffee (250 gm)	70

Wine is cheaper than in the UK, but a bottle of Scotch whisky would cost over DKr200. Cigarettes are expensive. Clothes are dearer than in the UK and so are most consumer goods, so it is not advisable to buy locally.

Accommodation is relatively inexpensive but difficult to find. An unfurnished two-bedroomed flat in Copenhagen would cost DKr3500 to 5000 a month. It is very hard to find apartments in central Copenhagen at all, but houses can be rented 15 to 20 kms outside the city; a modern three-bedroomed bouse in North Zeeland would cost around DKr10,000 per month furnished. Unfurnished flats and houses are slightly cheaper. In addition, DKr600 to DKr1000 per month should be allowed for electricity and heating. That is an average figure. Heating oil costs over DKr4000 a month at winter consumption rates. As far as owner-occupied accommodation is concerned, Denmark has experienced a slump in house prices and, as in the UK, housing is very much a buyers' market.

Copenhagen has an international airport (Kastrup) with frequent flights to European cities and to internal centres. Rail transport is efficient and reasonably priced – there are numerous concessions, eg for a man and woman travelling together, not necessarily husband and wife.

Driving is on the right, and the roads are reasonably good. As in other Nordic countries, there are strict regulations against drinking and driving.

The standard of medical treatment in Denmark is high. Health services have recently been remodelled on British NHS lines, with the emphasis on group practice and preventive medicine. Most treatment is free.

Education is compulsory from the ages of 7 to 17. English is taught in all schools. In Copenhagen there is an International Junior School for 4–14 year-olds and an International School for 15–19 year-olds, with an international/US curriculum; Rygaards School at Hellerup offers a UK or US curriculum for the age range 5–16. The Education Act of 1975 reformed the existing system and placed greater emphasis on teacher/parent relationships. The Danes pay great attention to adult education and vocational training. There are three main universities and two university centres, and a number of higher technical and scientific institutions.

The Danes are extremely hospitable, and many speak excellent English. They are more sophisticated and informal than the Swedes. Their liquor laws allow drinking at most hours. Beer and schnapps (akvavit) are the most popular drinks, often taken with open sandwiches (smorrebrod).

Copenhagen has a reputation of being one of the most permissive cities in Europe. It is also one of the most beautiful and lively, with facilities for shopping and entertainment, and a large number of restaurants, theatres, cinemas and concert halls, as well as open-air activities. The Tivoli amusement park in Copenhagen is a 'must' for visitors.

France

Background

With a population of 55 million and an area of 213,000 square miles, France is at the heart of Europe. Its neighbours are Belgium, Luxembourg, Germany, Italy, Switzerland and Spain; the Rhine, the Channel, the Atlantic, the Pyrenees, the Mediterranean and the Alps are its natural boundaries.

France's population, which declined in the inter-war years, has since grown rapidly as a result of a high post-war birthrate and immigration. However, this growth has now levelled off. Greater Paris has the largest concentration of population, with just over 10 million inhabitants, of whom more than 2 million live in Paris itself. Other important cities are Marseilles (1 million) and Lyons (1.2 million), Lille, Bordeaux, Nantes, Nice, Toulouse, Grenoble, Rouen and Strasbourg.

The French are intensely patriotic and proud of the country, its language, culture and achievements. There are wide inter-regional variations and differences in attitude and character. The inhabitants of Brittany, Provence, Corsica, French Catalonia and the Basque region are not at all like the Parisians; many have their own language and support federalism or even separatism.

France is a democratic republic with a written constitution. The present minority socialist government under the presidency of François Mitterrand and the more recent premiership of Edith Cresson is well established and has achieved a record of success in managing the economy.

Exchange rate: Fr10.00 = £1.

The economy

After years of steady anti-inflation policy, prospects for the French economy are encouraging, even though the Gulf War will inevitably have some impact on growth and inflation. Several years of rapid economic growth, low inflation and a strong franc have left France well-placed to weather a period of downturn or even a full-blown economic crisis.

France is well off for natural resources, with coal, natural gas, iron ore, potash, bauxite and fluorspar. However, despite an ambitious nuclear power programme, a steep rise in the oil price could still wreak havoc.

Trade is primarily with EC countries, headed by Germany, with the UK as its third largest export market. Principal exports are food, wine and dairy produce, petroleum products, metals, steels, chemicals, cars, non-ferrous metals, and a wide range of consumer goods. Fashion and luxury items, and tourism, are also important sources of revenue.

Industry is fairly evenly dispersed, though Greater Paris has the largest and most heterogeneous concentration and some areas, such as Brittany and the south-west, are under-industrialised. Textiles, coal and steel have declined but new technologically advanced and science-based industries, such as chemicals, electronics and nuclear engineering, have been developed particularly in the Lyons-Grenoble region.

Agriculture, largely dominated by small family farms, is still of major importance and influence, even though the numbers working on the land have steadily fallen and there has been a drift to the towns and cities.

Unemployment is around 9 per cent, but this relatively high figure is partly attributable to demographic factors: there are greater numbers of young entrants to the labour market than in neighbouring EC countries.

Personal finance

The level of managerial salaries is around 20 to 40 per cent higher than in the UK. Employers' contributions to social security are among the highest in Europe, but direct taxation is relatively low. Secretarial salaries are much the same as in the UK. On a salary of Fr 400,000, a married taxpayer with no children would pay just under 30 per cent in tax and social security contributions.

Taxation

The French system seems immensely complicated, so it is advisable to check with your employer or the income tax people exactly what your liabilities are.

British subjects living in France are liable to the personal income tax (*impôt sur le revenu*) as are the French. There is a double taxation agreement between the UK and France.

Income tax is assessed on actual income, derived from all sources, eg salaries, dividends, profits, rents and also certain capital gains.

The global taxable income is charged at progressive rates starting at 5 per cent and rising to a maximum of 56.8 per cent.

For people with dependants, there is a complicated points system of relief. There is also a range of allowances and exemptions. The French Embassy may be able to offer assistance or put you in touch with the income tax inspectorate in France.

Working conditions

British citizens with valid passports endorsed 'right of abode' or with passports issued since 1 January 1983 where the holder is described as a 'British citizen', do not require work permits but do need *residence permits*, obtainable from the local police. They can be difficult to get unless one already has a job arranged. The 39-hour week is standard. French workers are entitled by law to five weeks' annual leave. There are 11 public holidays. Many firms and offices are shut for much of August.

Most wages are fixed by collective bargaining at national level. Equal pay is theoretically obligatory – the gap between men's and women's pay is narrower than in most EC countries. There is also a minimum legal wage.

Many fringe benefits are provided and most employers have to contribute to housing and welfare. The practice of a 13-month bonus is widespread and most manual workers are now paid monthly, instead of fortnightly, and enjoy staff status. French workers attach as much importance to social security and fringe benefits as to money wages.

Living conditions

France compares with Britain on cost of living, with Paris dearer than London for food prices. In Paris inner city transport (metro and buses) is relatively cheap and so are taxis. Prices outside Paris are considerably lower, apart from in the main tourist areas.

The following are sample prices in January 1991 at a *Uniprix* supermarket:

	Fr
Milk 1 litre; full cream, fresh	5.80
Milk, UHT, 1 litre	4.50
Butter (250 gm)	9.50
Eggs (12)	15.30
Margarine (250 gm)	from 5.50 to 9.00
Sugar (1 kg)	6.70
Chocolate (100 gm)	from 3.65 to 8.50
Tea bags (500 gm)	from 69.50
Coffee, ground (250 gm)	12.00
Long grain rice (1 kg packet)	18.40
Pasta (spaghetti) (1 kg)	7.90
Mineral water (1.5 litre)	3.50
Potatoes (2.5 kg bag)	10.90
Oranges (1 kg)	6.50
Apples (1 kg)	7.50
Red wine (11.5% proof) (70 cl)	16.80
Beer (Heineken 4-pack)	19.50
Whisky (70 cl)	78.50

There is usually no problem about hotel accommodation in Paris, except at peak tourist periods. A double room in a first class hotel costs about £160 a night, but there are plenty of smaller hotels where you get good value for money, and outside Paris prices are lower.

Household goods, such as refrigerators, electric cookers, vacuum cleaners and TV sets, are dearer than at home.

Houses and apartments can be found by personal contact, or through house agents and/or newspaper advertisements. Rents vary according to the district and have been increasing steadily. An unfurnished three-roomed flat in one of the less fashionable areas would be from £600 a month. Alternatively, it is possible to buy a house or flat – home ownership is becoming increasingly widespread in France. Prices for older property start at around Fr10,000 per square metre. Electric voltage is usually 220V but this may vary.

Some families have a domestic servant living in, but it is more usual to employ a *femme de ménage*, often foreign; domestic help is hard to get as so many women go out to work. If you or your wife do your own cooking, you will probably prefer to shop at local markets and round-the-corner shops rather than at bigger shops and supermarkets. The smaller shops shut for a long midday break and stay open until late in the evening, but are often more expensive than supermarkets.

There is a reciprocal health agreement with the UK. Medical attention is expensive but fees can be reimbursed up to about 75 per cent. Private treatment is costly. There is a British hospital, the Hertford, and a more expensive American one.

Some expatriate parents send their children to local schools, which are of a high educational standard and where they can acquire a good knowledge of French. There is free compulsory education from 6 to 16 and below that age there are many crèches and nursery schools. Secondary education is in two cycles, from 11 to 15 and from 15 to 18. Those who complete the second cycle can take the Baccalauréat examination before proceeding to university or institutes of technology. American and British schools in Paris cater for children of diplomats and businessmen. The British School of Paris is geared to the UK system; it takes pupils from 4 to 18 and offers boarding facilities. Consult the ECIS *1990 Directory* and the Council of British Independent Schools in the European Communities for details.

Main centres are linked by internal airways and there are airports at Lyons, Marseilles, Nice, Bordeaux, Strasbourg and Toulouse, as well as two in Paris: Charles de Gaulle and Orly. The railway network is highly efficient, with a number of express and TGV (260km/hour) trains. Fares are considerably cheaper than in the UK. The roads are good and there is a network of motorways on which tolls are payable. These can be expensive on a long journey. Driving is on the right. Paris is congested and parking difficult, but the traffic flows. If you take your own car you are obliged to have it fitted with yellow headlights for night driving and with seat belts back and front.

All makes of car can be bought new or second-hand. A small car such as a mini is useful for city driving. A Peugeot 405 would cost about Fr85,000. Petrol is around Fr6.00 a litre. Car repairs and servicing are comparable with London prices.

Most provincial regions have their own newspapers, but some Paris papers, such as *Le Figaro* and *Le Monde*, circulate nationally. There is a wide range of weeklies, the best known being *Paris-Match* and *L'Express*. TV is state controlled with limited advertising, although cable and satellite facilities are expanding rapidly. There are one state, four commercial and a number of local private radio stations.

Paris and the main cities provide a variety of entertainment and opportunities for leisure activities. Outdoor sports are available – shooting and fishing have always been popular and camping (in extremely well-equipped sites) is increasingly so. Paris is rich in theatres, music, cinemas, museums and art galleries, as well as in night-life and restaurants. You can eat well at reasonable cost in the smaller family-run bistros off the beaten tourist track. Life is very different – slower and more reserved in the provinces – and outside the cosmopolitan centre of Paris it is even more important to have a fluent command of the language as an *entrée* to local life.

The French spend about a quarter of their incomes on food and it is still an important part of national life, with each region producing its own specialities. Business is often transacted over a restaurant lunch but entertaining is increasingly done in the home. If you don't appreciate good food and wine, France is wasted on you!

Germany

Background

The German nation, reunited in October 1990, has a population of 79 million, made up to 63 million from West Germany and 16 million from the East. Its formal name is still the Federal Republic of Germany, but increasingly, it will simply be referred to as Germany.

The new Germany covers an area of 138,000 square miles. Berlin, with a population of 3,236,000, is by far the largest city, overshadowing Cologne (927,500), Frankfurt (614,700), Hamburg (1,593,600) and Munich (1,188,800). Bonn, with only 290,000 inhabitants, remains the capital despite the wishes of some Germans for the seat of government to be transferred to Berlin.

The number of Federal Länder (states) rises from 11 to 16, and doubts have been expressed as to whether the federal system, which allows each state a considerable degree of independence, will continue to work as successfully in the new, enlarged Germany as in the old.

Over the next few years the dominant task facing Germany's Christian Democrat government, led by Helmut Kohl, will be the integration of the two Germanies.

Exchange rate: DM2.96 = £1.

The economy

The German economy shows strongly diverging trends: while the West is booming, the East is struggling to adapt to a market economy. Monetary union, which preceded the political union of the two Germanies, immediately created enormous pressures in the East – ailing industries were exposed to the full blast of competition from advanced Western countries, whose goods flooded into the shops, while demand for indigenous products collapsed.

Inevitably, the result was rising unemployment and short-time working in the East, and this is expected to go on increasing for some time – one forecast is that 3 million (out of a total population in the former DDR of 16 million) could be either unemployed or on short-time by the end of 1991.

In the short term, therefore, prospects for the East are gloomy, and substantial numbers – around half a million – are expected to move westwards this year. However, the restructuring process is going to lead to rising living standards in the longer term: per capita income, which is currently only about half that of West Germany, is expected to increase to almost 90 per cent of the Western level by the year 2000.

The West, meanwhile, is working to full capacity, with shortages of labour (despite the influx of East Germans). Indeed, reunification has benefited industry, creating new markets for Western goods. Despite the burden of unemployment and restructuring in the East, Germany remains the strongest economy in Europe. Inflation, under 3 per cent in 1990, is expected to rise slightly, but this should not create difficulties.

Germany's wealth, originally based on coal, steel and heavy engineering, is now founded on a broad spread of modern industries, including petrochemicals, artificial fibres, electric and electronic equipment, machinery, machine tools, scientific instruments and cars. New industrial development has been particularly noticeable in the south.

For many years the West German economy has relied on migrant labour – particularly from Turkey, Greece, Yugoslavia and Italy – and has also had a liberal policy towards refugees, both from the East and from the Third World. The presence of large numbers of foreigners has created tensions in German society, and these are being exacerbated by the influx of East Germans. There is already a serious housing shortage.

In the light of these changes, it is doubtful whether less skilled British workers (eg construction labourers) will be as welcome as they were in the past. But prospects for technical and managerial personnel, and for teachers of English, should remain reasonable.

Personal finance

At managerial level, the Germans do considerably better than the British – gross salaries are 40–70 per cent higher and, even after tax, a typical German senior manager would take home over 50 per cent more than his UK counterpart. Secretarial and skilled worker salaries are not much higher than in the UK; however, one must remember that the cost of living is now *lower* in Germany than in the UK. The British-German Trade Council in Cologne publishes annual surveys of salaries and fringe benefits in Germany.

Taxation

Income tax is levied on a graduated scale ranging from under 20 per cent to a maximum of 53 per cent. There are also compulsory payments for health care, social security and unemployment insurance, but benefit levels are much higher than in the UK, and business deductions are more generous: for instance, the cost of journeys to work can be deducted by employees.

Working conditions

British and other EC nationals are free to enter and move about the country; they need a *residence permit*, obtainable on arrival from the local aliens authority.

The standard working week is 38 to 40 hours for five days in many cases. There is a minimum of 15 days' paid holiday but, in many cases, 25 days' holiday have now been negotiated. There are 10 to 13 public holidays.

Wages and salaries are determined by collective bargains which usually have the force of law. There are separate arrangements for senior executives (*leitende Angestellten*). Individual contracts are usually for an indefinite period and terminated by written notice, with compensation according to age and length of service.

There is a long-established and comprehensive system of social security, with benefits related to earnings. Employers may provide, by law or by custom, additional benefits, eg 13-month bonus and group/performance bonuses, and help towards housing, meals, transport and recreation.

Useful sources of information (in German) of professional and executive jobs are *Markt* and *Chance*, see page 46.

Living conditions

Germany is a high cost/standard of living country. Prices are similar to those in the UK.

Here are some characteristic food prices:

	DM
Steak (1 kg)	28.00
Chicken (2 kg)	14.00
Eggs (12)	3.50
Butter (250 gm)	2.40
Sugar (1 kg)	2.00
Milk (1 litre)	1.25
Potatoes (2 kg)	2.60
Coffee (ground) (500 gm)	10.00
Jam (500 gm)	3.20

A 75 cl bottle of Scotch whisky costs DM22. Wine and beer are cheaper than in the UK. A packet of 20 cigarettes will cost about DM4.40.

The price of clothes is rather higher than in the UK, eg a man's pair of trousers would be DM155 and a woman's summer dress DM250. Household and consumer goods are no dearer – DM1000 for a refrigerator and DM350 for a vacuum cleaner. A colour TV set (22") would be DM1500.

House prices vary according to region and district, being highest in cities. The monthly rent for an unfurnished three-bedroomed apartment in a good area in a major city such as Cologne, Frankfurt or Stuttgart would be upwards of DM2000. Electricity is 220V. Germans in cities live in flats rather than detached houses.

Medical treatment is of a high standard and most costs are met through insurance funds. Charges are made for dentistry, medicine, drugs and medical aids. Germany has the highest proportion of hospital beds per 10,000 inhabitants of any EC country.

Education is compulsory from 6 to 18 (although after 15 or 16 pupils may attend a vocational school on a part-time basis). The standard is high, and thorough, and many expatriate parents send their children to local schools. Others want their children to continue education in the UK. There are International Schools at Dusseldorf, Frankfurt, Hamburg and Munich. The British Embassy runs a preparatory school in Bonn for children from 4 to 13. Fees vary, so it is necessary to check (see the ECIS Directory and consult the Council of British Independent Schools in the European Communities). Schools for the children of British military personnel sometimes admit those of civilians.

There is a highly sophisticated network of air, rail and road transport, serving all parts of the country. All major cities are linked by motorways (*Autobahnen*). Every make of car can be obtained – German produced Volkswagen, Opel and Ford cars take the biggest share of the market. Driving is on the right.

There is always plenty to do, winter or summer. Often even the smallest towns have their opera and most towns have theatres, cinemas, concert halls, museums and art galleries. Hotels and restaurants range from the very expensive to the cheaper family *Gasthaus* types. German cooking is usually good, though sometimes on the heavy side.

There are abundant facilities for sport, rambling, riding, swimming and sailing, etc and some very beautiful country, especially along the Rhine and in the southern mountains.

Most Germans are well-disposed towards the British, and British people generally feel more at home in Germany than in Latin countries. There is a sizeable British community in most main cities, and the British-German Trade Council has seven regional groups of members. The Trade Council also provides a variety of useful publications: a magazine called *Trade Partners*, a *Members' Bulletin*, information papers and reports on doing business in Germany. You don't have to know German for business dealings but it would be difficult to live there for any length of time without being able to speak the language. The older generation tend to be formal and punctilious, but there are fewer inhibitions among younger Germans.

Greece

Background

Greece covers an area of 51,000 square miles, its islands accounting for nearly one-fifth of the total. It has common borders with Turkey, Bulgaria, Albania and Yugoslavia. The country is mountainous, and there is little flat or cultivatable land, apart from some areas in the north. The highest mountain is Mount Olympus. The climate is Mediterranean – hot and dry in the summer, though it can be cold inland in winter.

The population is almost 10 million. About one-third live in the Greater Athens area, which includes the capital city, the port of Piraeus and a number of suburbs. It contains about 50 per cent of Greece's industry and is the country's principal commercial, financial and diplomatic centre. Efforts have, however, been made to decentralise the economy and the second city, Salonika (Thessaloniki) with its major port, has grown rapidly in population and industrial development. Other important towns are Patras, Larissa, Volos, and Iraklion on the island of Crete.

Greece is a parliamentary democracy, currently led by a liberal conservative government which is introducing Thatcher-style economic and social reforms.

Greece has been a full member of the EC since January 1981.

Exchange rate: Dr319.80 = £1.

The economy

The Greek economy was traditionally based on agriculture, with small-scale farming predominating, except in a few areas in the north. In common with all developing countries, there has been a steady shift towards industry, and although agriculture still employs nearly 30 per cent of the labour force, it accounts for less than 20 per cent of GDP. The principal products are tobacco, cotton, vegetables, wines, fruits and olive oil. An important part is played by the fisheries.

Greece is fortunate in having considerable reserves of minerals and ores, including bauxite, lignite, nickel and magnesite. These resources have yet to be fully exploited.

In manufacturing, Greece's performance is hampered by the proliferation of small, traditional, low-tech firms, often run as family businesses. Food, drink and tobacco processing, textiles, chemicals, metal manufacture and engineering are the most important sectors. There are some steel mills and several shipyards. Shipping is of prime importance to the economy.

Greece has experienced severe balance of trade problems but to some extent these have been mitigated by healthy invisible exports, especially shipping, tourism and migrants' remittances. Over 8 million tourists visit Greece annually. Trade is mainly with EC countries.

The government's major concern has been to combat inflation, which is around 23 per cent. Wages and earnings, though well below the general EC level, have risen progressively.

Greece has been a large-scale exporter of labour, particularly to Germany, but, with many less-skilled jobs being taken by East Germans, there is now a net immigration of Greek workers. Lack of opportunities at home and the relatively low standard of living have been the prime reasons for emigration. Official unemployment figures, however, are relatively low, as people without jobs in the formal sector of the economy are often absorbed into family businesses such as agriculture and tourism.

Personal finance

The level of executive salaries is around 50 per cent lower than in the more prosperous northern EC countries. On the other hand, the cost of living is lower.

Taxation

Income tax is raised progressively on taxable income, allowances against which tend to be fairly generous. The top rate of tax is 50 per cent. On an average executive salary tax and social security payments would be around 30–40 per cent.

Working conditions

The EC provisions about free mobility of labour apply in Greece. You can freely take up employment, or enter the country to look for work. You do, however, need a *residence permit* for a stay of longer than three months.

Job prospects for foreigners are slim at present, the best being with British firms with branches or subsidiaries in Greece or with multinational companies, especially in technological fields. It is not very easy to find work and priority is given to Greek nationals. Opportunities for women are very limited.

Working hours are as in any hot country. In the summer (April to October) these are from 8.00 am to 2.00 pm and from 5.00 pm to 8.00 pm. Meals are eaten late and many people take a siesta in the afternoon.

There are 12 public holidays, including religious holidays.

Living conditions

Wages and salaries may be lower than the average EC rates, but the cost of living is also lower, though Athens is more expensive than the rest of Greece.

Here are some food prices in 1990

	Dr
Steak (1 kg)	1,500
Chicken (2 kg)	1,100
Eggs (12)	275
Butter (1 kg)	1,200
Sugar (1 kg)	150
Milk (1 litre)	150
Potatoes (1 kg)	55
Coffee (ground) (500 gm)	1,000

Wine is inexpensive and the local lager-type beer is recommended. The local aperitif is ouzo (like pernod) and most Greeks drink retsina, a slightly resinated light wine, white or rosé, with their meals. Both are acquired tastes.

The food is reasonable and most English people, accustomed to similar food in Greek restaurants at home, will find it palatable, though some say that too much oil is used in cooking. Restaurants range from the expensive establishments in Athens and Salonika to modest tavernas in villages. The same applies to hotels. A double room in a luxury hotel costs around £85 a night, but all hotels are graded and must, by law, display room prices.

Shoppers will find that fresh fruit and vegetables are the best buy. Canned goods and imported foods tend to be expensive. There are supermarkets and large stores in the big towns, but many people prefer to shop in local markets and smaller shops.

You can get quite a wide range of local clothing and you can have things made up by a local tailor or dressmaker. It is probably best to bring out your own electrical equipment. Electric supply in Athens and most of the country is 220V, 50 AC.

Despite a lot of building in the towns and cities, accommodation may be hard to find. A three-bedroomed apartment in a good area of Athens would cost around Dr180,000 a month to rent. Landlords usually ask for two months' rent as a deposit and one month's in advance. House prices are very high, and furnished accommodation rarely found.

It is possible to obtain domestic help but difficult to find anyone prepared to live in. You would have to pay Dr60,000 to Dr90,000 a month for a domestic servant.

Transport is on the whole efficient and reliable and you can choose between air, rail, sea or bus. Most international air flights are based on Athens, and there are also regular services to and from Salonika. Domestic airlines serving some 30 towns and islands are operated from Athens by Olympic Airways. The railways are efficient and serve the main centres north and south of Athens. Long-distance coach and bus services provide a means of seeing the country and many shipping routes connect the mainland with the islands.

Taxis and cars can be hired, though car hire can be expensive. ELPA, the equivalent of our AA, runs a national road assistance service. Like all European cities, Athens has its traffic problems. The main roads in Greece are good, but conditions on local roads can be difficult, especially in the mountains.

Cars and petrol are expensive.

Greece has a comprehensive social security system. The majority of employees are covered by the Social Insurance Institute, financed by employer and employee contributions. Benefits include pensions, medical expenses and long-term disability payments.

Public education is provided free of charge from nursery to university level. Because of language difficulties, expatriate parents tend to send their children to schools in the UK or, if they can get in, to an International School. The British Embassy school, St Catherine's, in Athens is a preparatory school for British children of 5 to 13 years. The American Community School caters for boys and girls from 4 to 18. The fees vary according to age. Campion School in Athens offers education in English and enters pupils for GCSE and A level examinations.

Greece is very beautiful and the climate is excellent, but Athens suffers from a yellowish smog. There is always scope for outdoor activity, with trips to the mountains or the islands, sightseeing or swimming from the many splendid sandy beaches. There are also conventional sports, such as golf, tennis and riding. It is not surprising, with all it has to offer and despite the relatively low salary levels, that many British people put Greece at the top of their choice for a country to live and work in.

Language may present a problem. Don't think that because you learnt ancient Greek at school that you will be able to make yourself understood. Modern Greek is very different. Learn it if you can, if you are staying for some time or living outside Athens in areas where English is not generally understood. At any rate get to know the Greek alphabet.

Italy

Background

Italy covers an area of 117,000 miles and has a population of some 57 million. Its regions vary widely in geography, development, tradition and culture.

It lies wholly within the Mediterranean region. In the north, the Alps constitute a barrier against the rest of Europe, and the Apennines form a backbone which runs down the whole length of the country from the plain of Lombardy and the Po valley to the 'toe' in the Messina straits.

The north, centred on Milan, Turin and Genoa (the respective capitals of Lombardy, Piedmont and Liguria), is highly industrialised and contains about half the total population. The south, by contrast, is underdeveloped and poor. Rome, the capital, in the centre, is the headquarters of government and many business organisations. It has about 3 million inhabitants. Milan, the commercial and industrial centre, has 1.575 million; Naples and Turin each have 1.2 million; Genoa, the main port, has 755,000. Other important cities are Bologna (482,000), Florence (475,000), Venice (366,000), Taranto (210,400) and Trieste (280,000). The Vatican City has 1000 inhabitants and the tiny republic of San Marino 19,000. The expatriate population in Rome is mainly diplomatic and NATO personnel predominate in Naples. Milan and northern cities are the main centre for business expatriates, who include many British.

There is little love lost between Rome and the provincial capitals, many of whose people still regard themselves primarily as Venetians, Neapolitans, Tuscans or Milanese. There are a number of non-Italian-speaking minorities – German is used officially in the Trentino-Alto Adige region; there are Slavs in the Trieste area and a kind of dog-Latin is still spoken in the interior of Sardinia which, like Sicily and Val d'Aosta, is autonomous.

The climate is hot in summer and mild in winter. It can be extremely hot in the plains of Lombardy during the summer.

Italy is a parliamentary democracy and has been governed since the end of the war by successive coalitions, with the Christian Democrats in the majority. The political situation has been and remains extremely unstable. The Communists dominate the trade unions, and there are many municipal communist administrations, particularly in urban areas.

Exchange rate: Lira 2190 = £1.

The economy

The Italian economy has been growing strongly in recent years and this trend seems likely to continue. However, unemployment is high at around 12 per cent. Inflation is around 6 per cent.

Italy has few mineral resources, apart from scattered deposits of sulphur, iron ore, zinc, lead and mercury, and is therefore dependent on overseas trade. Its main exports are machinery, cars, metal manufactures, iron and steel products, artificial fibres, knitwear and hosiery, and a wide range of luxury and semi-luxury items, including food and wine of which Italy is now a bigger exporter than France. Tourism, of course, is a major revenue producer and is one of the country's largest industries.

Industry is unevenly distributed. The northern triangle - Milan, Turin and Genoa - produces about one-fifth of the national output and incomes are well above the national average. There has been a steady migration of labour from the impoverished south, both to the more prosperous north and to other EC countries. Successive governments have aimed at developing the 'mezzogiorno', but, despite government and EC aid, the south has remained relatively poor.

Most enterprises are small or medium-sized, but larger units predominate in engineering and chemicals.

Many American and multinational companies operate in Italy. Most of the major British companies have branches or subsidiaries, based mainly in Milan and Rome.

Personal finance and taxation

Managerial and executive salaries are on a par with most EC countries, that is, about 30 per cent higher than in the UK.

Income tax rates in Italy begin at 10 per cent and rise to a maximum of 50 per cent. There are also local taxes. Italy, however, is where tax avoidance devices flourish and you should certainly seek qualified advice on your position if you are going there on a salary at the usual expatriate level.

Working conditions

Citizens of the UK and other EC countries can enter Italy freely to look for and take up a job; they do not need work permits, but need *residence permits* if they are staying over three months. They should register with the local police within three days of arrival. It is also necessary to obtain a tax number which will be asked for when registering a car, buying a flat or getting a job.

Given the high level of unemployment and language difficulties, not many British people find jobs in Italy unless they are working for Italian-based UK companies. A frequent complaint among expatriates is the difficulty of dealing with the well-entrenched bureaucracy. A personal visit to find a job may pay off.

The 40-hour, five-day week has become the general standard. Most collective agreements provide for 4 weeks' paid leave for wage and salary earners. There are also 10 public holidays. There is a growing trend towards accumulating public holidays for summer vacations, so as to minimise disruption. Most towns also have a holiday on the feast day of their patron saint, and there are a number of half-day holidays. Employers have to face many additional charges, including a 13-month or Christmas bonus; assistance towards housing, transport and canteens; children's nurseries and kindergartens. Most of these concessions, which are negotiated, are common among the larger enterprises, and, in the case of smaller firms, often arranged through consortia. Some firms have savings plans. There are works' committees in firms employing more than 40 workers. The trade union movement is divided on political and religious lines. The biggest group is Communist led.

Living conditions

The cost of living is higher in the cities than elsewhere, but on the whole Italian prices are lower than in most northern European countries. Food is more expensive than in the UK. Here are some examples of prices in 1990:

	Lira
Steak (1 kg)	18,000
Chicken (2 kg)	11,000
Eggs (12)	3,200
Butter (250 gm)	2,200
Sugar (1 kg)	1,400
Milk (1 litre)	1,450
Potatoes (1 kg)	700
Coffee (ground) (500 gm)	6,800

Pasta, in all shapes and sizes, is the staple diet of many Italians and is cheap. Wine and spirits are less expensive than in the UK.

It is not cheap to live in Italy; it can be very expensive, particularly in Rome and tourist centres such as Venice. But, with careful budgeting, good value for money can be had, particularly in comparison with Switzerland and Scandinavia.

The cost of eating out varies enormously. You can eat a good robust meal at an extremely modest price in a family run trattoria or pay huge prices at a slap-up restaurant. Cigarettes are cheaper than in the UK.

Clothing is good value. Women's outfits (dress, skirt, tights and shoes) can be bought in department stores for about the same price as in the UK. The same applies to men's clothing, which is cheaper than in other EC countries. But shopping in boutiques or high-fashion shops in Rome, Florence or other centres is extremely expensive.

The cost of most household goods is similar to that in the UK. Hire purchase facilities are available.

Houses are practically unobtainable in the main cities, since most people live in apartments. Some examples of annual rents are: unfurnished four-bedroomed flat in Milan, L6 million; three-bedroomed unfurnished house, also in Milan, L4.2 million; unfurnished three-bedroomed flat in central Rome, L3 million. Domestic electric voltages are nearly always 220V, AC 50 cycles; lamp-bulb holders are of the screw type, wall plugs of the round two-pin continental type. Some older properties may actually have electricity at two different voltages. It is important to check the wiring.

Rail fares are lower than in Britain, but some main-line trains require supplementary payments. The main cities are served by a network of toll motorways (*autostrada*), and other highways are in good condition. Petrol works out at L1500 a litre, and many filling-stations are open day and night. All makes of car are available from dealers, though there is a strict limitation on the number of Japanese cars. Needless to say, if you are living in Italy, a Fiat is the best bet from the point of view of servicing and running costs. Small cars are handy in the appalling traffic congestion of Rome and other cities. Driving is on the right. Taxis and self-drive cars are available in all centres. Long-distance buses and coaches offer admirable services and a chance to see the countryside in comfort.

Telephoning is relatively cheap and efficient, but posts are slow and subject to delays.

Health insurance covers the whole of the employed working population, including foreigners. Private treatment is expensive but most foreigners prefer it. Italy has the highest doctor/patient ratio in Europe. A number of hospitals are run by the Church.

There are both American and English schools in Rome, Milan and other major cities. Details can be found in the ECIS *Handbook*, which also lists COBISEC member schools. These schools have a specifically British curriculum and, additionally, are inspected by HM Inspectors of Schools. Full and associate members include St George's English School, Rome; The New School, Rome; Sir James Henderson British School, Milan; the International School, Milan. There are opportunities for UK teachers to find jobs in some of the many schools, though, as in other countries, would-be EFL teachers should beware of rogue employers (one sign of which is apparent unconcern with an applicant's qualifications to teach).

Quite apart from working in Italy, many British people settle there permanently because they like the country and its way of life. British residents include many retired people, artists, writers, etc.

It is impossible to be bored in Italy; there are numerous theatres, concert and opera attractions, cinemas, museums and artistic treasures. All Italian cities are within easy reach of beautiful parts of the country, eg Lake Como from Milan, Capri from Naples; expeditions for sailing, swimming, climbing, fishing and skiing in the north can be made at weekends or on holidays.

The Italians are friendly, gregarious and exuberant, particularly in the south. For anybody working and living in Italy, a knowledge of Italian is essential: it is not a difficult language to learn.

Luxembourg

Background

The Grand Duchy of Luxembourg covers only 999 square miles and has a population of about 378,400 of whom 27 per cent are foreigners. Luxembourgers have their own dialect, but French and German are the administrative languages. English is widely spoken and understood. The people have a strong sense of nationality and independence. They are proud of their traditions.

The Grand Duke is head of state. The Chamber with 64 deputies is elected every five years and the government is usually formed by a coalition.

Luxembourg has maintained its position as one of the richest countries in Europe. Its central location within the EC and a liberal fiscal climate has attracted a large service sector there, particularly in international banking and finance. To some extent this has compensated for the decline in manufacturing.

Exchange rate: LFr61.10 = £1.

Personal finance and taxation

Top executives are less well paid than in neighbouring countries though gross pay is 50 to 100 per cent higher than in the UK at senior levels; many enjoy company fringe benefits (eg car, house, etc).

The taxation system is separate from that of Belgium. There are three groups for income tax purposes – single, married, and those entitled to a child allowance, and there is a basic graduated scale of taxation ranging from nil on the first LFr153,600 of taxable income to 56 per cent on incomes over LFr1,198,800. Other taxes include those on capital yields and property. Reliefs are given for children, age and special expenses or extraordinary burdens.

Working conditions

Procedure for permits is as throughout the EC. A good knowledge of French and German would be valuable as both languages are widely used in business. All salaries and wages are tied to the cost of living index. The 40 hour week is standard.

Holidays are 25 days for all workers plus 10 public holidays. There is a bonus for each day's holiday on the basis of average daily pay for the previous three months. Most workers get an end of year bonus. Salaried staff sometimes get extra bonuses.

Living conditions

Living conditions are much as in Belgium, though prices of basic foods tend to be lower and clothes are cheaper. The overall cost of living is lower than in the UK. The rate of inflation is 3.4 per cent.

The following table lists some typical food prices in Luxembourg in 1990:

	LFr
Bread (1 kg)	51.00
Butter (1 kg)	196.00
Milk (1 litre)	32.00
Rumpsteak (1 kg)	608.00
Coffee (ground) (1 kg)	276.00
Beer (½ litre)	20.50
Cigarettes (20)	62.00

Purchasing power is high and Luxembourgers are among the best-off communities in Europe. They have more cars per 1000 people than any EC country and more telephones than any, except Denmark. The climate is temperate, but cold in the winter and in the higher altitudes of the Ardennes.

Food and drink are good, with moderately priced wines from the Moselle and local delicacies from the Ardennes such as ham and paté. Eating out is relatively expensive. Petrol works out at about LFr22 per litre. Annual rent for a small two-bedroomed unfurnished flat in Luxembourg City is around LFr380,000–420,000. House rents (unfurnished or part furnished) in the city are from 600,000 to 950,000. As one would expect, rents are lower in country areas. There are several letting agencies recommended by the Luxembourg National Trade and Tourist Office, which will supply their names and addresses on request.

Medical facilities are of a high standard but costly. Some doctors have been trained in the UK: many speak English.

There are two schools in Luxembourg which cater for non-national children and are English-speaking. The Ecole Européenne is intended for children of EC and ECSC personnel, but is open to others.

New building has kept pace with the influx of business people and EC officials. Shopping and business hours are as in Belgium.

There is plenty of social life among the foreign diplomatic and business communities, but less organised entertainment than in Brussels. Country-lovers will appreciate the beauties of the Ardennes, 'Little Switzerland', and the Moselle valley for walking, cycling or motoring. The airport, which is only 4 miles from Luxembourg City, is served by regular British Airways and Luxair flights from Heathrow.

The Netherlands

Background

The Netherlands is one of Britain's main gateways to Europe. Amsterdam is less than an hour by air from London and there are regular flights to many UK cities. The port of Rotterdam, the biggest and busiest in the world, is at the hub of the EC's trade.

The Netherlands is small but densely populated: 14½ million people live in an area of 16,000 square miles. The country is flat and low lying – a quarter of its territory is below sea-level, and the Dutch have had to wage an unremitting battle against flooding, through land reclamation and dykes drainage. Half the population lives in a narrow industrialised strip, known as 'Randstad', bounded by Amsterdam, Rotterdam, the Hague and Utrecht.

Amsterdam, with almost 1 million inhabitants, is the capital of the Netherlands, although the political and diplomatic centre is the Hague. Rotterdam and district (1.2 million) has become the most important industrial centre.

The Netherlands is a constitutional monarchy, with a two-chamber Parliament. Queen Beatrice became head of state in April 1980. There are a number of political parties, and the country has been governed by coalitions since the end of the war. The present government is a centre-right coalition, dominated by the Christian Democrat party.

Exchange rate: Guilder (DFl) 3.34 = £1.

The economy

The traditional image of the Netherlands as a land of bulbs, windmills and wooden shoes is perpetuated for the sake of tourists but, in fact, its modern industrial basis and rapid economic growth have placed the Netherlands in the forefront of Common Market economies. Industry accounts for nearly one-third of both the national income and the working population.

It has no natural resources, apart from natural gas and salt in the east. The Netherlands is thus highly dependent on foreign trade and experiences recurrent balance of trade problems. The Netherlands is dependent on overseas suppliers for oil, but has stepped up its natural gas production to counteract this. Inflation is around 2 per cent.

Agriculture, though its percentage contribution to GNP has fallen relative to industry, is still important and very efficient. Production continues to rise, with cattle and dairy products, fruit, vegetables and flowers as its principal products.

The main industries include electrical and mechanical engineering, textiles and clothing, steel, shipbuilding, processed foods, and chemicals, with diamonds and furs in the luxury range. Oil refining and the rapidly expanding petrochemicals sector dominate the Rotterdam area. The electrical and electronics industries are highly sophisticated and produce computers, telecommunications equipment and precision instruments. Coal mining, after being progressively run down, has ceased completely.

That the Dutch are internationally minded is shown in their industrial structures. The multinationals include Philips, the electrical giant, Unilever, Shell and other major oil companies. Joint German/Dutch enterprises have been set up in some sectors. Foreign investment is welcomed, particularly in the development areas in the north-east and south, where generous incentives are offered. The UK heads the list of foreign investors, with the USA second. Many of the large British companies have Dutch subsidiaries.

Traditionally a free trade/free enterprise economy, the state role is limited to setting a favourable climate for growth and investment.

Personal finance

Executive salaries are about 25 per cent higher than in the UK; secretarial salaries are roughly comparable.

Taxation

There is a range of tax-free personal allowances – amounts depend on such factors as age, marital status and number of dependent children.

After the relevant allowances have been deducted and all other applicable deductions have been made, rates of tax on the remaining amounts vary from 35 to 60 per cent.

Social security payments which have to be made by individuals in the Netherlands are very high – but so are the benefits, should you need to call on them. There is, however, a very important concession made to qualifying expatriates as far as tax on income derived in the country is concerned. If you are working for a non-Dutch company your Dutch income is reduced by 35 per cent for tax assessment purposes, though some fringe benefits are taxable as income. Furthermore, no Dutch tax is levied on income derived from outside the Netherlands nor on the interest on deposits in Dutch banks.

Working conditions

Many British people put the Netherlands at the top of their list of preferred locations overseas. It is near home, most people speak English and the way of life is not unlike our own. But it is not easy to get a job, and unemployment is high. An official statement points out: 'In view of considerable unemployment, a seemingly permanent housing problem and the increasing density of the population, immigration is not encouraged.' If, in spite of this chilly attitude, you still want to find work in the

Netherlands, the procedure is as in other EC countries – no visa is required for stays of up to three months but you need a *residence permit* from the local police. After five consecutive years a permanent residence permit can be granted.

A legal minimum wage is fixed for all workers aged 23 to 65 and is reviewed at least once a year in the light of movements in average earnings and the cost of living index. Apart from this, wages are determined by collective agreements – the practice of plant agreements has grown with the increase in the size of firms.

Collective agreements usually lay down procedures for dealing with disputes and provide for reference to arbitration boards in the event of failure to settle. The country has been relatively strike-free. Most contracts are written and provide for a two-month trial period. Dismissals and resignations come under government supervision; length of notice is governed by the terms of individual contracts and length of service – for managers the notice period is usually three months. In most industries the 40-hour week has become standard.

Workers are entitled to three weeks' paid holiday and most get more through collective bargaining. Four to five weeks is normal for managerial staff.

Most companies provide canteens and many subsidise transport and give some form of housing assistance. Some grant education and study allowances.

Living conditions

The overall cost of living is now lower in the Netherlands than in the UK. Here are some typical 1990 food prices:

	DFl
Steak (1 kg)	30.00
Chicken (2 kg)	15.00
Eggs (12)	3.30
Butter (1 kg)	10.00
Sugar (1 kg)	2.30
Milk (1 litre)	1.20
Potatoes (1 kg)	1.00
Coffee (ground) (500 gm)	6.00

Wine and whisky are a little cheaper than in the UK. Most consumer goods are fairly expensive, eg a refrigerator would cost DFl 1200 and a colour TV set DFl 1660. The price of clothes and personal services is, on the whole, a little higher than in the UK.

Apartments are hard to get in spite of a massive house-building programme. A furnished two-bedroomed flat in central Rotterdam costs about DFl 1000 per month. There are few detached houses in the country:

those that exist are very large and very expensive. Semi-detached and terraced houses are the norm for those who do not live in blocks of flats. Mortgage interest is tax-deductible and mortgages easily obtainable from banks, which offer lower interest rates than in the UK.

A new 1600cc Opel would cost around DFl 34,000.

Eating out is expensive, but less so than in Belgium or Scandinavia. There are many moderately priced restaurants in Amsterdam. Domestic help is difficult to find in the big cities. Electricity is supplied at 220V, 50 cycles.

The cost of living is relatively low in comparison with other northern European countries. The 'social wage' in the Netherlands is among the highest in the EC: unemployment benefit, for instance, can be over £200 per week – far more generous than in the UK.

The Dutch health service is based on a mixture of compulsory and voluntary schemes. The compulsory scheme covers about 70 per cent of the population. Private medical treatment is expensive. The Dutch are healthy, and have the longest life expectancy of any EC nationals. There is a reciprocal health agreement with the UK.

Education is free and compulsory from 6 to 16, with part-time schooling for a further two years. There are state schools and state subsidised denominational schools. Primary schooling lasts six to seven years, followed by different types of secondary education – general, vocational or gymnasium (grammar-school type). There are universities at Rotterdam, Utrecht, Leiden, Groningen, Maastricht, Nijmegen and Amsterdam and a number of technical colleges. There are International Schools in Rotterdam, Amsterdam, the Hague, Beverweerd, Arnhem, Brunssum, Ommen and Eindhoven, and British Schools in Amsterdam and the Hague.

The British School in the Netherlands is in the vicinity of the Hague and provides for children between 3½ and 18 years. The fees compare favourably with other International Schools in the Netherlands.

There is a British Primary School in Amsterdam and a number of other International and American Schools in the major cities – details of these can be obtained from ECIS and COBISEC.

Internal and urban transport are very efficient. Frequent train services link the main centres and there are country-wide bus services. The roads are good and not over-congested. Nearly everybody in Holland cycles and there are special cycle paths on the main roads.

British people like living in the Netherlands, both because there are few language obstacles and because the way of life is attractive. The Dutch are very hospitable and welcoming to foreigners, particularly the British. Most speak English, but it would be as well to learn the language. The Hague is more formal than Amsterdam, which is completely free and easy. There is plenty to do, particularly in Amsterdam, with theatres, art galleries, concert halls, cinemas and many good restaurants. There is scope for outdoor sports, including swimming and sailing, and the Dutch coast with its long stretches of sandy beaches provides a perfect holiday for people with children. On the debit side, some areas suffer from mosquitoes and many residents complain of frequent outbreaks of flu in the cities.

Norway

Background

Norway is the fifth largest country in Europe and the least densely populated – just over 4 million people live in its 123,000 square miles. The country is long and narrow, and its 1700 mile-long coast is indented with fjords. Nearly three-quarters of the total territory is mountainous and uninhabitable, and about half lies within the Arctic circle. The vast majority of the population live in the southern half, which includes Oslo, the capital (449,337 inhabitants), Bergen (208,000) Stavanger (92,000) and Trondheim (135,000). In the far north, as in Sweden, there are communities of Lapps, with their own language and culture.

Norway has longer summer daylight and longer winter darkness than any inhabited country in the world. The Gulf Stream keeps the temperatures higher along the Atlantic coastline than in the more easterly parts.

Like the rest of Scandinavia, Norway is a constitutional monarchy, with a one-chamber Parliament (*Storting*), elected every four years. The present minority government is a coalition of centre right parties.

Norway actively supports the United Nations (it provided its First Secretary General, Trygve Lie) and belongs to NATO. EC membership was rejected in the referendum of 1972, but has been the subject of continuing political debate.

Exchange rate: Krone 11.56 = £1.

The economy

The exploitation of oil deposits in the North Sea revolutionised Norway's economy and transformed its entire industrial and social structure. Thousands of workers left their traditional occupations in farms, fisheries and forests to find work in the rapidly developing oil sector, leading to severe pressure on housing and other social resources.

The government, anxious to avoid too much disruption and the development of a 'gold rush' mentality, proceeded cautiously, limiting rates of production and exploitation, and taking care of the pollution and preservation aspects. It participates in operations, through its ownership of Statoil and heavy taxation of companies. Nevertheless, the collapse in oil prices in 1986 hit the Norwegian economy hard. Recovery took some time but there is now a healthy balance of payments surplus, helped by higher oil and gas prices and increased production.

Oil apart, Norway is rich in mineral resources and has taken advantage of its cheap and abundant water power (which meets virtually all electricity requirements) to develop modern electro-metallurgical and electro-chemical industries.

The most important of these are aluminium (based on imported bauxite), ferro-alloys and nitrates. Other valuable minerals include iron ore (the basis of Norway's steel industry), copper, zinc, nickel, dolomite and titanium. Fishing and forestry, together with the production of timber, paper and pulp, are important, though relatively declining, sectors. Shipbuilding has steadily expanded, and has increasingly turned to the production of oil rigs and platforms. Consumer and service industries have developed, eg food and fish processing, clothing and textiles, but half the nation's food still has to be imported. Unemployment is around 4 per cent – relatively low by EC standards, but the highest rate experienced by Norwegians since the 1930s.

The state plans and regulates economic development. The steel industry is dominated by the state-owned concern in the far north. In some cases, the state is the majority shareholder, but most manufacturing, eg shipbuilding, is in the hands of private enterprise. The government welcomes regulated foreign investment, offering special incentives for underdeveloped and underpopulated areas. Inflation is around 5 per cent.

Sweden is Norway's major trading partner, but trade with the EC – particularly the UK, Germany and Denmark – makes an important contribution. Tourism is a useful revenue earner and many visitors are attracted to Norway by the midnight sun and the open-air, away-from-it-all life.

Personal finance

Managerial salaries are about 10 to 15 per cent higher than in the UK, but their purchasing power is lower because of the high cost of living.

Taxation

As in other Scandinavian countries, Norway's citizens have a heavy tax burden to bear for their welfare state and social services. Both state and local taxes are graduated according to income.

Expatriates, however, get 15 per cent of income tax free; rates of tax on the remaining amounts vary from 35 to 60 per cent.

Working conditions

Foreigners, apart from people from the Nordic countries, need both a *work permit* and a *residence permit*. Work permits, issued initially for one year, should be obtained before arriving in Norway, and the applicant must show a firm offer of employment and satisfactory housing arrangements. Residence permits are obtainable from the local police.

There is a temporary embargo on immigration. It applies, with some exceptions, to everyone who would normally need a work permit, but not to workers employed on mobile drilling vessels on the Norwegian continental shelf. Specialists, technically trained personnel and key personnel considered absolutely necessary to an undertaking may be exempted.

The normal working week is 37½ hours and overtime is limited. All employees have four weeks' annual leave, and there are up to 10 public holidays. Both sides of industry contribute towards a jointly managed training fund.

Living conditions

Oslo is the most expensive capital in Europe, and it is difficult to obtain personal and domestic services. The cost of basic foods is much higher than in the UK. Here are some typical food prices:

	NKr
Eggs (12)	24
Butter (500 gm)	17
Cheese (500 gm)	33
Milk (1 litre)	7
Jam	28.00
Coffee (500 gm)	30.00
Bread (1 kg) (1 loaf)	21.00

Clothes are a little more expensive than in the UK. Cigarettes and drinks are very much dearer.

Consumer durables and services are expensive. Rents are about the same as in Sweden, and slightly more than in Denmark.

Scattered settlements, and the country's topography, make transport and communications difficult and expensive. Regular shipping services serve the coastal towns throughout the year. There are regular sea/rail links with Europe, and Norway cooperates with Sweden and Denmark in SAS, which operates regular air services internally and externally. Apart from the south-east area, roads are inadequate. Foreigners must be particularly aware of Norway's very strict 'drink and drive' laws. Anyone caught driving with more than 0.5 per 1000 ml alcohol in the blood must reckon with an almost automatic prison sentence plus suspension of licence for at least a year.

Social life in the main towns and cities is very like that of Sweden, though the Norwegians are less formal. Their command of English is impressive. Conditions in the remote areas, particularly in the north where it is dark most of each day in the winter, are severe, but housing compares well with the south. Warm clothes are needed in the winter.

Norway has unlimited facilities for outdoor sports, such as sailing, fishing, camping, riding and skiing (until April), and the country is wild and beautiful. But facilities for culture, such as theatre and music, are comparable with smaller UK cities only, and you may find the long dark evenings wearisome. TV entertainment includes Sky Channel as well as the Norwegian TV channel, with Swedish TV in the east.

Portugal

Background and the economy

Portugal, like its neighbour Spain, has become a popular holiday destination for tourists over the last 30 years. The most favoured spot has been the Algarve in the south, but the rest of the country is also attractive and has great areas of fertile land. The climate is mild throughout, though warmer and drier in the south.

Portugal has a population of around 10.5 million, a higher proportion of whom are engaged in agriculture and fishing than in most European countries – nearly as many as are employed in industry, much of which is 'low tech' and labour intensive. But the biggest single sector is services (including public administration) which accounts for over 40 per cent of the working population. This probably explains Portugal's relatively low rate of unemployment and reflects a political situation in which various slightly right of centre governments have had to make economic sacrifices in the interests of political stability. Inflation at 12 per cent is high by current European standards.

Portugal has long-standing historical ties with Britain, going back to the fourteenth century when King John I of Portugal married Phillipa of Lancaster. Portugal has also been a member of the EC since 1986 and this has been followed by a growth of economic activity in the country and a liberalisation of the labour laws.

Exchange rate: Escudos ($) 256.10 = £1.

Personal finance and tax

Portuguese nationals are poorly paid by international standards – a managing director of a medium-sized firm earns £20,000–£25,000 a year and a secretary no more than £5000. However, expatriates could expect to be paid about 25 per cent more than the equivalent rate for the job in the UK. An expatriate executive would be paying income tax and social security at 35–45 per cent. There is a double taxation agreement with the UK.

Living costs and conditions

Rents vary considerably. In Lisbon, for example, the annual rent for a part-furnished three-bedroomed flat could range from Esc 1.5 million to 3.75 million. Houses are usually let unfurnished and in Lisbon rents could be anything from 3 to 5 million Esc per annum. It is possible to buy property, but buying a house is a complex process, riddled with legal pitfalls for foreigners and should not be undertaken without trustworthy local professional help. More information is given in *Living and Retiring Abroad: The Daily Telegraph Guide*, 5th edn, Kogan Page 1991.

Food costs are seasonal and, as in other expatriate locations, it is much cheaper to buy in street markets than in supermarkets. By the same token, one can eat well and cheaply in restaurants frequented by locals or pay international prices and get what is often indifferent quality in those favoured by foreign tourists or business visitors on expense accounts. In the shops meat and dairy foods are expensive, but fruit and vegetables are cheap. Overall it is estimated that the cost of living in Lisbon is about 20 per cent less than in London. Some other costs are:

	$
Family car (Toyota Corolla 1.6)	3,200,000
Petrol (litre)	150

There is a sizeable British community in Portugal, a couple of British schools and a British Hospital in Lisbon.

Spain

Background

Of all European countries, Spain is perhaps one that British people think they are most familiar with, but this familiarity is generally limited to small and in many ways uncharacteristic strips of the Mediterranean coast. Spain is, in fact, a large and varied country – the second largest in Europe. It has a population of about 38 million, the main centres, apart from Madrid, being Barcelona (1.75 million), Bilbao (880,000), Seville (650,000) and Malaga (400,000).

Since the death of Franco, Spain has been a democracy with the king, as head of state, playing a limited but effective political role. The moderate Socialist government enjoys widespread support, but there are still stresses in the country of which the most visible signs are the activities of the Basque and Catalan separatist movements and the periodic stirring of right-wing feeling in the army and the Guardia Civil.

The other cause of stress is economic. Though inflation, at 7 per cent, is lower than current UK rates, it is coupled with a low growth rate and high unemployment. The immediate economic prospect is not very good, though tourism continues to flourish and the level of foreign investment is satisfactory. The motor industry is also doing well. Spain joined the EC on 1 January 1986.

Exchange rate: Pesetas 182.35 = £1.

Personal finance

The principal jobs available for expatriates in Spain relate to employment with a multinational firm. Here international salary standards apply and prospective expatriates at executive levels should be looking to earn at least as much as in the UK, plus removal and other disturbance costs.

There are complicated provisions governing convertibility of income arising in Spain, but basically residents can remit 50 per cent of Spanish earnings (subject to the employer's written confirmation).

Taxation

Spain is no tax haven, and income tax rates go up as high as 56 per cent. Taxes are levied at two levels: national and local. National taxes include corporate income tax, personal income tax, VAT, wealth tax, inheritance and gift tax. Local taxes are: property taxes, municipal gains tax, and various licence fees.

Liability for income tax depends on residence (irrespective of whether a person has a work permit or residence permit); an individual is regarded as a resident if he or she is physically present in Spain for at least 183 days in the year. Residents pay tax on their world-wide income.

A typical expatriate employee with a dependent spouse would pay 30–40 per cent of gross salary in tax and social security contributions.

Working conditions

Working conditions in Spain increasingly resemble those in other European countries, with city offices abandoning the time-honoured siesta. The EC rules about free movement of workers will not apply in Spain until 1993, so *work permits* are still needed.

Living conditions

Most of Spain has a hot dry summer, intensely so inland, where winters can also get very cold. Northern Spain is cooler and wetter and many Spaniards actually prefer to spend their holidays on the Atlantic rather than the Mediterranean side.

Prices in Spain are now much the same as in the UK. The following are examples of food prices in 1990:

	Ptas
Steak (1 kg)	1,430
Chicken (1 kg)	280
Eggs (12)	220
Butter (1 kg)	1,000
Sugar (1 kg)	140
Bread (1 kg)	260
Cheese (1 kg)	1,200
Milk (1 litre)	100
Potatoes (1 kg)	50
Coffee (ground) (500 gm)	390

Although English is much more widely spoken than it used to be, it would be very difficult to get by without a good knowledge of Spanish, and even then there are some pitfalls for the foreigner. It is advisable to appoint a personal agent (known as a *gestor*) to deal with legal matters and licence applications. Particular care has to be exercised in buying property, since Spanish property tenure is very complicated. The naive or unwary may find themselves buying a property hedged about with so many legal encumbrances as to be practically worthless. The monthly rent on a furnished four-roomed flat in a good area would be £1200–£1500.

Personal effects can be imported duty-free by foreigners intending to establish permanent residence in Spain, and by foreign owners of holiday accommodation, if they guarantee to keep it in their possession for at least two years. A British national can also bring in a car, free of duty, provided the car has been registered in his name for at least six months.

There are estimated to be at least a quarter of a million British residents in Spain and these have created a market for private English-speaking schools which exist in most of the main cities – Madrid, Barcelona and along the east and south coasts and in the Balearic and Canary Islands. Up-to-date information on fees can be obtained from Mr A Powell, Chairman, National Association of British Schools in Spain, c/o Runnymede College, Arga 9 (El Viso), 28002 Madrid.

Sweden

Background

Sweden, covering 174,000 square miles, is nearly twice as large as Britain, and is the fourth largest country in Europe. It has only 8.6 million inhabitants and the lowest population density in Europe: 90 per cent of the

Swedes live in the urbanised south, and Greater Stockholm has 1,402,000 inhabitants. The port cities of Malmö and Gothenburg in the south have 453,000 and 730,000 inhabitants respectively, including suburbs. Main towns in the centre are Uppsala, Västeras and Norrköping, and Umea and Lulea in the north.

The Swedes are a homogeneous Nordic race, except for about 15,000 Lapps who form an ethnic minority within the Arctic circle and are largely nomadic, and about 405,400 immigrants.

It is a land of lakes and forests, flat along the coastal plain and particularly in the south, where most of the population is concentrated. The north is mountainous and thinly populated.

Sweden is a parliamentary democracy. The king is head of state, but has no political power. Its one-chamber Parliament (*Riksdag*) is elected every three years. It is the archetype of neutralism and has not been involved in a war since 1814.

Sweden has applied to join the EC; if its application is accepted, it could become a member by 1995.

Exchange rate: Krona 10.55 = £1.

The economy

Sweden is one of the world's most prosperous and politically stable countries, rich in natural resources and with a highly diversified manufacturing sector. Its economy is mixed with a considerable element of state ownership. The standard of management is probably the highest in Europe, and the emphasis is on technologically advanced and science-based industry.

The government encourages foreign investment and offers special incentives for its northern and western development areas. UK companies are second to those of the USA, both in number and in the total of employees. Immigrant workers represent about 5 per cent of the labour force, nearly two-thirds coming from other Nordic countries which form a common labour market. There is a shortage of some skilled labour. Sweden has suffered from inflation, with steep price and wage rises. Inflation is now around 11 per cent.

Personal finance and taxation

Wages and salaries are higher than in Norway. However, tax rates are also very high, and rise progressively. A new, revised tax system came into force on 1 January 1991; details are available from the Swedish Embassy in London.

Working conditions

Sweden is not yet a member of the EC, so foreigners need both *residence* and *work permits*. The latter should be obtained (from the Swedish Embassy in London) before arriving in Sweden, with proof of employment and housing. Residence permits should be obtained beforehand. These are valid initially for six months, and renewable. Five years' residence and renunciation of your British citizenship are required for Swedish citizenship.

Although Sweden has been, and still is, short of skilled manpower, it adopts a cautious attitude towards the employment of foreigners. As in Norway, people who possess exceptional technical qualifications, considered absolutely necessary to an undertaking, may be admitted. Most British people work in a managerial or specialist capacity in a subsidiary or branch of a UK company.

The 40-hour, five-day week is standard, though hours may be slightly shorter for salaried staff. Opportunities for overtime are limited. Swedish workers are entitled to five weeks' annual holiday with up to 12 public holidays. (There is no substitute day if the holiday falls on a Saturday or Sunday.) Periods of notice according to age and length of service are laid down by law in agreements. Employer-employee relationships are highly egalitarian both in practice and in terms of legislation. Possibly for this reason, industrial disputes are rare.

Many employers provide subsidised canteens and contribute towards transport, holidays, health and leisure facilities. They are obliged in certain circumstances to provide language teaching, as well as housing, for immigrants. They bear a heavy proportion of contributions towards social security.

Living conditions

Sweden has one of the highest standards and costs of living in Europe. The table below lists food prices in 1990:

	Kr
Steak (1 kg)	150.00
Chicken (1 kg)	45.00
Eggs (12)	22.00
Butter (1 kg)	44.00
Sugar (1 kg)	7.60
Milk (1 litre)	7.00
Potatoes (1 kg)	6.00
(Instant) Coffee (250 g)	68.00

A bottle of wine costs Kr50, a bottle of Scotch Kr200 or more, and a packet of cigarettes Kr23. Clothes are expensive – to buy an off-the-peg summer dress would cost Kr850 and a man's off-the-peg suit about Kr2800. Prices of consumer durables are variable and it pays to shop around, but the cost of such items is certainly higher than in the UK.

The housing shortage, particularly in Stockholm, remains a problem for many people. Accommodation is often expensive, though less than in several other European countries. Housing exchanges in most towns help with finding accommodation. Two-thirds of all Swedes live in apartments, but there has been a popular movement against high-rise blocks in city suburbs.

The level of health care is high, and charges are generally modest. There is a fee of Kr 105 for a visit to the doctor; house calls, however, can be expensive. The fee also applies to out-patient hospital treatment, but once you are admitted to hospital your treatment is free. Medication for hospital patients is free, but out-patients and those who are prescribed medicines by their GP must pay prescription charges.

State education is free, and of a high standard. A third of pre-school children go to nursery schools run by the communities. Children of foreign residents have special courses in the Swedish language if they attend Swedish schools. There is an International School in Stockholm for children from 4 to 14. The syllabus is American up to junior high school level. The school caters for about 300 pupils.

Public transport is clean, efficient and universally available.

The Swedes drive on the right. The roads are mainly good and there are some motorways between the main cities in the south. UK and international driving licences are accepted; after two years you must obtain a Swedish licence. The main car manufacturers are Volvo and Saab. A 1600cc car would cost Kr100,000 approximately. Petrol costs Kr6.3 a litre. If you import a car from the UK it must pass the very strict Swedish roadworthiness examination which includes tough exhaust emission tests. It can be very expensive to bring a car up to the required standard if it fails. Seat belts are compulsory and the laws on drinking and driving are very strict.

The Swedes are very hospitable and enjoy parties. Most of all they enjoy their outdoor life. Many of the Stockholm business community have lakeside villas or cottages and there are ample facilities for sailing, fishing and swimming, or skiing in the winter. The Swedish winters are long, cold and dark and it is important to have plenty to occupy yourself with in the evenings.

Switzerland

Background

Switzerland is a small (16,000 square miles), land-locked country in central Europe. A land of mountains – the Alps and the lower-lying Jura, which comprise 70 per cent of the land area – and a central plateau with its lakes, it is very beautiful and has a large tourist trade, particularly in the winter when its skiing resorts are full. The population is about 6.7 million of whom 1.1 million are foreigners.

Switzerland has a strong democratic tradition and this is reflected in the jealously guarded liberties of each of the 26 cantons of the confederation. Caught between the traditional great powers of Germany, France, Italy and Austria, it has wisely steered a course of political neutrality in the last 150 years. As the standard bearer of internationalism, it has become the home of bodies such as the Red Cross and various UN agencies.

Exchange rate: Swiss Francs 2.48 = £1.

The economy

Switzerland is prosperous commercially, and the main cities of Zurich, Basle, Geneva and Berne are leading European banking and commercial centres. Agriculture is efficient and economic progress has been sufficient to attract large numbers of migrant workers, particularly from Italy. Apart from tourism and banking (crucial 'invisibles' which help to offset the visible trade deficit) Switzerland's main manufactured exports are machines and metal products, chemicals and pharmaceuticals, electrical goods, precision instruments, textiles, clothing and watches. Its main markets are the EC, the USA and Austria. The country is politically stable, highly developed industrially and commercially and strong enough to insulate itself from the worst effects of recessions. It has one of the lowest unemployment rates in the world. Inflation is currently around 6 per cent.

Language in Switzerland reflects its position as a former client state of the great powers: 65 per cent of the population speak German, 18.4 per cent speak French, 9.8 per cent speak Italian and 6.7 per cent speak other languages as a first language. In practice, many people are bi- or tri-lingual, and most members of the business community are fluent in English, French and German.

Personal finance and taxation

Managerial salaries are among the world's highest. The managing director of a typical medium-sized firm would be earning £95,000, as opposed to around £60,000 in the UK. Skilled workers would expect upwards of SFr5000 a month, and a trilingual secretary would earn about the same amount. Income tax is progressive and our managing director on £95,000 would receive net pay of around 65 per cent of gross salary. Most expatriate employees will be subject to tax, though some categories of foreign teacher are exempt. Guidance on tax matters should be sought from the Federal Tax Administration in Berne, the local tax authorities or a Swiss tax consultant (*Steuerexperte*).

Working conditions

The Swiss government is at present reluctant to grant visas to foreign workers, and has imposed numerical limits on long- and short-term labour permits. In general, long term permits are available only to people with special skills or qualifications who have been offered a position by a Swiss employer. Unsolicited applications are, therefore, not encouraged and have little or no chance of success.

Similarly, the government has reduced the number of seasonal permits (ie work permits covering periods of less than one year). Employment opportunities have been correspondingly reduced, though there are still opportunities in the hotel and catering trades during peak tourist periods.

It is useless to go to Switzerland and then start to look for work. The Swiss Embassy's leaflet on employment states that: 'Applications made by or on behalf of persons who have entered Switzerland temporarily as visitors, tourists or on business will be refused and reconsidered only after the applicants' departure from the country.'

It is clear, therefore, that the best chance of long-term employment is with a British or American firm, or international agency with offices in Switzerland. Once you have obtained a position with a Swiss employer, or UK company based in Switzerland, your prospective employer must obtain the labour and residence permits you need. On entering the country you will need to produce a valid passport and an 'assurance of residence permit' or a visa from the Swiss consulate.

Cost of living

If you succeed in finding long-term employment, remember that prices in Switzerland, particularly in the major cities, are high. Though prices have increased more rapidly in the UK than in Switzerland in the last few years, the latter is still more expensive.

The following table gives average prices of various foodstuffs in 1990:

	SFr
Milk (1 litre)	1.85
Butter (250 g)	4.80
Eggs (12)	7.00
Bread (1 kg)	4.80
Rice (1 kg)	3.60
Beefsteak (1 kg)	55.00
Bottle of wine	12.00
Petrol (litre)	1.12

Private boarding school education is expensive as is membership of sports clubs. Facilities for winter sports are, of course, excellent.

Living conditions

Communications in Switzerland offer no difficulties except in the upland region where, in winter, snowfalls are hazardous. The railway and air networks are dense and highly efficient. So too is the road system, despite the difficult terrain. The price of a new Toyota Corolla 1.6 is around SFr 21,000. Banking is highly developed and it will be easy to find a bank which will carry out transactions with your UK bank. Swiss currency can be freely exported.

Accommodation is not easy to find, and rents in good parts of the main cities are high. Ideally, your employer should look for good accommodation for you. For a reasonable, four-roomed unfurnished apartment, you might expect to pay £640–£1000 a month. (Furnished apartments are almost non-existent in Switzerland, so you will have to arrange to bring your furniture with you.)

Expatriates are strongly advised, in their own interest, to join a health insurance scheme from the very beginning. You should seek information from your employer on this point. The insurance should comprise not only medical and hospital treatment but also adequate sickness benefit, since employees have only a limited claim to payment of wages in the event of illness. Most people in Switzerland are insured against illness and accidents through various kinds of insurance scheme. The most popular ones, the so-called 'Krankenkassen', try to exert control over physicians' fees. For private patients and patients covered by other types of insurance, physicians usually charge more, according to income. Specialists, as a rule, charge significantly more than general practitioners.

Social insurance agreements between Switzerland and various other countries make it easier to join specific health insurance schemes and in certain circumstances shorten the waiting period. Under some agreements, moreover, the Swiss employer is required to make sure that an employee coming from the country concerned is insured for medical care (doctor and hospital) and, if he is not, to take out an adequte insurance for him; he can deduct the contributions for this from the employee's wages. In cases of doubt inquiries should be addressed to the appropriate consulate or to the Bundesamt für Sozialversicherung, 3003 Berne.

Information on English-speaking schools can be obtained from COBISEC which has two excellent (but expensive) member schools.

The Swiss have a reputation for insularity and coolness, but this is misjudged. Expatriates will, for the most part, find them good colleagues and warm friends. Living standards are high and opportunities for recreation and entertainment are plentiful (though playing membership of, say, a golf club near one of the main cities would be very expensive). Your business and social life is greatly eased and improved if you can speak one or more of the indigenous languages, and few employers now send people to Switzerland who do not have some proficiency in French and/or German.

The Middle East

The risks faced by expatriates in this region were brought home forcefully by the events leading up to the Gulf War. The long-term effect of these events is uncertain but, as pointed out in the Introduction, expatriates will need to be more rather than less sensitive to local cultures.

The Arab Countries: Some Notes on Etiquette

One of the things that worries expatriates about living and working in the Arab world is the idea of having to conform to a society whose customs and etiquette are very different from our own. All sorts of stories circulate about niceties of social behaviour, failure to observe which will mortally offend the Arabs, but most Arabs you are likely to meet will have travelled or studied in the West and be quite used to Western ways. Of course if, while talking to an Arab, you lounge in your chair in an arrogant or disrespectful fashion, it will not go down well. Nor will it be appreciated if you smoke, eat or drink in the presence of Moslems during the holy month of Ramadan, the time when their religion enjoins abstinence from such activities. But what one is really talking about then is simple good manners, and simple good manners will take you a long way in contacts with members of your host country.

This is not to say that there are not some points of etiquette that you should bear in mind on such occasions as you come into social contact with local people. If you are invited to dinner in an Arab country you will be expected to arrive on time (although Arab guests to your home will be much more casual about punctuality). You should be very careful about admiring any object in the house in which you are a guest because your host may press you to take it as a present, but he will, in due course, expect a present of at least similar value from you. When food comes, you will have more heaped on your plate than you can eat. It is not considered bad manners to leave most of it, rather the reverse, because to leave nothing on your plate suggests you think the host has not been sufficiently generous. If food is being eaten with the fingers (or indeed when you are offering anything to an Arab), use your right hand only; the left is considered impure, since it is associated with what one might politely call the exercise of intimate bodily functions.

If there are long periods of silence over dinner, do not consider yourself a social failure. Arabs do not regard constant talk as a social necessity. Nor should you be taken aback if they ask you rather personal questions – this goes for talk between women in particular. They are not restrained as we are, about the things concerning other people that we are dying to know but are always too polite to ask – while hoping they will come back to us in the form of gossip. Nor should you feel the evening has gone badly if your Arab guests leave immediately after dinner. This is customary, and they expect you to do likewise. Incidentally, few Arabs, except the more westernised and sophisticated, will bring their wives in response to an invitation, and neither will they expect the guest to do likewise.

There are other points of social etiquette as well, and if you are being asked into an Arab home or vice versa, you should certainly get advice from someone who knows the local scene. It is worth acquainting yourself before your departure with the dos and don'ts of everyday behaviour. For instance, all Arab countries, even the more liberal ones, frown on what the Americans politely call 'public displays of affection' between the sexes. Women wearing revealing clothes are apt to attract attention which varies, according to the country, from what would be described in the UK as rude stares to being told by the police to go home and put on something more suitable. It is unwise to argue with the police in an Arab country since the processes of justice are, to say the least, different from those in the West. This does not mean, even in Saudi Arabia, that they will cut off some valued part of your anatomy if you are found guilty of a crime; but they will unceremoniously put you on the next plane out of the country if they do not like your behaviour. The public flogging incidents which have received so much publicity are extremely rare (as far as Westerners are concerned). This sort of punishment would only be put into practice in the face of the most open and provocative breaches of the law. However, in countries where Koranic law is strictly observed, particularly in Saudi Arabia, there is no right to representation in court and lengthy periods of arrest before trial can occur. On the positive side Islamic law lays great emphasis on the fulfilment of contractual obligations – by both parities.

Drinking is severely punished in the various countries where alcohol is forbidden and it is criminal and foolish to try to smuggle it in. This does not mean to say that smuggling of alcohol does not go on. There are few places where whisky is not available, at prices of up to £80 a bottle. But it is best to leave smuggling to others; and if you do get offered smuggled booze be very discreet about drinking it – no raucous parties and avoid being seen under the influence in public.

The maxim about good manners getting you a long way also applies to business etiquette. There will be some things about business contacts that you will find frustrating or annoying but you will just have to accept them with good grace. For instance, Arabs are lax about keeping appointments; and when you do get to the person you may have waited hours or even days to see, all sorts of individuals will probably pop into his office while you are there and interrupt your conversation for minutes on end. This is just where Arab customs are different from ours, as they are about the acceptance of gifts. This is a tricky one for businessmen, but a lot of what we could castigate as bribery is the normal custom in an Arab country. This is not to say that you should go about trying to bribe people to get favours – this is generally considered to be a bad idea, because as a Westerner, you would not know who to bribe and how to go about it for a start – but if you are offered a present in a business context you should not refuse it, unless it patently *is* a bribe. To a Moslem, the return of a gift implies that it is unworthy of the recipient and can be a tremendous slap in the face for the giver. It is difficult to tread the narrow path between integrity and self-righteousness, but then few things about leaving home to go and work in another country are easy – though they are nearly always interesting.

One final question that tends to be asked now is whether and to what extent the backlash against Western ways and influence which marked the Iranian Revolution has spread to other Moslem countries. Certainly, extremists seem to have seized on the furore caused by Salman Rushdie's book, *The Satanic Verses*, to advance the cause of fundamentalism, which means there is unlikely to be any loosening up of observances regarding alcohol consumption, dress, religious holidays and so on. But while the possibility of upheaval can never be entirely discounted in countries going through a period of such radical changes as at present, informed opinion regards them as unlikely.

Egypt

Background

Egypt is about four times the size of Great Britain, but about 95 per cent of the country is virtually uninhabitable desert, a fact which gives cause for alarm about its rapidly growing population, estimated at 48.5 million and increasing annually at about 3 per cent. An estimated 12 million people live in Cairo and another 4 million in Alexandria. The rest are concentrated largely in the Nile valley and delta.

Politically, Egypt is a democratic socialist country. President Muhammed Hosni Mubarak, who succeeded President Sadat, was re-elected for a six-year term in 1987.

During the past few years, support for Muslim fundamentalism has grown in Egypt, particularly among the poorer sections of the community, who see the establishment of a wholly Islamic state as a remedy for the country's economic and social problems. Both prominent Egyptians known to be opposed to Islamic fundamentalism and symbols of Western influence, such as liquor stores, have been the target of terrorist attacks. To compound the country's problems, worsening economic conditions have led to strikes and outbursts of civil unrest.

Exchange rate 5.54 Egyptian pounds (LE) = £1.

The economy

The need for development aid is focused on the problem of housing and feeding Egypt's large, impoverished population. The potential for instability has been brought to the fore on a number of occasions in the shape of serious rioting. Worrying factors are high inflation, a fall in oil revenues and a sharp reduction in the inflow of money from Egyptians working in other Arab countries. Theoretically, with its large population, Egypt could become the manufacturing centre of the Middle East. It is here, in construction and in oil and water exploration, that most of the development is going on and where European expatriates are mostly employed.

Personal finance and taxation

Foreigners living in Egypt are liable to income tax, but allowances are generous and tax on an average expatriate salary would be around 30 to 35 per cent. Salaries for expatriates should be at least 50 per cent higher than in the UK and some companies pay well over 100 per cent more to attract highly qualified personnel. Arrangements should be made to have some of this paid outside the country, since although in theory up to 75 per cent of one's Egyptian income can be remitted out of the country, in practice this is reported to be very difficult. A further advantage in having part of one's salary paid outside the country is that it is not then liable to Egyptian tax. It is, in fact, common for expatriate salaries to be paid in hard currency outside Egypt, with only as much as is required for living expenses being brought into the country.

A *work permit* is needed, which must be arranged by the local employer. It is advisable to take a plentiful supply of passport photos and duplicates of essential documents as bureaucracy in Egypt is an industry in its own right and there are many occasions on which form filling, supported by documents, is called for. Reserves of patience are also advantageous, for the Egyptians, though extremely nice people to deal with, are not noted for speed or efficiency.

Living conditions

The two main cities are Cairo and Alexandria. Both have long hot summers, where the temperature averages 90°F and frequently goes over 100°F, and short winters. These run from November to March and though mild by European standards they do require warmer clothing and a certain amount of indoor heating on colder days. In upper Egypt temperatures are much higher, though it is a dry heat. Alexandria, on the other hand, is inclined to be humid because of its position by the sea.

Egypt need not be an expensive country to live in, provided one does not rely on imported food. Local fruit and vegetables are cheap and good, though it is essential to wash them if eaten fresh – preferably in boiled or filtered water, since tap water is not recommended. Overall, food is much cheaper than in the UK, though prices at the big hotels are geared to international standards. Current annual rents in Cairo for a three-bedroomed unfurnished flat range from US$20,000 upwards; rents are lower in Alexandria. Many expatriates, however, are employed on remote sites (usually on single status contracts), with purpose-built accommodation provided.

In finding accommodation (if it is not provided by the employer) it helps greatly to work through an agent, whose guidance on local practice and general know-how should be well worth the 30 per cent of one month's rent he takes in commission. Two important and sometimes overlooked requirements to brief him on are the orientation of the windows – they should not face the sun during the hottest hours of the day – and the availability of a telephone, which otherwise can take months or even years to instal.

Air-conditioning, though generations of expatriates lived without it, is considered essential for modern standards of comfort. Like other household effects air-conditioning equipment can be bought locally, but it is generally advisable to bring it with you. Electricity is provided at 220V 50 Hz AC, but frequent power cuts and unevenness in supply can play havoc with equipment. Plugs are usually the 2-pin, round variety. A device called a voltage stabiliser is therefore an essential adjunct to any electrical goods you bring with you. There is little difference between the price of electrical goods in Egypt and the UK, so they are probably best bought locally.

Efficient household equipment is all the more necessary because good servants are increasingly difficult to find, though wages of LE80 a week for cooks and LE50 for a maid are very reasonable. They work from 7.30 am to 3.00 pm and expect overtime for longer hours plus a modest yearly bonus. Dry cleaning is available only at the major hotels.

Locally assembled cars can now be bought and a locally produced Fiat will cost from LE18,000. Because of import restrictions, second-hand cars can be as expensive as new ones. The state of the roads is very poor, so cars need to be serviced every 1500 kilometres or so.

The local situation regarding schools is quite good but they are expensive. Medical attention is also good in theory – Egyptian doctors are much sought after throughout the Middle East – but the standards of hygiene in hospitals can leave something to be desired. As far as recreation is concerned, Egypt has plenty to offer. Social life is much more relaxed and varied than in other Middle Eastern countries. There are no constraints on the consumption of alcohol and the practice of Islam, though universal, is not exercised with any degree of fanaticism.

The Gulf States

Background

Bahrain

Bahrain is composed of a group of 33 islands in the Arabian Gulf with a total land area of some 230 square miles. The capital city and chief business centre of the country is Manama, which lies at the north-east end of the main island, with Isa Town, a largely residential area, situated seven miles south of the capital. Oil was first commercially exploited in Bahrain in 1932 and now provides 75 per cent of export earnings. Owing to the gradual decline in crude oil production during the past few years and the fact that present reserves are forecast to last only until the late 1990s, the government is actively encouraging foreign investment in diversified industrial development – with some success. Recent estimates put the population at 430,000, increasing at a rate of 3 per cent a year.

Bahrain is governed by an hereditary Amir who is advised by a Cabinet of Ministers. Arabic is the official language but English is widely spoken, particularly in commercial circles. Although the usual Moslem observances are kept, Bahrain is generally thought of as one of the more progressive, relaxed and hospitable Arab states to which expatriates should have little difficulty in adjusting.

Exchange rate: BDinars 0.62 = £1.

Oman

The Sultanate of Oman runs in a 1000-mile-long narrow strip around the south-eastern corner of the Arab peninsula. Its most northern point is separated from the rest of the country by the United Arab Emirates. The total area is about the same as that of the UK, but 97 per cent of the country is desert or mountains. Statistics differ about the population size, but it is generally thought to be 1.5 million of whom 250,000 live in the area of the capital Muscat and its neighbouring port, Mutrah, which is also the commercial centre.

Oman is an independent state, ruled by Sultan Qaboos bin Said. Politically and economically it is favourably disposed towards the UK, which is also its biggest single source of imports. This fact is reflected in the relatively large British community. It is fairly stable politically.

The official language is Arabic, but English is widely understood in business circles.

Exchange rate: Omani Rials 0.64 = £1.

Anyone going to Oman, even on a non-business visit, must previously obtain a 'No Objection Certificate' issued by the Sultanate immigration authorities and obtainable in the country by the employer or a local sponsor who should allow at least six weeks for that process. The NOC is necessary in order to obtain a visa even for family visitors. This proviso does not apply, though, to business visitors born in the UK, who can obtain visas in London.

Qatar

Qatar, which is one of the smaller OPEC countries, consists of a narrow peninsula of some 4000 square miles which juts northwards 100 miles into the Arabian Gulf with Saudi Arabia, Bahrain and Abu Dhabi as neighbours. Situated on the east coast of Qatar is the capital city and chief commercial centre, Doha, a fast-developing modern metropolis from which 1080 km of excellent roads radiate to the rest of the peninsula. Other important urban centres are Umm Said, also on the east coast, which is the centre for industrial development and on the west coast, Dukham which is a major oil-producing centre.

The population of Qatar is estimated at around 371,860 of which about 80 per cent live in Doha. Qatari nationals constitute about half the total with large communities of Indians, Pakistanis, Northern Arabs, Iranians and Gulf Arabs. The British community is thought to number about 6000. The official language of Qatar is Arabic, but English is widely spoken in business and professional circles.

Qatar is governed by an hereditary ruler, His Highness The Amir, who presides over a Council of Ministers which is assisted by a 30-man Advisory Council drawn from leaders of the community. The ruler takes a keen personal interest in the economic development of the country as a whole, the aim being to make it much less dependent on oil revenue through the establishment of other types of industrial activity. The government of Qatar has a reasonably progressive reputation and although the country is a Moslem state in which the strict Wahhabi sect flourishes, this only makes for austerity in public life, and provided the usual Moslem etiquette is observed (for example, both men and women should dress modestly in public), most Western expatriates will find their private lives are not markedly affected. The country is politically stable.

Exchange rate: Qatari Riyals 6.07 = £1.

United Arab Emirates: Abu Dhabi

Abu Dhabi is the largest and richest of the seven Emirates which make up the UAE. Its ruler is also President of the UAE. It has a population of about 670,000 of whom only 22 per cent are Abu Dhabians, the rest being Arabs from other countries, Indians, Pakistanis and Europeans, of whom there is a sizeable community.

The main population centre is Abu Dhabi town, which is on an island 10 miles long and which until relatively recently was little more than a fishing port. There are some handsome buildings, a choice of Western-style supermarkets, several sports clubs, and a surprising amount of greenery planted along boulevards and in parks.

A three-lane ring road including an airport link and down-town tunnel is under construction. Most of the rest of the Emirate, which is about the size of Scotland, is desert. The oasis town of Al-Ain, 100 miles inland, is a fast-growing population centre, however, and is the site of the UAE's university. Oil in large quantities has been found both on and offshore, the centre of the offshore oil industry being Das Island, about 80 miles out in the Gulf

United Arab Emirates: Dubai and Sharjah

Dubai and Sharjah are the two neighbouring Emirates to the north of Abu Dhabi. The population of Dubai is over 400,000 and of Sharjah, about 270,000. Most of them live in towns of those names, though Dubai actually consists of twin towns: Dubai and Deira. Sharjah town is only some nine miles from Dubai. In both of these Emirates oil has been discovered only in the last few years, though Dubai was an established commercial centre as an entrepot for Middle East trade for a century before.

Dubai is generally considered a more pleasant and sophisticated place to live in than Abu Dhabi.

Kuwait

Kuwait lies at the head of the Arabian Gulf and is bordered to the north and west by Iraq and to the south by Saudi Arabia. Its land area, of some 6900 square miles, includes the Kuwaiti portion of the former neutral zone, a territory of some 2000 square miles partitioned between Kuwait and Saudi Arabia, in which both countries continue to share equally in the exploitation of oil and natural resources. The capital and commercial centre of the country is Kuwait City which is situated on Kuwait Bay. Kuwait, liberated from Iraqi occupation in February 1991, is also one of the Gulf States. The rebuilding of Kuwait is confidently expected to generate renewed opportunities, but at the time of writing the situation remains too confused for comment. Certainly, it is not likely to attract any but the toughest, single status, pioneering-minded expatriates – though for them the rewards may well be considerable.

Exchange rate: UAE Dirham 6.12 = £1

Economies

Oil is the salient factor in the economies of all the Gulf States, although the level of reserves varies. Most of these countries are making efforts to diversify into other activities and to invest oil revenues in the creation of infrastructure. Bahrain is developing large-scale industrial enterprises, including aluminium smelting and shipbuilding; it is also an important offshore banking centre and is emerging as a regional centre for technology and light industry. Oman, whose oil reserves are modest by Middle Eastern standards, is developing copper mining and smelting, cement production and fisheries; it also has a programme to expand health, education, communications and public services such as electricity and water. Qatar produces fertilisers and cement, and is also making rigorous efforts to develop its agricultural industry. In the UAE, Dubai is an important banking centre, and its harbour is one of the largest in the Middle East. Abu Dhabi has invested in building up its infrastructure – roads, schools, housing, hospitals, hotels – and developing the harbour. Water is in short supply, so the development of desalination plants is another area of investment.

Personal finance

Expatriates should be earning considerably more than the equivalent UK salary, with generous fringe benefits: certainly free or heavily subsidised accommodation; provision for medical treatment; payment of school fees or help with them; six weeks' home leave a year, with air fares paid in the case of married men and spells of two to three weeks' leave every four months for bachelors; and probably provision of a car and, in the case of a managerial job, at least one servant.

Taxation

At the time of writing there is no personal income tax in any of the Gulf States.

Working conditions

Work and residence permits are required in every state.

Anyone going to Oman, even on a non-business visit, must previously obtain a 'No Objection Certificate' issued by the Sultanate immigration authorities and obtainable in the country by the employer or a local sponsor who should allow at least six weeks for that process. The NOC is necessary in order to obtain a visa even for family visitors. This proviso does not apply, though, to business visitors born in the UK, who can obtain visas in London.

Throughout the Gulf, you would be well advised to take a supply of passport photos with youu, to help speed up the process of obtaining official documents. You should also check for last-minute changes to visa requirements, which are apt to be brought in with minimal notice.

Living conditions

The region is characterised by hot and humid summers, with temperatures over 100°F. Air conditioning and lightweight clothing are essential, and you should bring a good supply of the latter with you, because you will probably find that you have to change at least once a day. It is more comfortable, in local conditions, to wear cotton clothing, rather than synthetics, and it is sensible to take garments which can withstand frequent washing.

From November to April the climate is pleasantly warm; it can at times be sufficiently chilly to warrant wearing an overcoat. In Bahrain, where rain falls during the cooler season, expatriates are advised to include among their clothing a waterproof coat and wellingtons as unmade roads rapidly turn into quagmires after heavy rainfall.

It may be possible to find local tailors who will make copies of Western clothes at a reasonable price.

With most expatriate postings, free or subsidised accommodation is usually offered along with the job, and it is usually of a high standard, fully furnished and air conditioned. Good servants are difficult to find and many expatriates do without them – if a servant is essential, it is easiest to find Indians, Pakistanis or Filipinos.

A car is essential, and new models can usually be bought at prices slightly lower than in the UK, although not all British makes are available. Petrol is, of course, cheap. Check with the local police about driving licence regulations; you may be able to drive on an international licence, or you may have to apply for a local licence (usually obtainable without too much difficulty).

Food prices are generally higher than in Britain, although you should be able to save by shopping in local markets.

On the thorny matter of alcohol, exercise discretion. Non-Moslems are usually able to buy alcohol for private consumption, but in most of the Gulf States it is necessary to obtain a liquor permit, either from the police or, in Qatar, from the British Embassy in Doha. Bahrain, with its licensed shops, is comparatively liberal and permits are not required.

Alcohol apart, there is usually a lively social scene in the form of parties and dinners. Leisure naturally centres on the outdoor life – bathing and fishing at the beach, picnicking and camping in the desert during the cooler part of the year. Facilities for organised sports such as golf or tennis are available through clubs or hotels, but they tend to be expensive.

Most expatriates in the Gulf belong to private medical schemes, funded by their employers. However, state-run facilities are generally of a high standard, and some provide free care, even for non-nationals.

There are a number of British and International schools, although in view of the volatile situation in the region, many parents prefer to send their children to boarding school in the UK.

Libyan Arab Republic

Background

The Libyan Arab Republic (officially known as the Socialist People's Libyan Arab Jamahiriyah) is about six times the size of the UK and its population is estimated to be no more than 3.2 million. Most of the country is desert and until the 1960s it was one of the world's poorest nations. The discovery of oil and gas in vast quantities inland between the two main cities, Tripoli (988,000) and Benghazi (650,000), made it immensely rich, but the drop in oil prices has since sharply reduced earnings. Agriculture and industry are encouraged. Because of the small population it relies heavily on foreign labour and employs large numbers of workers from poorer Arab countries, especially Egypt. Skilled professional people are also recruited from these countries, as well as from Europe, but the number of British people declined after the Libyan Embassy siege in London and even more so after the American air raids in 1986. British diplomatic interests are looked after by the Italian Embassy though commercial contacts have been maintained.

Although British expatriates and business visitors still go to Libya, they do so literally at their own risk. The gloomy comment of one expatriate is that it should be considered as a short-term measure at a time of dire financial need – if at all.

The country is ruled by a military dictatorship, the Revolutionary Command Council, headed by Colonel Gadaffi, a man who combines puritanically traditionalist Moslem fervour with revolutionary socialist views. Thus all enterprises above a certain level of turnover are state-owned and many prices are controlled. Religious festivals, such as Ramadan (the annual month-long semi-fast, when eating, drinking and smoking is forbidden to Moslems between dawn and dusk), are rigorously enforced. Not only is Arabic the official language, but all street, shop, traffic and other public signs are displayed solely in Arabic and all correspondence from Libyan public bodies is in that language. Needless to say the sale, import or consumption of alcohol is strictly forbidden. All this, combined with wide-ranging political and moral censorship, makes Libya a difficult country for some expatriates to adjust to. On the positive side there is very little crime and conditions for women are less restrictive than in other Moslem fundamentalist countries.

Exchange rate: LD0.49 = £1.

The economy

As indicated above, the salient fact of the economy is oil, but the government, which is committed to a comprehensive policy of nationalisation, is making considerable efforts to diversify by building up a variety of secondary manufacturing industries, particularly in food processing, building materials, steel, clothes and footwear; by looking for other minerals; and by investing a lot of money in agriculture and fishery research. There is also a great deal of construction activity particularly in housing and in improving roads, harbours and other forms of transport and communications, though activity in these areas has slowed with the decline in oil revenues.

Personal finance

As a rule of thumb, you should expect to be earning double your UK salary, plus the usual fringe benefits. Because of the stresses of living in Libya previously referred to, generous paid leave terms are normal. They average about 40 days a year, taken either in one spell or, more usually, on an arrangement providing for a break every three months. People working on the oilfields inland and in intense heat are generally given one week's foreign leave in every four, though it can be more depending on how badly your skills are needed and where you are based. Accommodation, which is very scarce and expensive, is either provided or subsidised. Most people would consider that working for the Libyan government is a course of action most likely to appeal to the young and adventurous or those committed on the political left – and probably both!

A typical package of benefits advertised by the Oasis Oil Company (Libya's National Oil Corporation) is as follows:

Furnished married/single housing provided in Tripoli town.
Free meals and housing plus desert allowance for field-based personnel.
Vacation: Tripoli based – 30 days' annual leave with paid air fares to point of origin plus 7 days' interim leave after 6 months' service with paid air fares to Europe plus per diem allowance.
Field based – 30/20 commuting schedule with 7 round trip paid air fares per year to point of origin.
Free medical attention and BUPA cover.
Attractive provident fund plan.
Low cost accident insurance plan.
School facilities and children's education assistance for Tripoli-based families.

Taxation

Income tax is on a graduated scale and is based on salary plus housing allowance. There is little in the way of allowances for dependants, so tax rates do not vary much within the salary bands. A person with two children earning an expatriate salary of LD15,000 would pay about 40 per cent of this in tax and social security contributions.

A tax clearance certificate has to be produced before leaving the country if you are resident there.

Working conditions

The working week runs from Saturday to Thursday (Friday being the Moslem holiday) and hours generally run from 8.00 am to 2.00 pm. Shops are open in the evening with a break in the middle of the day.

Work permits, which have to be obtained by the employer, are needed for a stay of more than 30 days and must be obtained in advance of your arrival. But whatever your length of stay, your passport must carry an Arabic stamp, showing all personal details in Arabic. Without this you will not be allowed into the country.

You can change jobs while in Libya on a work permit, provided your employer there does not object and that your tax and social insurance contributions are fully up to date when you switch. If you leave the country and have a work or residence permit you have to obtain an exit and re-entry visa to enable you to resume employment when you go back. When you finally leave Libya you must have a final exit visa, showing that all taxes and bills for public services (eg gas, water, electricity) have been paid. Once you have obtained a final exit visa, you have to wait for six months before returning to Libya to work for another employer. As the reader will by now have gathered, the time-consuming and bewildering (because apart from anything else they have to be conducted in Arabic) bureaucratic procedures in Libya are a major drawback of life there. It is recommended that you get a 94 page passport because of the amount of documentation needed every time you enter and leave the country.

Dependants may also be allowed to work provided their employer gets a work permit for them, but in order to get such permission it is necessary to produce evidence of relevant qualification (nursing, teaching, secretarial, etc) as well as a marriage certificate. Working opportunities for qualified wives are reportedly excellent.

There are restrictions on remitting money out of the country, 90 per cent of annual salary may be remitted if you get a housing allowance but otherwise the permitted maximum is 60 per cent. There have been recent problems in getting full settlement on completion of contracts. It is now recommended that employment offers from all but the largest companies should be treated with great caution.

Living conditions

There is a brief cool winter when it occasionally rains heavily (causing flood hazards on the many ill-laid roads) from November to early March. Winter nights can be very cold. The summers are dry and hot; temperatures rarely exceed 100°F but are trying because of the high humidity. New houses are not built to take into account extremes of temperature, so both heating and air-conditioning are a necessity, which means that quite high fuel bills have to be reckoned with. Light-weight clothing is also essential and, though dutiable, should be bought in the UK, since in Libya it is expensive and of poor quality.

Accommodation, unless it is provided by a European company, is let unfurnished and in view of the mountainous difficulties involved in bringing possessions into Libya, the easiest way is probably to buy household goods once you get there, if you are working for a local concern or the Libyan government. It is possible to buy second-hand from expatriates returning home if you establish the right contacts. However, state control of retail outlets also means that new goods are extremely cheap, lower than so-called duty-free prices in places like Hong Kong. Electrical fittings are of the continental type, but what is more important is that the electricity supply, theoretically provided at 125V and 220V, AC, fluctuates considerably, so it is necessary to buy a regulator to protect the equipment. Standards of repair and service are poor.

Used personal effects are not dutiable, but customs clearance on unaccompanied baggage is apt to be a protracted business which includes checking that imported goods are not on the Arab blacklist. To this end you need to have a certificate of origin, authenticated by the Libyan embassy or that of any other Arab league nation. Because of these complexities, men with families would be well advised to travel ahead and count on having to live in a hotel for three or four weeks to prepare the ground. Hotels cost about £50–£90 a day, exclusive of meals, but it is essential to make sure that your prospective employer or a reliable local agent has confirmed hotel arrangements on the spot, since desk staff are apt to deny all knowledge of you when you arrive, even if a firm booking has been made by post.

The majority of expatriates in Libya live in company-owned compounds. Rented accommodation is scarce and prohibitively expensive.

There are some favourable seasonal variations in locally grown food and petrol is very much cheaper than in the UK. The government's policy of nationalisation has led to a drastic decline in the number of shops offering any wide range of goods. The European-style supermarkets which stocked – at a price – almost everything you could obtain in the average British high street (apart from alcohol) have virtually disappeared, and the standard of restaurants has also deteriorated sharply; on the positive side, however, what you can get in the shops is reasonably priced. Since there is not a lot to spend one's money on in Libya it is a good place to go if you want to build up some savings. There are now quite serious shortages of food and commodities. For this reason it is best to take with you even the less obvious things such as books, toys, and a food processor.

Domestic help is unavailable officially. Some Europeans bring au pair-type domestic help with them.

Cars are essential since public transport is virtually non-existent and taxis extremely expensive. They can only be imported as company vehicles – individuals are not allowed to import cars. Spares are a problem and standards of repair and servicing poor so, while second-hand cars can be bought, keeping them on the road can be risky. They are also very expensive and often in poor condition. You need to have a Libyan driving licence, though you are allowed three months' grace during which you can drive on a UK licence. However, you should begin to take steps to obtain a Libyan licence as soon as you arrive. Like other bureaucratic processes in Libya, it is a time-consuming and trying business. Comprehensive insurance is advisable and third party insurance is required. Although traffic in the towns is not too bad, standards of driving and observance of road discipline by both drivers and pedestrians are poor.

Facilities for leisure and entertainment are limited, though there are excellent beaches and good fishing in places. You can also play tennis and golf (of sorts, in view of the sandy terrain). The beach club in Tripoli is a place where women can wear bikinis without attracting unwelcome attention. Otherwise revealing clothing and 'permissive' behaviour should be avoided in public. Noisy late-night parties are also frowned upon, and may attract police attention. There is very little social contact between Libyans and expatriates.

Both Tripoli and Benghazi are rather clean and quite pleasant cities, with good health records. Medical and dental attention is provided by the Libyan government, but standards of care and staffing are reputed not to be high and expatriates use private health services. In Tripoli, the Oil Industry Medical Society, while theoretically confined to oil industry employees, is open to outsiders on payment of a (quite large) annual subscription by their employers, with further fees per individual consultation for medical or dental treatment. In Benghazi Europeans use the Ageco clinic. However, serious or prolonged illnesses need to be treated abroad.

The oil companies maintain a primary school in Tripoli.

Saudi Arabia

Background

Saudi Arabia occupies about 80 per cent of the Arabian peninsula and shares borders with many Arab countries – Jordan, Iraq, Kuwait, Qatar, UAE and Yemen. It covers about nine times the area of the UK, but a large part of it is desert. No exact population figure exists, but it is probably around the 11 million mark, about a quarter of whom are nomadic or semi-nomadic. Two-thirds of the remainder are urban dwellers, mostly living in the larger cities; the capital, Riyadh and Jeddah, the chief port and commercial centre (1 million each), the sacred cities of Mecca and Medina (500,000 and 350,000 respectively), Al Khobar (45,000) and Dhahran, in the centre of the oil industry (60,000). That industry is situated in the eastern province along the Gulf. Saudi Arabia is the world's second largest oil producer and new oilfields are still being discovered.

The country is ruled by its royal family, headed by King Fahd. The rulers' sympathies are strongly with the West, particularly with the USA, and this relationship has been intensified by the Gulf War, with Saudi Arabia playing host to the largest concentration of US and allied forces to be assembled since the Second World War.

The presence of non-Moslem troops has caused considerable unease in a country which is traditionally ultra-conservative and adheres to strict codes of conduct in moral and religious matters. Some Saudis fear the presence of Westerners so close to the holy cities of Mecca and Medina. There has also been concern about the presence of US women soldiers;

however, most of them are deployed in the desert or in bases at Dhahran, so they are hardly visible. Saudis are also worried about the possibility of the troops bringing in alcohol, and holding Christian religious ceremonies on Saudi soil, but so far the allied troops have acted with tact and discretion.

Nevertheless, there is consensus that the war will bring permanent changes to Saudi society. A recent protest by Saudi women, who are still not allowed to drive, was quashed, but there are influences at work which are bound to affect the Kingdom in the longer term. Among educated Saudis, the crisis and war have started debate about the role of the royal family, the lack of democratic institutions, freedom of the press and women's rights (or lack of them). Balanced against these more liberal elements in Saudi society are the religious zealots. The eventual direction of Saudi Arabia will depend on which side gains the upper hand – and this depends on whether a permanent American presence is established in the post-war period.

Exchange rate: Saudi Riyals 6.25 = £1.

The economy

Saudi Arabia's wealth is almost literally limitless and it has monetary reserves second only to those of West Germany. The backbone of the economy is, of course, oil. It is also thought that the country may be rich in other minerals. Although little has yet been done to exploit them, there are now plans to develop other mineral resources over the next few years. Gold, silver and copper are now being produced. The income from oil has been largely devoted to improving the country's infrastructure (roads, ports, airports, telecommunications and all kinds of construction). There are plans for a wide range of projects for individual development. These range from the obvious ones of petrol refining, gas liquefaction plant and other petroleum-based activities to the expansion of a wide range of manufacturing industries. There has also been a good deal of investment in agriculture, which employs about a quarter of the Saudi labour force. Agricultural products, however, are far from sufficient to meet local demand. Since they depend on the availability of water – one resource which is critically scarce in this arid country – another major form of investment has been in various measures of water conservation and deployment and in investigating possibilities for desalination.

Apart from water, Saudi Arabia's scarcest resource is trained manpower and the country is heavily dependent on foreign skills. For this reason a great deal of money is being put into education at all levels. In the longer term, this may reduce Saudi reliance on foreign labour, and already Saudi graduates have, to some extent, taken over middle-level posts in banking and administration which were previously held by Indians and Pakistanis. But at the extremes of the labour market – highly skilled technicians and professionals, and labourers – it seems unlikely that reliance on foreign

workers can be reduced for some time to come. Inflation is around 2 per cent.

Personal finance and taxation

You could expect to more than double your gross UK earnings in the more arduous inland posts. Elsewhere salary differentials between Saudi Arabia and the UK are not as high as they were, but you could still expect to increase your UK gross salary by about 60 per cent.

These high salaries are accompanied by generous fringe benefits, which include furnished accommodation, ample home leave with air fares paid, a car, medical attention, and free or subsidised education for children in the case of more senior jobs. The level of remuneration reflects the rather arduous social and climatic conditions in the country, which women in particular find hard to take.

There is no income tax in Saudi Arabia; an attempt to introduce it led to a threat by foreign workers to resign en masse, and the proposal was abandoned.

Working conditions

Work permits must be applied for by your Saudi agent, employer or contact in the country. When this is forthcoming you must supply its details to the Saudi Embassy which will issue a visa. This is apt to be a lengthy procedure and plenty of time must be allowed for the documentation to come through. It is a good idea to have smallpox and cholera vaccinations, and polio, TAB and antitetanus are also advisable.

A particular point to bear in mind is that, if you arrive in the Haji (pilgrimage to Mecca) time, special precautions against cholera have to be taken and certified. Check details before leaving as conditions are sometimes changed without notice.

The working week runs from Saturday to Wednesday. Work starts early in the morning, at 7.00 or 8.00 am, but there is a long break in the middle of the day.

Telephone services, internationally and between towns, are improving, as are the posts. Deliveries are made to box numbers at the main post offices, except in the case of hotels and government offices.

Foreigners should carry their ID, driver's licence and residence permit at all times. It should also be borne in mind that exit visas are required to leave the country and these sometimes entail bureaucratic delays before you get them. You also need a letter of release if you are changing employers within Saudi Arabia. The conditions under which you can terminate your employment should therefore be clearly set out in your contract.

Many jobs, particularly at more junior levels, are single status. Where accompanying wives are allowed, you are advised to bring copies of your marriage certificate.

Living conditions

For most of the year the places where expatriates are likely to find themselves in Saudi Arabia are extremely hot and temperatures of 100°F are usual. Around Jeddah and the eastern province oilfields, humidity is high as well. The interior is dry and, though equally hot in summer, can get very cold in winter (December to March). Thus warm clothing is necessary in winter in places like Riyadh. There is little rainfall anywhere and although irregular heavy showers do occur in the winter months, the average annual rainfall is only five inches.

Clothing is available locally, but the range is limited and expensive, so it is best to take it with you. Take plenty of lightweight articles and a few medium weight things for winter wear.

In spite of the heat, you have to be careful about clothing etiquette. Men should not wear shorts in public and there are very severe restrictions on what is considered proper for women in public. Thus, no 'revealing' dresses (décolleté or see-through), no hems above the knee, sleeves at least to the elbow, trousers only if worn with a top that goes below the thighs and, on the beach, one-piece bathing costumes only.

Clothes and other personal effects can be shipped in duty-free, and shipping times have improved enormously. The formalities are complicated and it is best to use a clearing agent.

It is also best – and not too expensive – to buy electrical equipment locally. Electricity is supplied at 110V or 220V, 60 cycles AC and many places have facilities for both. Refrigerators and air-conditioners (or air coolers) are essential.

Nearly all jobs advertised for Saudi Arabia offer free accommodation, usually furnished.

If you have to travel out ahead of your family or are otherwise in the position of waiting for accommodation, bear in mind that a good hotel will cost about SR300 a night.

Executive jobs tend to include domestic help as a fringe benefit, though you will first have to find your servant. Saudi women are not allowed to work and the personnel available are Arabs from other countries, Filipinos, Indians, Pakistanis and North Africans. Ethiopians and Sudanese are considered the best bet, but you should try to get someone recommended to you by another expatriate. Although members of the business community speak English, servants seldom do so and a basic knowledge of Arabic is therefore useful, as well as being a courtesy much appreciated by your Arab contacts. It is advisable to insure servants against injury as employers can be held liable for damages, and it is a good idea to get them to take a medical before you employ them.

All kinds of food are available in the large city supermarkets, including baby products. Imported foods are, naturally, expensive though bulk-buying can cut the cost considerably. Local meat is not good by European standards and should never be eaten rare, though an inspection system has now been introduced. Vegetables and fruit are varied, plentiful and reasonably priced but should be washed in disinfected water if eaten fresh. Imported foodstuffs, whether frozen or canned, have to come a long way (a lot of the meat, for instance, comes from Australia) so check for spoiled items when shopping.

Shopping is, for women, an ordeal. It is usual to carry cash, and cheques are rarely accepted. Women are not allowed to drive which means that they must either walk or take a taxi, unless they are lucky enough to have a chauffeur. In fact, although cars are essential and petrol is comparatively cheap, owning one is not without its hazards. Driving standards are poor; there is no legal insurance requirement, but the compensation that has to be paid for an accident involving loss of life is high. Maximum comprehensive cover and third-party liability are most strongly advised. However, the consequences of being involved in a traffic accident are always serious and the Saudi police are not famous for their lenient treatment of foreigners.

A wide range of models is available but, alas, British cars are not really a good buy. Japanese ones, ranging at medium price levels from SR30,000 to around SR40,000, are the most popular. A car usually goes with the job, in any case with executive or supervisory posts. You will need a Saudi licence which at present can be obtained, with a three-month delay, on production of a UK one.

Facilities for recreation in Saudi Arabia are extremely limited, and boredom, particularly for wives, is a major problem. On the whole, single women would be ill-advised to go there, however tempting the salary, though in practice jobs for them very seldom come up. There are no tourist-associated facilities and with the exception of restaurants, there are very few facilities for public entertainment, not even cinemas. A few of the big corporations' expatriate townships have their own private recreational arrangements, but these are also very limited. There are, however, some good places for swimming and other kinds of water-based pursuits. Saudi television has an English-language channel. It is generally possible, also, to pick up English TV channels from Bahrain and other countries in the Gulf. Video rentals are popular.

The health situation is good, though intestinal upsets are not uncommon. Some places are supplied with potable water, but in other areas it should be bought in bottled form. Expatriate jobs generally include free medical attention, and hospitals in the main centres are extremely good. Private treatment, of course, is very expensive – even an ambulance journey to hospital costs around R600. Oculist service is not well catered for, however, and if you need glasses you should bring spare pairs with you. Sunglasses are also a good idea, because of the strong glare.

Educational facilities are very limited, though there are several expensive international and American schools for children up to the age of 15. There are British private primary schools in Jeddah, Riyadh and Al Khobar. Below this level there are play schools run by expatriate wives. On the whole, taking children of school age to Saudi is not a good idea and in any case places are very hard to get.

Africa

Kenya

Background

Kenya is one of the most important and advanced countries on the African continent. It lies within the tropics and has long coastline borders on the Indian Ocean. It covers 225,000 square miles and has over 23 million inhabitants with a rapidly rising birthrate and a very young population. Nairobi, the capital and chief political and commercial centre, has over 1 million inhabitants and is a modern, prosperous and sophisticated city. It is followed in size by the port of Mombasa, with some 500,000 inhabitants.

Kenya has borders with Sudan and Ethiopia to the north, Somalia to the east, Uganda to the west and Tanzania to the south. Over half the land is arid, but the south and west are fertile and cultivable, with plateau and upland country rising to high mountains – Mount Kenya is about 17,000 feet high, and Nairobi is 5432 feet above sea level. Its climate is pleasant and invigorating, whereas it is hot and humid on the coast. The main rainy season is from April to June.

The population includes Europeans, Asians and Arabs. There are some 35 tribal groups. The national language is Swahili and a working knowledge of this language is advisable, although English is used everywhere. There are Anglican and Catholic churches in most towns and other Christian denominations, as well as Moslem faiths.

Kenya, first colonised by the British in the 1880s, achieved independence in 1963, and is a republic within the Commonwealth. Daniel Arap Moi succeeded Jomo Kenyatta as President on the latter's death in August 1978, and was re-elected in 1983 and 1988. Moi is President of the ruling party, KANU.

Exchange rate: Kenya shilling 46.32 = £1. (Though not an official unit of currency it is common practice to refer to a Kenya pound – symbol £K – to denote 20 Kenya shillings (KSh). There are 100 cents to the shilling.)

The economy

Kenya is best known for its tea and coffee, which form the backbone of the economy. Other crops include sugar, sisal, cotton, maize, fruits and vegetables. Tourism is one of the most important sources of foreign exchange, though its growth is thought to have been affected by the spread of AIDS, now a considerable health hazard in East Africa. Eighty per cent of the population derive their livelihood from agriculture, which accounts for 70 per cent of exports. Most farms are on a subsistence basis and a few large estates account for about 40 per cent of the marketable output for coffee and tea.

There are few mineral resources, but the government is encouraging exploration. The manufacturing sector is being expanded – it includes food processing, chemicals, drink, tobacco, car assembly, paper and printing, metal products, textiles, clothing, footwear and cement. An oil pipeline links the Mombasa refinery with Nairobi.

The government welcomes foreign investment, with or without Kenyan participation. Many enterprises are jointly owned by government or quasi-government institutions and foreign investors, who consider the Kenyan atmosphere a favourable one.

Economic development is based on national planning, with emphasis on agriculture and manufacturing and on encouraging export and labour-intensive industries.

Britain and Germany are the principal trading partners and the UK is the major individual provider of external aid, particularly in sending experts, teachers and technical advisers.

There are serious balance of payments imbalances and inflation is around 17 per cent. Unemployment and under-employment have remained serious problems, particularly among the young. These are exacerbated by Kenya's rapid population growth – the world's fastest.

Coffee, which is of high quality, is Kenya's major crop, but has suffered from unstable prices and rising costs. Tea has also suffered from the same problems, and only a permanent recovery of tea and coffee prices would significantly reduce the strain on the economy. The government has decided to modernise coffee production, mainly carried on in small farms on the slopes of the mountains, and improve harvesting and distribution methods.

Despite deriving much power from hydro-electricity, Kenya has suffered because of rises in the price of oil. This has been accentuated by fluctuations in coffee prices and the effects of drought which also created poor economic conditions in Kenya's neighbouring export markets in East Africa.

Personal finance and taxation

Most employers provide housing and make allowances for children's education, cars, etc. Currency control is strict and it is advisable to seek advice on exchange and currency controls from your bank or a financial adviser.

Income tax is charged on total income, (including benefits in kind). Personal allowances are given for single and married people, but there are no allowances for children. The following table shows the percentage of income a married man would pay in income tax (assuming he was on a two year tour with income fully taxable):

Gross pay per annum	*Percentage tax*
200,000 KSh	25
400,000 KSh	34
600,000 KSh	38
800,000 KSh	39
1,000,000 KSh	40
1,200,000 KSh	41

Working conditions

A valid passport is needed, but Commonwealth citizens do not need a visa, except Australian, Sri Lankan, Indian and Nigerian citizens and British passport holders of India, Bangladeshi or Pakistani origin. Entry permits vary according to the type of employment. Applicants must show that they have adequate financial resources and that their activities will benefit the country. It is advisable to check immigration regulations with the authorities, as these are liable to change.

A *work permit* must be obtained by the employer from the Principal Immigration Officer in Nairobi (PO Box 3019) before the employee leaves Britain. The PIO's permission is needed for dependants to work. Work permits for wives, unless they are professionally qualified, are hard to obtain.

Working hours are as throughout tropical Africa, eg 8.00 am to 5.00 or 5.30 pm. There are 10 public holidays, both religious and official.

Living conditions

Most people find Kenya fairly expensive, owing to inflation and import restrictions, but there is a wider choice of things to buy than in most developing countries. Generally speaking, basics are cheaper, luxuries more expensive than in the UK. You can save money, and vary your diet, by shopping in local markets for meat which is usually of good quality, fish, dairy produce, vegetables and fruit.

Examples of food prices in 1990 were as follows:

	KSh
Butter (1 kg)	52.00
Sugar (1 kg)	10.50
Rice (1 kg)	19.50
Coffee (ground) (1 kg)	80.00
Cooking oil (1 litre)	35.00

Milk, fresh (1 litre)	9.00
Eggs (12)	24.50
Cheese (1 kg)	140.00
Pork chops (1 kg)	89.00
Chicken, fresh (1 kg)	72.00
Potatoes (1 kg)	8.40
Beer, bottled (50 cl)	12.80
Scotch whisky (bottle)	500.00

There are occasional shortages of certain canned goods. The quality of meat is said to be good but often spoilt by bad butchering. Most people drink beer. The local tipple, Kenya cane, a cross between vodka and rum, sounds as if it should be avoided.

Prices of standard household goods are very much as in the UK, but those of imported consumer durables are considerably higher. A refrigerator, for instance, would cost nearly three times as much as in the UK.

Imported European and American clothes are expensive, but locally made clothes are sufficient for casual wear. Tailoring and dressmaking are usually of good standard, but it is advisable to bring as much as you need from home – light-weight clothes plus woollies for high altitudes.

There is no shortage of housing in Kenya, not even in Nairobi, where increasing numbers of international organisations are establishing headquarters. Most employers supply accommodation, whether part or fully furnished, but it may be necessary for a newcomer to stay for several weeks in a hotel before a house or flat becomes vacant. It is probably advisable for the husband to travel out alone and send for his family later. Security is a problem. Burglary and more violent crimes are not uncommon and it is advisable to keep children playing at home rather than, for example, in the street or in public places.

There are excellent hotels in Nairobi and in the main tourist areas, guest houses and game park lodges. Prices at Nairobi hotels are around £65 a night, with meals extra. Advance booking is essential during the high season (December to April). Details of hotel and guest accommodation can be had from the Ministry of Tourism, Utalii House, off Uhuru Highway, PO Box 30027, Nairobi, or from the Kenya Tourist Office, 24–25 New Bond Street, London W1.

Electricity is supplied at 240V, 50 cycles AC in most centres and the supply is reliable. Lamps are mainly bayonet fitting, plugs three-pin square 13 amp in modern buildings. Water is drinkable in the towns.

Most household and electrical goods can be bought in the main stores, and the range of locally produced articles is steadily rising. But it is probably cheaper to bring as much as possible – check that electrical equipment from the UK is suitable for Kenya.

Most expatriates employ one or more domestic servants, who often live in, and wages are low (averaging about KSh 1400 a month).

Housebreaking, car thefts, pickpocketing and pilfering are on the increase, so it is essential to take precautions. Mugging is also becoming increasingly common, particularly in Nairobi and Mombasa.

Shopping hours in the main stores are from 8.00 am to 5.00 or 6.00 pm. There are numerous banks, and they are open from 9.00 am to 1.00 pm Monday to Friday and 9.00 to 11.00 am on Saturday. Personal services such as dry-cleaning and hairdressing are fully available in Nairobi and Mombasa. Well-known brands of toilet articles and cosmetics can be bought, but at twice the UK price.

International and national air services operate from Nairobi International Airport. The main railway line runs from Mombasa to Nairobi and beyond and services include sleeping compartments. Local rail and bus travel are usually avoided. A private car is essential for people staying any length of time and should be tough enough to withstand difficult conditions. New and secondhand cars can be bought locally, but are about twice as dear as in the UK. Servicing facilities are adequate in Nairobi, but if you are taking your own car it is advisable to contact the manufacturer beforehand about spare parts, etc. Roads are of fairly high standard. Driving is on the left. There are facilities for car hire. There is an AA of Kenya with headquarters in Nairobi. A valid British or international licence, which should be endorsed at a police station on arrival, is accepted for up to 90 days, thereafter exchanged for a Kenyan one – no test is imposed. The AA and RAC have reciprocal arrangements with the Kenyan AA.

Outside the cities, roads are poor. It may be necessary to have a Landrover-type vehicle there. Many expatriates have two cars, though cars are very expensive. If you have to buy your own it is best to go for a cheaper model; otherwise they are difficult to re-sell when you leave the country. Petrol costs about KSh 11 per litre.

Airmail from Europe takes about four days; surface mail six to ten weeks. There are full facilities for telephoning and telex.

Kenya is, in general, a healthy place in which to live, apart from the risk of AIDS and the usual tropical hazards, particularly along the coast. Anti-malarial drugs should be taken. Medical standards are high, particularly for private facilities in Nairobi. The main government hospital is the Kenyatta National Hospital in Nairobi, which has 1500 beds, including some semi-private amenity wards. Doctors' fees and medicines are expensive, however, so bring out what you need. Hospital fees can be reduced through the National Insurance fund but, where insurance is not provided in their contract, many expatriates subscribe to a locally available scheme.

There is a network of district hospitals, clinics and dispensaries, and also mission hospitals. Very remote areas are served by a flying doctor service, which requires a small annual subscription.

Most expatriate parents send their children to private primary schools, but many of these have long waiting lists. There is generally no problem about placing children in nursery schools and kindergartens. The Nairobi International School takes in children for both primary and secondary schooling, though fees are high. It follows the US curriculum but most private schools are geared to that of Britain. There are schools in Mombasa and most other centres; some schools take boarders. There are a number of convent schools. Nairobi University, the Strathmore College of Arts and the Kenya Polytechnic admit students of all nationalities.

The main English language newspapers are the *Standard, Daily Nation* and *Kenya Times*; there are several weeklies and monthlies and most UK papers can be bought in Nairobi and Mombasa. There is one national radio station in Nairobi with provincial sub-stations in Mombasa, Kisumu and Mount Kenya. There are two TV stations in the country.

About 25,000 British people live in Kenya, mainly in Nairobi and Mombasa. There are also communities of Americans and other Europeans. Life is more cosmopolitan and sophisticated, as well as more relaxed, than in many African countries. A number of clubs provide social and recreational facilities (many employers pay your subscriptions) and there are opportunities for sports, including motor and horse racing. Most towns have cinemas, libraries and swimming pools and Nairobi has a great variety of restaurants, of all nationalities and at all prices. It has a repertory theatre and a music conservatory. There are many local amateur dramatic and musical activities. In general, Western influences are inherent in the arts.

Most people spend their weekends and leave periods exploring the country, going on 'safari' to the nature and wildlife reserves, camping, bird watching, riding, fishing, photographing or swimming and surfing at the coast. The wildlife, country and the coast are unbelievably beautiful.

British people in general feel at home in Kenya, where the climate is very agreeable and life is not so different from the UK as in some West and East African countries. The Kenyans are hospitable and mix easily with Europeans. There would seem to be fewer frustrations in day-to-day life than in many developing countries. Kenya has been one of the most politically stable countries in Africa, maintaining good relations with all nations and, despite its current problems, has made considerable economic progress.

Nigeria

Background

Nigeria, with its estimated population of 110 million, is the largest and most influential state in black Africa. Despite the economic problems of the past few years, it still employs a considerable expatriate managerial and technical force from both European and Asian sources.

The country falls into two geographical parts: the southern tropical rain forest area that includes the coastal area, and the more arid northern plains that stretch to the fringe to the Sahara desert. Temperature in the south is generally about 84°F with a humidity almost as high. The rainy season begins in April/May and continues until September/October with a short break during August. Temperatures in the north are sometimes above 90°F and rain is restricted to the midsummer months. The harmattan, a dust wind from the Sahara, can be a nuisance to air traffic and is prevalent from November to February. The ethnic groups of the north, the Fulani and the Hausa, are mainly Moslem, while the people of the south are mainly Christian.

The commercial capital, Lagos, is in the south of the country, as are the other major ports of Port Harcourt, Warri and Calabar. A new federal capital is in the course of construction at Abuja, almost in the centre of the country. Transfer of administration to Abuja started in 1982, but completion of the project has been delayed by economic problems.

The British administered the country from 1914 to 1956 and granted self-government in 1956 and independence four years later. English is the *lingua franca* and a very substantial amount of goodwill exists between Nigeria and Britain. There are estimated to be over 8000 British expatriates living there. Half of the total foreign investment in Nigeria is of British origin. American influence has grown in recent years.

Nigeria has had a chequered political history since independence. The present military government of President Ibrahim Babangida, which took power in 1985, is committed to a policy of returning to civilian government in 1992.

Exchange rate: Naira 13.32 = £1.

The economy

Nigeria is a major oil producer, but during the 1980s much of its oil wealth was squandered and a huge external debt built up. To cope with the crisis, austerity measures – endorsed by the IMF – have been implemented since 1986. The reform process is not yet complete, and meanwhile Nigeria's economic prospects remain disquieting. Corruption is endemic, reforms difficult to implement, the infrastructure is deteriorating and unemployment rising.

Under current plans, the government is aiming to diversify the economy away from oil, to encourage the development of agriculture and industry, and to overhaul the infrastructure – particularly transport, power supplies and water. Increased spending on social services is also planned, to ease the adjustment of an urban population which has experienced falling living standards over the past few years. However, popular discontent with the government's austerity measures calls into question the feasibility of peaceful transfer to civilian government in 1992.

Personal finance and taxation

Income tax is progressive, at rates varing from 10 to 55 per cent. More important to the expatriate is the amount of salary that can be remitted home in foreign exchange, which is currently 25 per cent of net salary. Recently many expatriates have had difficulty getting their money out through the Central Bank on completion of their contracts, especially if they have no one remaining behind in the country to look after their interests. The advice now being given is that expatriates should remit the maximum amount and not hold any more Naira than they need for living expenses. If part of the salary is paid offshore, this avoids difficulties over remitting money from Nigeria. Another reason for holding as little Naira as possible is the frightening rate of inflation – the latest available figure is 32 per cent.

Working conditions

All visitors except nationals of certain neighbouring countries require a visa (easily obtainable for nationals of Commonwealth countries). A visitor's permit will last for a maximum of three months. Expatriates working in Nigeria require a *resident's permit* and this is obtained by the employer within the quota allowed to the company.

Nigeria acknowledges both Christian and Moslem holidays as well as National Day (1 October).

Living conditions

Petrol is cheap at about 3.5p per litre, but motor maintenance and spares are very costly. Comprehensive insurance may be about N1,600. In Lagos road conditions have improved considerably, although there can be long delays at peak periods. Meals out are expensive. A meal at one of the few good restaurants will start at £20. Lebanese and Chinese restaurants provide the best food.

Most manufactured goods are imported and are therefore expensive. There is, however, a vigorous black market in smuggled goods which may cost less than their UK equivalents.

Housing is expensive and difficult to find. Typical rents for an unfurnished three- to four-bedroomed house will be N250,000 a year in a good part of Lagos, though much cheaper elsewhere. Many companies, particularly construction companies, build and provide their own housing in company compounds for both single and married employees. While this has the added advantage of security, it does limit social contact with the indigenous population. Domestic electricity supply is 230V, 50 cycles AC, when available. You need a standby generator because of the supply situation. Household goods are also very expensive locally and your contract should include a substantial air baggage allowance. Surface mail takes months.

Most expatriates employ a cook/steward, a driver, a nanny and a nightwatchman. A cook/steward's wages would be N360 plus accommodation in the south, but much less in the north.

Because of the conditions of working in Nigeria, leave tends to be generous, particularly with companies who operate in other overseas markets. Three tours of three months a year with the one month's leave after each tour is not uncommon, although a tour of six months is more normal.

Anti-malarial pills should be taken regularly starting two weeks before each tour and continuing for four weeks after. It is also advisable to obtain immunisation against yellow fever, typhoid, tetanus, polio, cholera, hepatitis A and B. Water should always be boiled and fruit and salads carefully cleaned. Swimming pools can be a health hazard and advice should be sought from residents. Exposure to the sun can be a danger, particularly in the north. If there is a need to be hospitalised it is best to return home if possible. Blood transfusions and injections should be given only at clincs recommended by an authoritative source because of the AIDS virus. State hospitals have difficulty in maintaining international standards of hygiene while private hospitals tend to be expensive and commercially orientated.

Credit cards are not generally used in Nigeria and are accepted in only one or two hotels in Lagos. Credit is not usually given. Hotels require a deposit covering all likely expenditure in advance and in cash and payment by non-residents has to be made in hard currency. All retail purchases are made in cash. It takes a considerable amount of time, up to three months, for a cheque to be cleared from a bank in a different part of the country. Only 'certified' cheques, or bank drafts, are accepted as currency. Cheques tend to be used only to draw cash from one's own local branch. Banking hours are 8.00 am to 3.00 pm on Mondays and 8.00 am to 1.00 pm Tuesdays to Fridays.

A double room in a good hotel in Lagos will cost from £60 a night. Most hotels are air-conditioned but the equipment may not be functioning. There is often a shortage of water and electric power. Hotel food is generally poor.

Trunk roads linking the various state capitals have improved considerably in recent years. A motorway runs from Lagos to Ibadan, and from Lagos to Benin. However, within Lagos itself traffic conditions are horrendous. For instance, you have to allow about four hours to get out to the airport. Poor road maintenance can cause some hazards, and road accidents in Nigeria are very frequent. It is not safe to drive after dusk because of the risk of accidents and highway robbery. Driving is on the right.

Most state capitals now have airports, the most recent addition being Makurdi, Benue State. Regular services are frequent, but delays can occur because of poor weather conditions. Bribery, known as 'dash', may be necessary to clear customs and immigration. In the north, a private airline links the state capitals, in competition with Nigeria Airways, and has a good reputation.

Nigeria Airways and British Airways provide daily flights from the UK to Nigeria, and most continental airlines have a weekly or bi-weekly service. There are three international airports: Ikeja, 17 miles from Lagos; Kano, in the north; and Port Harcourt, 22 miles from the town of Port Harcourt. Where airports are some distance from the town only taxis operate. Care should be taken to ensure the taxi is properly marked and that a reasonable fare has been agreed upon before the journey begins. Ideally, visitors should always be met at the airports.

The telephone system is notoriously inefficient. While it is now possible, within Nigeria, to call most of the major cities direct in theory, in practice it requires a lot of patience, due to the overcrowded telephone system. International direct dialling services are being introduced and calls can be made direct to the UK from certain phones, including those at the offices of NITEL (Nigerian Telecommunications).

International post takes a minimum of six days (airmail) and four to six weeks by surface mail. Documents are better despatched by courier, particularly as some mail does get mislaid. Internal post takes about 7 to 10 days.

Telex is fairly reliable, though this depends on an efficient and keen operator at the Nigerian end and also on a source of electric power, which on occasions can be unobtainable.

The newcomer to Nigeria should understand that, while with care he will probably have a trouble-free tour, there *is* a crime problem in Nigeria. This takes a variety of forms: car thefts, usually only of new Peugeot cars, housebreaking, mugging and highway robbery. While appropriate precautions will vary from time to time, it is generally not considered safe to travel out of town at night.

Most state capitals still have the old British clubs and these now provide opportunities for swimming, tennis, golf, squash, etc and for meeting both Nigerians and other expatriates. Membership of one club provides affiliated membership to the others. There are swimming pools in all the major hotels. Cinemas are to be found in most of the clubs and also in some of the larger hotels.

Most expatriates send their children to UK boarding schools at an early age and certainly for secondary education. There are private International Schools in Nigeria, often staffed by Europeans, which cater well for the ages of five to nine and provide a congenial atmosphere. There are International Schools in Lagos, Ibadan, Kano and Kaduna. Fees tend to be somewhat higher than in equivalent schools in the UK.

South Africa

Background

South Africa's most recent census gave a population figure of 23 million, with a further 10.6 million in the 'homelands'. Most of the white population of around 4.6 million live in the four main industrial centres: an area within a radius of 100 miles around Johannesburg; Durban; Port Elizabeth; and the Western Cape. Although South Africa is principally thought of in terms of mining – and the country has large reserves of virtually every mineral with the significant exception of oil – it does in fact engage in a broad range of industrial activities. The newcomer will see, in this respect, few differences between South African cities and those of any other industrialised nation.

The differences lie under the surface – though not very far – and are a product of racial tension and the political system which has been evolved to control it. South Africa is ruled by a parliament predominantly elected by the white population, which is in a 1:5 minority of the total racial mix of Europeans, Africans, Indians and people of mixed blood. Racial segregation is now being dismantled, although vestiges remain.

President de Klerk claims a mandate to carry out a policy of 'orderly reform'. With the unbanning of the ANC and talks between de Klerk and Nelson Mandela, there is now hope (despite continuing violence in the townships) that peaceful change is possible in South Africa.

Financial exchange rate: Rand 5.59 = £1.

The economy

The economy is in difficulties. Inflation is high (around 14 per cent), living standards are falling and unemployment rising rapidly. South Africa has been hit not only by sanctions (particularly those imposed by the international banks) but also by the falling price of gold, its principal export.

Personal finance and taxation

South Africa has lately been declining in the world salary league table. Taxes are now relatively high, and there are few concessions in the way of rebates. Thus, in the case of a married man with two children, some 35 per cent of an R100,000 salary would go in tax and other payments to the state. For a single person the figure would be just under 40 per cent.

Fringe benefits are not a significant part of remuneration, although managerial jobs generally earn a car and holidays tend to be generous, six weeks a year being frequently quoted. Free or subsidised medical aid schemes are frequently offered to more senior people. If these are not available such costs should be borne in mind in assessing the true value of the remuneration package. However, the most daunting factor now is the fluctuating value of the Rand (due to South Africa's uncertain political future).

There is a wide variety of indirect sales duties, the most significant of which is on cars. The remission of duty on personal effects is marginal and it is not worth bringing a car into South Africa. A new car in the 1.6 litre range costs, on average, around R30,000. You can drive on a UK licence for the first six months of your stay, but after that you have to apply for a South African one, which is normally granted to anyone with a recognised overseas licence.

If you are an approved immigrant you may, however, import one motor vehicle per family under full rebate of customs duty (but subject to sales duty), provided that the motor vehicle has been owned and used by you and registered in your name, in your country of residence, for at least 12 months before your departure and before the date on which it was shipped to South Africa.

There are no restrictions on the amount of foreign currency you can bring in, but strict exchange control regulations are in force on taking money out of South Africa. For this reason, it is advisable to transfer no more of your assets than you absolutely need to South Africa unless you are absolutely sure you want to stay there. You have to declare the existence of overseas assets to the bank when you get to South Africa, but they will normally allow you to keep them abroad, subject to your making certain undertakings. For instance, you must not make them over to a South African resident, as this would be an obvious way of circumventing the regulations.

Working conditions

At executive and professional level, working conditions (ie hours and leave) are very similar to those in the UK. There has been little industrial unrest in South Africa, though it has increased recently. Wages are fixed by industrial councils and vary according to occupation and region. Welfare benefits are minimal compared with the UK, although numerous private schemes for medical care, pensions, disability, etc do exist on a contributory basis and about 85 per cent of the white population belong to a scheme of some kind.

There is quite a generous assisted immigration scheme and most UK professional qualifications are recognised in South Africa. The scheme is selective, the criteria being primarily the state of the economy at the time and the extent to which the applicant's qualifications fit in with its needs. However, immigrants are not allowed to change occupation without approval for three years after their arrival in South Africa and there are also some restrictions on change of residence. This is related to the availability of work. It should be noted, however, that to have worked in South Africa may make if difficult to move to another African country thereafter. Prospective immigrants should write to the Counsellor (Migrations), South African Embassy, Trafalgar Square, London WC2N 5DP for further information. If you are thinking of working in South Africa for a more limited period, application for a *work permit* has to be made to the Consul-General, Consulate-General of the Republic of South Africa, 16 Charles II Street, London SW1. In this connection, you should be aware that, even as an immigrant, you may be called up for military service.

Although opportunities in the private sector are very similar to those in Europe or America, the public sector is somewhat different. The crucial factor here is that the Afrikaners – whites mainly of Dutch descent – largely make up the party that has ruled South Africa for nearly 40 years. Their appointees dominate the public sector and, though the position is beginning to change, it is still rare for a non-Afrikaner to be found in a senior position in any official job. Similarly one suspects the ultimate opportunities for a foreigner in an Afrikaans-owned firm would be limited. Afrikaners, who are increasingly found in business nowadays, have a highly developed tribal sense and, other things being equal, would tend to give jobs (and contracts) to their own kin or at least to people willing to learn the language. A knowledge of Afrikaans – not a difficult language – would be very useful to acquire if you are proposing to stay there for any length of time.

Living conditions

South Africa's climate is excellent, though by no means uniform. There is quite a difference at all times of the year between semi-tropical Natal, the Mediterranean climate of the Western Cape and the dry, cold winters and hot, thunderstormy summers of Johannesburg. These varied conditions make it possible for all foodstuffs to be grown locally, though they are no longer particularly cheap. All in all, and allowing for variations such as the fact that there is no National Health Service in South Africa, the cost of living is a good deal less than in the UK bearing in mind the low international value of the Rand. A refrigerator would cost R1100, a washing machine about R1100, and a colour TV set R2000. Food prices in 1990 were as follows:

	R
Steak (1 kg)	17.50
Butter (500 gm)	3.60
Eggs (12)	2.20
Bread (loaf)	1.90
Apples (1 kg)	2.40
Wine (bottle)	9.00
Petrol (1 litre)	1.15

As in any move to a new area, it is unwise to plunge into buying a new house without first disentangling the subtleties of congenial and uncongenial neighbourhoods. Rented accommodation is, however, in fairly short supply. House prices are lower than for similar properties in the UK. As in this country, it is highly advisable to consult a solicitor before signing either a lease or a deed of sale.

Many people in South Africa employ servants, who normally receive free meals and accommodation in separate servants' quarters in addition to their wages. Check with neighbours about going rates and administrative procedures connected with employment of non-white labour.

Education in state schools is free, but schools are allowed to charge a small fee to cover miscellaneous expenses. There are, of course, plenty of private fee-paying schools as well. Children who will not have reached the age of six before 1 July of the year of admission will not be allowed to attend school, even if they have done so previously. The school year begins after the Christmas holiday.

Afrikaans is a compulsory subject, though this requirement is relaxed for pupils attending South African schools for the first time in their last two years of school. It should be noted that the syllabus and atmosphere of South African schools is markedly more traditional and restrictive than is the case in most other countries. University education is not free.

Zambia

Background

Zambia is over three times the size of the UK and its population at the latest estimate is about 8.3 million and growing rapidly. It includes about 20,000 expatriates, mainly Europeans.

The country is landlocked, bordering on Tanzania and Zaire to the north, Malawi and Mozambique to the east, Zimbabwe, Botswana and Namibia to the south and Angola to the west. Most of the land is plateau, with an elevation of 3500 to 4500 feet, intersected by rivers, of which the Zambesi is the most important. There are high peaks in the Muchinga mountains to the north-east.

Zambia is the most urbanised country in black Africa and more than a million people live in the Copper Belt. The capital, Lusaka, is a rapidly expanding city with more than 921,000 inhabitants. In the Copper Belt, Kitwe is the main city (395,000) with Ndola (467,200) on its outskirts. Livingstone (102,300) is the main centre in the south.

English is the official language. The principal African languages are Nyanja, Memba, Tongu, Lozi, Lunda, Luvale and Kaonde. Christians make up 80 per cent of the population, but there are Moslem and Hindu minorities, and some Africans follow traditional beliefs.

Because of its altitude, the climate is temperate, with extremes of heat and cold in summer and winter. The rainy season is December to March.

Zambia became independent in October 1964, after the breakdown of the Central African Federation. The United National Independence Party (UNIP) waged a successful campaign against the CAF and its domination by white Southern Rhodesia. Zambia's President is Kenneth Kaunda, leader of UNIP since 1958. Zambia is a member of the Commonwealth, the UN and the Organisation of African Unity (OAU).

The administration is divided into nine administrative provinces: Lusaka, Central, Copperbelt, Eastern, Luapula, Northern, North Western, Southern and Western.

Exchange rate: Kwacha 93.40 = £1.

The economy

The economy is based on copper, which accounts for about 95 per cent of foreign exchange earnings, and is highly sensitive to fluctuations in world copper prices. As a result of falling world copper prices Zambia has faced serious economic difficulties and a huge balance of payments deficit.

About 70 per cent of the people are engaged in agriculture, the main crops being tobacco, sugar and maize. Farming is on a subsistence basis. Like other developing countries, Zambia has adopted national plans to develop and improve its farming, encourage diversification and reduce its dependence on imports. The scale of manufacture is still small, but a wide range of industries has been, or is being, established, such as food and tobacco processing, grain milling, production of steel sheets, cotton, furniture, clothing, plastics, cement, beer, soap and detergents, fertilisers and copper products, and vehicle assembly.

The government pursues policies of rapid 'Zambianisation' of jobs and of state ownership of and/or participation in enterprise. It holds a 51 per cent share in copper mines. Non-Zambians are debarred from certain spheres.

The aim is trade with all and sundry and international competition in investment – West Germany, China and Italy have all contributed towards major projects. Britain, however, has contributed most aid, mainly in technical assistance and experts. There is still a shortage of technical and qualified manpower. Many white mining technicians have left the country to work in the Middle East or South Africa and new recruitment has become increasingly difficult in the prevailing economic problems.

Zambian wages and salaries are higher than in surrounding countries, owing to the relatively high level of pay in the mines. Outside the Copperbelt and the main towns there is little paid employment and considerable poverty.

Personal finance and taxation

Expatriate employees of overseas companies usually receive benefits such as a car, a house, travel and education allowances which vary from company to company.

Contracts should include an *inducement allowance*, paid in US dollars and remitted monthly, an *end of contract gratuity*, paid in US dollars, and a local salary. The inducement allowance and end of contract gratuity are tax free: the local salary is taxable, and none of it may be remitted (there are strict exchange controls).

Working conditions

Visas are not required by holders of valid UK passports but those with passports containing South African residence stamps will need a visa, although this requirement is presently under review by the Zambian government. Expatriates need a *work permit*, obtainable by the prospective employer from the Chief Immigration Officer (PO Box 31984, Lusaka). Dependants are not allowed to work without his permission. There are limited opportunities for women to work as doctors, nurses and teachers, but the authorities can be reluctant to issue work permits to expatriate wives. Voluntary work, however, is possible.

Working hours are as in other parts of tropical Africa, ie 8.00 am to 4.00 or 5.00pm. There are 10 official public holidays. Leave arrangements for expatriates are negotiated individually.

Expatriates are usually expected to train Zambians working under them to acquire higher skills. This may not be explicitly stated, but it is assumed that sooner or later a job will be 'Zambianised'.

Living conditions

Inflation, security fears and scarce transport make Zambia an expensive and difficult country in which to live. With the easing of import restrictions, the supply of goods has improved, although at times it can be difficult to buy many items, particularly those that are locally produced such as cooking oil, sugar etc. Here are some examples of prices in 1991:

	Kwacha
Bread (loaf)	60.00
Sugar (1 kg)*	80.00
Rice (1 kg)	160.00
Tea (250 gm)	74.00
Coffee (ground) (250 gm)	200.00
Milk, fresh (1 ltr)	36.00
Cooking oil (750 ml)	256.00
Eggs (10)	60.00
Cheese (1 kg)	400.00
Steak, fillet (1 kg)	250.00
Chicken, fresh (1 kg)	150.00
Potatoes (1 kg)	70.00
Beer, bottled (500 ml)	50.00

*at present only available on the black market

Meat is readily available and is of good quality as are local fruit and vegetables which are in plentiful and varied supply. Household necessities tend to be expensive, particularly of the imported variety. There is a limited choice in household furnishings, particularly electrical, and prices tend to be about double those of the UK. Most expatriates bring their own equipment with them. Locally produced clothing items are of poor quality and imported items expensive, however, local tailors are quite skilful at making and copying clothes. A sample of 1990 prices is shown below:

	Kwacha
Men's two-piece suit	from 3500.00
Trousers	from 900.00
Shirt	from 795.000
Shoes	from 1000.00
Dress	from 1000.00
Jeans	from 1500.00

Informal dress – shorts for men, cotton dresses for women – is preferred. Men usually wear suits or safari suits to the office. The golf clubs demand long trousers or shorts with long socks for men and both women and men must wear tops with collars. Temperatures drop rapidly at nights and warm clothes are also needed in the cool season.

It is almost impossible to find accommodation for oneself. Housing *must* be provided with the job. The shortage of accommodation is so great that many newcomers often have to spend a long time in a hotel.

Electricity is supplied at 230V, 50 cycles AC and is available in towns; many people in country areas use bottled gas or paraffin.

Most expatriates have domestic help. Wages are upwards of K1600 per month for house servants but are rising rapidly in line with inflation. Check the going rates with the local labour office. Servants also expect to be provided with housing, free utilities and uniforms, together with a bag of maize meal (the local staple) and/or ration money monthly.

Many families employ a day or nightwatchman and many also use the services of a security company such as Securicor. Housebreaking, burglary and petty theft have increased alarmingly. Thefts include cars and car fixtures, refrigerators and electrical equipment. Mugging and pickpocketing are also prevalent.

Hotels tend to get heavily booked, particularly in Lusaka. Prices in 5 star hotels are around US$110 per night for a single room plus service and sales tax (10 per cent each), which must be paid in hard currency for non-residents of Zambia. Tipping is illegal. Hotel prices are lower outside Lusaka. Accommodation can sometimes be found in government rest-houses.

There are internal air services serving 19 centres. Zambia Airways operate flights to the UK and leading African countries. There is a single-track railway system from Livingstone to the Copperbelt, and the Tazara railway, covering nearly 1600 miles, serves 147 stations between central Zambia and Dar es Salaam in Tanzania. The daily express trains are good, but other cross-country rail travel is not recommended.

Most main roads are tarred, though secondary roads have gravel or earth surfaces. Express buses link Lusaka with Livingstone and the Copperbelt, but urban transport is not much used by Europeans. Taxis and self-drive cars can be hired in Lusaka and other towns.

The Zambians are exuberant drivers and have one of the world's highest accident rates. New arrivals in the country would be well advised to hire a car with a driver. Indeed, some companies employ drivers for their staff and these drivers' services may be available, for an additional payment, out of office hours.

If you wish to drive yourself, you might consider bringing your own car, but make sure you meet it on arrival. Be prepared for duty and surcharge of at least 150 per cent of the value of the vehicle. (Advice on exporting a car can be obtained from the RAC.)

A few Japanese imports are available, at around K1.1 million for a Toyota Corolla 1.3. There are also locally assembled Peugeots and Fiats. However, if you buy a car on arrival, planning to sell it before you leave, you may have difficulty in repatriating the proceeds of the sale. In order to drive in Zambia, you will have to take the Zambian driving test; this takes a long time to arrange and there is a high failure rate. An international permit is valid for one year. Be careful about security – car thefts are frequent.

Zambia is a healthy place, in part because of its elevation. Hospital and medical treatment is free, but there is a severe shortage of doctors, nurses and medical equipment. Dentists are few and far between. Private hospital treatment can be arranged through the Zambia Medical Aid Society. The mining companies have their own hospitals and provide medical services for their personnel and families.

Education

Zambia has given high priority to its educational programme, and has had a long way to catch up. When it became independent, there were only 100 university graduates in the country and illiteracy was widespread. Now it has a number of teacher training colleges; the aim is universal education and an expansion of secondary education. State education is free.

Zambian State schools are geared towards Zambian needs and classes are often overcrowded. For expatriates in Lusaka there are four private schools, all of which have long waiting lists:

The International School is for children of 5 to 18 years. The curriculum is basically American but pupils are prepared for GCSEs and A levels. The school has two free scales – one for kwacha earners and one for foreign exchange earners. Fees per term range from K23,000–K30,000. The foreign exchange fee scale is considerably higher than the former.

The American School is kindergarten to Grade 8. All fees are payable in US dollars. Fees, including registration, range from $3000 to $4800 per year. Lake Road School (primary and secondary) and Nkwazi (primary) are both trust schools, run and owned by ZCCM, who also subsidise fees. First option for places is given to 'mine' children. Fees range from K5500 to K7500 per term. There are also privately run Italian, French and Scandinavian schools and a limited choice of nursery schools for which there are long waiting lists. Elsewhere throughout Zambia there are a few other private schools and in the Copperbelt there are also trust schools and two private schools: Simba and Lechwe in Ndola and Kitwe respectively. Most expatriates send their children to be educated in the UK from the age of 10, although some use home teaching methods.

Social life is what you make it, as there is little organised entertainment. This is usually done at home, with lunch, supper or cocktail parties – barbecues ('braai') are very popular. Dress is informal. Clothes should be light weight and loose fitting, and sandals or canvas shoes are best.

There are plenty of clubs and sports facilities and most employers help with entrance fees. There is excellent fishing in Kariba lake and other waters and hunting is allowed outside game reserves. Camping and trekking are popular. Many expatriates take their weekend leave in neighbouring Malawi or Zimbabwe.

Most towns have cinemas and there are local amateur dramatic and music groups, some assisted by the Zambia Arts Trust. There are English broadcasts on Radio Zambia. The two main newspapers, the *Times of Zambia* and the *Daily Mail*, are government papers.

Expatriates often complain about the frustrations of daily life and about bureaucracy. Specific grievances concern housing, shortages and burglaries.

For people who live near the Malawi border there are opportunities for trips to its well-stocked shops to make up deficiencies. (But beware the restrictions on dress in Malawi. Women may not wear trousers or shorts, and skirts must come below the knee. Men's hair must be short.) Most expatriates advise people to bring with them all necessary electrical goods, sports equipment, cooking utensils and gardening tools.

It is said to take about six months to get used to living in Zambia, but, once the adjustment has been made, most people find it an interesting and stimulating country. The Zambians are friendly and tolerant and there are no problems of race relations.

Zimbabwe

Background

Zimbabwe, formerly Rhodesia, has an area of 151,000 square miles. The country is landlocked, bordering on Botswana to the south-west, Mozambique, north and east, South Africa, south, and Zambia, north.

Most of the country lies 1000 feet or more above sea level and 80 per cent is above 2000 feet. The highest land is in the mountainous district near the Mozambique border, where mountains reach nearly 8000 feet. Because of its elevation the climate is healthy and pleasant, with daily maximum temperatures of 80° to 90°F for most of the year. The rainy season is from November to March; it is warm and dry from August to October and cool and dry from May to August. There is no need for air-conditioning.

The population is 9.4 million and is increasing at a rate of 3 per cent per annum. Seventy-five per cent of the population live in the rural areas through urbanisation is now proceeding rapidly.

Harare, the capital, has a population of 680,000 and Bulawayo, the second largest city, 413,000. Both cities have mixed racial populations. Other towns include Mutare (Umtali), on the Mozambique frontier, Gweru (Gwelo), in the centre and Whange (Wankie) near the Zambian border.

Zimbabwe's first black government came into office in 1980, following elections supervised by the British. Robert Mugabe's party won a sweeping victory, gaining 57 out of 80 seats, and Mugabe became Prime Minister. Mugabe's instincts have been shown to be pragmatic and he has encouraged Europeans to stay in the country, though many have emigrated to South Africa. Some of them are actually returning, as conditions stabilise in Zimbabwe but become more unsettled in South Africa. Mugabe's re-election in 1985 was interpreted as a popular mandate for a one-party state. In theory, the constitution still provides for a multi-party system, but the main opposition party, Zapu, led by Joshua Nkomo, merged with the ruling Zanu PF in 1987. Nkomo and other Zapu members were appointed to posts in the Zanu-controlled government, a government which is committed to the creation of a socialist society by gradualist means.

There are three official languages: Chishona, Sindebele and English.

Exchange rate: Zimbabwe $5.03 = £1.

The economy

The mainstays of the economy are minerals and agriculture, dominated by tobacco, the major export crop, but the country produces wheat, cotton, oilseeds, maize, cane sugar and beef and is self-sufficient in food. About 1.4 million Africans are occupied in agriculture, mainly at a subsistence level and there are 4000 to 5000 white farmers, many of whom employ efficient methods. Just over 2 per cent of the total population are employed in manufacturing and nearly 1 per cent in mining and quarrying (coal, copper, chrome, asbestos, nickel and gold). The rate of inflation is around 15 per cent.

With its plentiful resources and the Prime Minister's policy of 'stability and unity' and intention of promoting gradual, rather than revolutionary, change, there is every reason to hope that Zimbabwe will re-emerge as a leading political and industrial force in southern Africa; but this, it must be said, is a long-term goal. At present the country is experiencing rapidly increasing unemployment (despite an acute shortage of skilled labour) and progress on the economic front has been disappointing.

Personal finance and taxation

Wages and salaries are highest in the mining sector and are above the African average. There is, of course, a very wide gap between the pay of blacks and whites, but this presumably will be reduced as a result of the policy of promoting Africans to positions of responsibility.

A PAYE system of taxation is in operation, at rates rising from 20 per cent to a maximum of 60 per cent. The remittance of funds is restricted to one-third of income, subject to assessment by the authorities (who are anxious not to lose foreign currency and are particularly worried that white emigrants will remit their capital). It is possible to have salary paid into a UK or US offshore bank, while having a local living allowance.

Working conditions

UK nationals do not need a visa. The term 'expatriate' is not popular with the Zimbabwean authorities and it is preferable to use the expression 'employee under contract'. Contract employees are recruited from outside Zimbabwe to fill vacancies in areas where there is a manpower shortage. They are normally recruited for a maximum of two years, with the option to extend their contracts for a further one year. The consent of the Ministry of Manpower and Planning Development is required for recruitment of contract staff. Conditions are covered by collective bargaining through industrial councils. There is provision for redundancy and severance pay.

There are no restrictions on women's employment and it should be possible for expatriate wives to find jobs in teaching, nursing and secretarial work, as well as in voluntary work. Business hours are normally 8.30 am to 2.00 pm and 8.30 to 11.00 am on Saturdays.

Living conditions

Zimbabwe has a high standard of living by African standards, though it is not so high for the majority black population. Here are some examples of prices in 1990:

	Z$
Cheese (500 g)	5.40
Bread (1 loaf)	0.80
Butter (500 gm)	1.85
Eggs (12)	2.50
Sugar (1 kg)	0.80
Tea bags (250 gm)	5.25
Potatoes (1 kg)	0.85
Coffee (ground) (500 gm)	7.25
Rice (1 kg)	2.00
Toothpaste	4.00
Marmalade (500 g)	2.00
Steak (1 kg)	10.50
Chicken (1 kg)	4.50
Cigarettes (20)	1.10

Housing does not present a great problem; indeed, the wide choice of properties left by the considerable number of Europeans who have emigrated is one of the principal advantages of being there. The power supply is reliable (voltage 220–230 AC). Tap water is potable. Harare is a sprawling city in which parks and gardens abound. The majority of villas have their own swimming pools and tennis courts. Most suburban families employ one or more servants. A house servant, living in, would be paid at least Z$150 a month.

There are good hotels in Harare and Bulawayo, at prices from about Z$75 single and Z$90 double. There are restaurants both in the hotels and outside. Make reservations in advance.

The shops are usually well stocked, though there are occasional shortages. It is advisable to bring as many household goods as possible with you. You need receipts of purchase because duty is charged on items less than six months old. Shopping hours are from 8.00 am to 5.00 pm, although some stay open longer.

Medical services are adequate but some Zimbabweans prefer to go to South Africa or Britain for more advanced treatment and there have been some recent shortages of medical drugs. There is a medical aid health system and there are both nursery schools and private schools, fees for which vary considerably. There is no waiting list for local expatriate schools.

There is an excellent system of main and feeder roads, with traffic control in cities and suburbs. Rail connections link the country with South Africa, Mozambique, Botswana and Zambia and there are international flights connecting with the UK and South Africa, as well as domestic services from Harare to Bulawayo, Kariba, Hwange and Masvingo. A private car is, however, essential. Many models can be bought locally and there is a wide choice of French, German and Japanese cars. It is advisable to take a valid international driving permit. However, if you hold a valid British licence, you will probably be issued with a Zimbabwean licence without having to take another test. Automatic cars are also available and taxis are reliable.

There are two English language daily papers, the *Chronicle* and the *Herald*. Internal and external phone and postal services are good.

What of the future for the whites? It has been argued that Mugabe needs a white presence. He has urged Europeans to stay and has followed a far more moderate line than many predicted. Antagonisms within the cabinet, tribal hostilities and economic and political uncertainty remain, but Mugabe has cleverly and capably steered a middle course and, despite the fact that many whites have emigrated since he came to power, his policy is showing signs of succeeding.

The American Continent

Canada

Background

Canada is the second largest country in the world in area, although its population is only some 25 million, most people living in a 200 mile wide strip along the southern border. Over 25 per cent of the total live in the three main cities: Toronto, Montreal and Vancouver. The northern areas of the country – 40 per cent of Canada's land mass is in the Arctic – are bleak, bitterly cold for most of the year and almost completely unpopulated except for isolated settlements. Only some 17 per cent of the land surface is arable, but a third of this is very high quality indeed. Canada also has large areas of forest, mainly in British Columbia, Quebec and Ontario.

Canada, like its dominating neighbour, the USA, in the past pursued an 'open door' policy towards immigration. The result was a large-scale influx from all over Europe, but predominantly from the British Isles; around 40 per cent of the population are of British origin. English communities are in the majority and the main provinces in central and western regions are English-speaking. Immigrants came from over 100 countries besides Britain and France, making up 30 per cent of the population. There are large German, Dutch and Ukrainian minorities. There are also ethnic minorities of Indians and, in the far north, Eskimos (or, properly, Inuit). But the biggest single population group, after those of British origin, is French, accounting for 29 per cent of the population. Nearly 6 million French live in Quebec and they form a sizeable minority in several other provinces. Canada is bilingual in the federal parliament, civil service and courts and from time to time nationalist agitation for a separate Quebec resurfaces. The majority of French speakers, however, accept that their close proximity to the USA means that the use of English is essential for business.

There are two main tiers of government – federal and provincial. The provincial governments, by and large, are responsible for regional affairs, but where these overlap with federal interests (eg environmental matters, health and welfare) programmes are planned jointly.

Like other countries, Canada has shifted to the right in recent years, under the leadership of the Conservative, Mr Brian Mulroney.

Exchange rate: \$1.93 = £1.

The economy

Canada is basically a very rich country, but its economy in recent years has been rather patchy because of the varied nature of what it does. This variety can be illustrated by looking at the country's five main regions.

1. *The Atlantic provinces.* Largely involved in fishing and agriculture and to some extent in mining and manufacture. Oil and gas have also been found.
2. *Central Canada.* Contains some of the major cities and most of Canada's industrial and mineral capacity.
3. *The prairie provinces.* The principal sources of wealth are wheat, oil potash and natural gas. There are also large uranium deposits.
4. *The Pacific province.* Main product is timber. Also important for fishing.
5. *The northern territories.* Contain much of Canada's vast and largely unexploited mineral wealth. Also large deposits of oil and gas.

Immediate economic prospects look sluggish, with projected GDP growth of only 1 per cent in 1991. Inflation, which fell to 4 per cent in 1990, is widely expected to rise again, and the 1991 unemployment rate is forecast to increase to over 9 per cent, as compared with 7.6 per cent in 1989.

Personal finance

An average executive job, requiring graduate or professional-level qualifications and some five years or so of experience, would command an annual salary of between \$70,000 and \$80,000. A senior managerial job would be worth \$120,000 plus. However, and unlike many other countries, cars are not normally provided as an executive fringe benefit, unless they are actually an integral part of the job. A skilled worker could expect to earn something in the region of \$40,000. A university professor would be paid from \$60,000.

Taxation

Normally, while you are living in Canada, all sources of revenue, whether from inside or outside the country, are liable to federal and provincial tax whether or not you are a Canadian citizen. As a separate rate of income tax is levied by each province, the total tax paid will vary somewhat, but, to take a fairly typical example, for a married employee with two children, earning \$60,000, total deductions for tax and social security would come to just under \$19,000.

Your identity as a taxable person (and also as a beneficiary of social benefits) is established through your Social Insurance number and you should apply for this as soon as possible after you arrive in Canada.

Working conditions

The general working atmosphere and corporate style in Canada closely resemble those of the US, but Canadian society is more stable, with lower crime figures. If you go to Canada intending to stay more than three months, you have to register this fact on arrival.

Modest increases in immigration levels are to be allowed over the next few years as a result of Canada's ageing population and falling birth rate. It is, however, still quite difficult to emigrate to Canada. Many potential British immigrants fall into the 'family class' category, with either close relatives already in Canada, or a Canadian spouse. Otherwise, they come into the 'independent' category, and have to fulfil specific criteria: there should be a demand for their skills and they should be able to support themselves. A job offer from a Canadian employer makes a great deal of difference, as does higher education. Professional groups that are in demand include mathematicians, sales and advertising personnel, chemists and physicists. It is also possible to immigrate if you have capital available and intend to run a business in Canada.

In the public services preference is given to Canadian citizens and here, as well as in many private sector jobs, a knowledge of French is essential for civil servants dealing with French-speaking people and areas. It should not be assumed that the status of French in Canada is merely a nationalistic gesture. It is the mother language of many Canadian citizens. However, people who do not speak it may still enter public service, as provisions will be made for them to learn the language subsequently.

People who want to exercise professional skills will have to apply to the appropriate professional bodies and institutes to make sure that their qualifications are recognised. The Canadian High Commission in London will advise you of the appropriate addresses. In some cases where training to achieve the qualifications in question is substantially different in Canada, further examinations may have to be taken to achieve recognition. In all instances, though, documentary proof of degrees, etc should be taken with you, as well as such personal documents as birth and marriage certificates. Information on visa requirements and employment opportunities in Canada is available from the Canadian High Commission at Macdonald House, 38 Grosvenor Street, London W1X 0AA.

Living conditions

It should be remembered that Canadian winters are much colder than anything one is accustomed to in temperate zones, although similar to Scandinavia. This is true even in the population centres in the southern part of the country. If you are to arrive in Canada any time between

October and March make sure you have plenty of warm clothes with you, especially outer garments, because they will cost you a lot more if you have to buy them there in a hurry. They will not be needed indoors, as most apartments and offices are centrally heated. On the other hand, the summer (June to September) can be very warm, with temperatures averaging around 90°F in mid summer in southerly places like Toronto.

You will also have to take account of the fact that heating bills are a considerable part of the winter budget and that adequate central heating will have to be an essential feature of any house you buy. However, while you are finding your way about it is better to rent accommodation, although the availability and cost of this varies widely. Most apartments are unfurnished and a three-roomed flat in Toronto would cost from $600–1200 a month. This would include heating, hot water, electricity, fridge and a stove, though it is obviously vital to check what exactly you are getting for your money when you sign a lease. Prices in major cities are in line with this figure, but it is obviously lower as you go out into suburban and country districts.

Buying a house in Canada can be expensive, although average house prices still compare favourably with prices in many parts of the UK.

Many newer houses include ready-installed cookers and refrigerators as part of the price. Electricity in Canada is supplied at 110V, 60 cycles and conversion from other voltages is not really possible. Do not bring UK electrical appliances such as TV sets with you.

Food prices vary from province to province, but some typical recent averages are:

	$
Chicken (1 kg)	4.80
Cheddar cheese (500 g)	5.70
Sugar (1 kg)	1.25
Eggs (12)	1.60
Potatoes (1 kg)	1.00
Butter (250 g)	1.85
Cooking oil (1 litre)	3.70
Scotch whisky (75 cl)	21.00

One of the principal differences between the USA and Canada is the latter's adherence to the welfare state concept. Social benefits in Canada are widespread. There is a compulsory national pension scheme with contributions related to income up to a modest index-linked maximum. There are fairly generous allowances for each child (these count as taxable income), and there are various forms of unemployment and disability benefit. Most important, though, is the fact that Canada operates a national health insurance programme, which is administered by the provinces, for both hospital and ordinary medical (though not dental) care. In all provinces except Quebec and British Columbia, which impose a brief residence qualification (though in the case of Quebec only for hospital insurance), these are available to immigrants immediately on arrival and you should be sure to obtain details of registration and premium payments as soon as possible. Many employers pay the employee's contribution as part of the remuneration package and this is a point worth checking in any job offer.

Education in Canada is compulsory from 6 to 16 (14 in some provinces) and is free to the end of secondary schooling. Educational methods are progressive and akin to those in primary and comprehensive schools in the UK. There are also a small number of private schools. In Quebec and French speaking Canada the medium of instruction in many schools is French, and the teaching of French is an important part of the curriculum.

Post-secondary education is not free, but repayable loans are available from the province, and there are various other forms of monetary assistance including scholarships for able students. University fees are low.

Social life in the cities near the US border is very like that in America and, even in the remoter regions of the north and west, many of the same features prevail: for example, the widespread use of credit facilities, shopping at drive-in self-service supermarkets on the outskirts of towns, the high standard of material efficiency and comfort and the ubiquity of the motor car.

Conditions vary enormously between the different provinces and between urban and country areas.

Canadians do a great deal of entertaining in their homes. Many have lakeside or country cottages (perhaps built by themselves) and to have one is the ambition of most families. The scope for outdoor activity is unlimited, whether organised sport (ice hockey, Canadian football and baseball) or individual pursuits such as sailing, swimming, fishing, hunting, canoeing and mountaineering. Soccer is increasingly popular.

Liquor laws vary from province to province. In some they are pretty strict, prohibiting drinking on Sunday. There are few pubs in the British sense but plenty of bars in the cities. The Canadians are easy going and informal and most British people who have settled there would probably take a great deal of persuasion to accept the fall in living standards which coming home would involve.

Mexico

Background

Mexico is the largest Spanish-speaking country in the world and the third largest country in Latin America. In area it is about eight times the size of the UK. Estimates about the population vary but it is believed to increase by 2 million a year and is generally thought to be about 83 million, of whom over 20 million live in and around the capital, Mexico City. Other main centres are Guadalajara, population about 4 million, some 400 miles north-west of Mexico City and a centre for light industry; and the heavy industrial centre near the US border, Monterrey. A significant socio-political fact of life in Mexico, as in other Latin American countries, is rapid migration from the country to the cities and a birth rate which, though falling, is still too high in a country where poverty, unemployment and underemployment are endemic. The country is, however, quite stable politically – it has been governed by the same party since 1929. The current President, Carlos Salinas de Gortari, has held office since December 1988.

Exchange rate: Pesos 5004 = £1.

The economy

Mexico, as a major oil producer, is one of the few countries likely to benefit from the Gulf War, and even before hostilities began, the national oil company, Pemex, had stepped up production.

The legacy of the Mexican debt crisis of the early 1980s remains, and strict control of public finances is still essential. Nevertheless, there are signs of recovery – not only in the oil sector, but also in manufacturing, where exports have been increasing at a rate comparable with SE Asia, and in the growth of the *maquila* (in-bond) industry, which involves the use of cheap Mexican labour to assemble components into finished goods for export.

Annual growth rates are expected to rise from around 3 per cent to 6 per cent by 1994; inflation, however, remains a serious problem.

Working conditions

Expatriate salaries in Mexico correspond to US levels. A *work permit* is needed which has to be applied for by the local employer; it is not easy to get because strong preference is given to Mexicans. The employer has to pay a deposit of US$2000, returnable on the employee's departure. Documentation plays a large part in the settling-in process and it is a good idea to get all major documents (eg birth and marriage certificates) certified by the Mexican Consul at this end before you arrive. Clearly, in a country where inflation is over 30 per cent, it is absolutely vital that your salary should be expressed in a strong foreign currency. Tax rates start at 3 per cent and rise to 35 per cent. Foreigners employed under a technical assistance agreement are not liable to income tax.

Living conditions

The climate in Mexico is mainly hot and dry, though Mexico City is cooler because of its high altitude where the level of air pollution is high. Altitude does produce problems of breathlessness, insomnia, etc, and those suffering from anaemia or who are overweight may encounter particular difficulties. Notoriously, also, Mexico has a reputation for giving foreigners stomach upsets – 'Montezuma's Revenge' and 'Mexican Foxtrot'. But in the writer's experience, the hazards of diarrhoea are no worse than in any other hot country and, though ultimately unavoidable at some point, can easily be kept in check by common sense about what you eat and drink. For more serious ailments, Mexico has a good state medical service although the degree to which it is free of charge depends on your local employer's contributions to the social security system. Since such contributions are not mandatory it is important to know where you stand in respect of medical treatment.

An unfurnished detached house (three bedrooms) would cost about US$2000 per month.

There are fluctuations in the electricity supply (100–127V, 60 cycles) so as well as checking that your equipment is adapted to these voltages you should also bring a 1KW transformer. For any portable valuables you would be well-advised to take out a world-wide all-risk insurance policy, since burglary in Mexico is not uncommon.

Among the good things to buy locally is pottery, which is attractive and cheap and makes an excellent present to bring home for people who appreciate such things. But in order to shop in markets and indeed to live in Mexico at all you will need to learn Spanish, preferably before you get there. This is in fact true of all the Latin American countries (though, of course, for Brazil read Portuguese rather than Spanish). Servants, if they have worked for an English speaking family, can often be a source of informal language lessons, especially for children. Wages are around P120,000 per week for a general servant.

For people who do take children to Mexico there are a couple of good English schools in Mexico City which go right up to A level, but fees are high. Because of the unstable currency position fees are subject to rapid fluctuations and it is advisable to check the latest position.

As far as leisure is concerned, there is a great deal to see and do in Mexico, ranging from splendid unspoiled beaches to magnificent archaeological remains, though Mexico City itself is wildly overcrowded and slum-ridden. Roads are good and petrol is cheap by European standards. British cars are not readily available and cars are expensive – prices are among the highest in Latin America; British or international driving licences are valid when driving cars registered abroad, but a Mexican licence is essential to drive cars registered in Mexico. Standards of driving are not good and third-party insurance, though not compulsory, is advisable.

The United States of America

Background

Whether you look at it in terms of size and population, or of wealth and power, everything about the United States is big. It is a continent, rather than a country, and contains wide differences in geography, climate, people and customs.

There are about 245 million inhabitants living in a total area of 3.6 million square miles. The country as a whole is sparsely populated, with a density of only 64 inhabitants per square mile, but in some areas on the eastern seaboard (eg New Jersey) it is over 900 to the square mile.

The USA is bordered by the Atlantic, the Pacific and the Gulf of Mexico and has common frontiers with Canada and Mexico. There are wide differences in climate. During July and August the country is very hot: Washington is also humid and New York can be unbearable. The winters everywhere are cold, except in the deep south and the south west.

The Americans are essentially urban dwellers and about 70 per cent of the population live in towns and cities. Many of the major cities are densely populated. Washington DC, the US capital, has only 638,000 inhabitants but it is the centre of government and of political and diplomatic activity. New York with about 7 million citizens (1.5 million in Manhattan alone) is the leading port and financial centre. Chicago has 3 million and Los Angeles 3 million. Altogether 26 other cities have populations of over a million. The most congested part is a wide belt in the north-east stretching from Boston to Washington. Other concentrations of population are round the Great Lakes and on the west coast, associated with Chicago and San Francisco respectively.

Between the east and west are the vast underpopulated wheat belt and plains of the mid-west, the Rocky Mountains and the desert land of Utah, Colorado and New Mexico.

The population comprises a rich variety of ethnic groups. There are about 22 million black Americans – racial discrimination is barred and equal opportunity stipulated under the law. Successive waves of immigration brought Irish, Italians, Germans, Poles, Chinese and Jews and more recently the inflow has been from Asia, the Caribbean and South America. While keeping alive their traditions, customs and sometimes their own languages, the immigrants have been absorbed down the years into the vast melting pot of American society.

The USA is a federal republic with 50 federated states. Each state (except Nebraska) has its own governor, senate and house of representatives and exercises considerable autonomy over its internal affairs. The federal government is responsible for foreign policy, defence and monetary affairs. The President is elected for a four-year term, and he may not run for more than two terms. Congress consists of the Senate and House of Representatives.

Exchange rate: $1.67 = £1.

The economy

The USA is the richest and most successful economy in the industrialised world. There are certainly longer-term economic problems embedded in the USA's big deficits and mountainous defence spending, financed by high interest rates, which President Bush is having to come to terms with. However, the sheer size of the American market and the natural wealth of the country make it almost independent of the world economy. At the same time, there are shifts within the US economy which affect expatriates - principally the growing importance of the 'sunbelt' states in the south with their 'sunrise' high technology industries and the relative decline of the old industrial north. Inflation is currently between 5 and 6 per cent.

Personal finance

American salaries are around 40 per cent higher than in the UK but there is nothing like the range of benefits and degree of employment protection that you get in Europe. People intending to take up employment in the USA should bear in mind that state health schemes are limited to the elderly and that medical treatment is very expensive. If insurance is not included in the remuneration package this could make quite a hole in an imposing salary. It may not be, because American executive salaries are less perk-laden than those in some other countries: for example, very few American executives get cars unless their job necessitates it.

Job advertisements in the USA, certainly at executive level, tend to demand a lot from the applicant but to be rather coy about what he or she is going to receive. Salaries, for instance, are rarely stated. It is as well to get advice from someone who has worked in the USA before accepting any offer, unless it is from a multinational, where conditions are usually fairly standard.

According to one recent survey, a typical middle management salary would be around $60,000, with more senior posts in the $100,000–$150,000 range; bear in mind that the cost of living in the US is now around 20 per cent lower than in the UK. However, pay rates vary around the country, with higher salaries in Boston or California than in Chicago or Dallas. In practice, an expatriate is most likely to find a job in the USA with a multinational unless he or she has special skills in engineering, computing, R&D or electronics, or a reputation in an academic discipline.

There is some evidence that US firms are now seeking British managers with international experience, to establish and run European manufacturing bases. There are also opportunities with US companies that have investments in the UK.

Taxation

If you think making tax returns is complicated in the UK, you are in for a shock in the USA. The American tax system is built round the idea of self-assessment, which requires a smaller bureaucracy than ours but also places more of a burden on the person making the tax return. In fact, most people consider it impossible to complete the US self-assessment forms without professional advice.

Even wage and salary earners come under the self-assessment umbrella, because, although their tax is deducted initially under a form of PAYE, eventual adjustments in the form of rebates or further payment demands are based on the self-assessment return which is monitored by spot checks and computer matching with previous returns. Penalties for cheating are ferocious, but allowable deductions are rather more generous than in the UK; and federal tax rates are lower than UK taxes – they range from a basic 15 per cent to a top rate of 28 per cent. However, there are also state income taxes, so what the individual actually pays varies from state to state. Some cities also have income tax, notably New York City.

There is no VAT in the USA but there are sales taxes which vary from town to town – rates are generally between 2 and 10 per cent. Since they are not shown as part of the price of the goods, as VAT usually is, this can mean a nasty shock when you get your bill for an expensive item.

Working conditions

Visitors to the USA, on business or holiday, no longer need a visa for a stay of less than 90 days.

How you set about applying for a visa that enables you to work in the USA, however, is a matter that requires a good deal of caution. Visas for permanent immigration are extremely hard to get unless you have close family ties there. Furthermore, if you make an application of this kind and get turned down, it then becomes extremely difficult to get a visa of any kind – even as a visitor – because the presumption is that once you get to the USA you will find some illegal way of remaining there.

If you are going to work for the British subsidiary of an American firm, or vice versa, the task is relatively easy. Your firm would apply for an L1 visa which would grant you residence for up to three years. Similarly, if you are proposing to invest substantial sums, at least $200,000, to start up a business venture in the USA, you could apply for a treaty investor's or trader's visa, designated by the number E1 or E2.

People who merely want to go to the USA to take up a job offer must get their employer to file an application for a temporary worker's H1 or H2 visa. If you are going to the USA to look for a job, you have to ask the employer to do this as soon as he makes you an offer. These applications are processed within a matter of a few weeks.

You are allowed to take into the country your personal effects, for example household goods which have been used for at least a year, professional books and tools of trade, cars, etc and antiques more than 100 years old.

Although the 35-hour week prevails, working conditions are a great deal more strenuous and exacting than in some firms here. American employers expect results and are fairly ruthless about removing people who do not deliver them. Senior executives come and go and it is not unusual for a shake-up at the top to work its way right down the ladder. In some firms considerable conformity with the image of the company in relation to dress, life-style, etc is expected, even in the private lives of their employees.

Living conditions

The overall cost of living is now lower than in the UK, although food costs rather more. Here are some 1990 prices:

	$
Fresh fish (1 kg)	11.50
Cooking oil (1 litre)	2.50
Tomato juice (½ litre)	1.20
Cigarettes (20)	1.80
Cheese (500 gm)	4.20
Pork (1 kg)	7.00
Steak (1 kg)	10.50
Chicken (1 kg)	2.50
Bananas (1 kg)	1.15
Apples (1 kg)	2.30
Beer (1 litre)	2.10

Some other significant prices are:

	$
Good quality cotton dress	95–140
Man's shirt	35–50
Ready-made suit	300–400
Purchase price, house in a good area	170,000 upwards
Rent of a two-bedroom furnished flat in a good area	1000 a month upwards

If you can wait for sales time, you will find that quality goods – not buy-ins, but brand names – are marked down by as much as 50 per cent and more. In fact even at ordinary shopping times, US department stores have bargain offers, particularly in clothes.

Restaurant meals can be astronomically expensive, particularly in pretentious 'French' restaurants (there are some good ones, but many more are over-priced and of poor quality). On the other hand, the average restaurant meal is quite good and moderately priced. Standards of service in public places generally are friendlier and better than in the UK. Hotels have increased in price recently, particularly in New York, where decent hotels now cost from $150 upwards per night for a single room, though in smaller towns, less frequented by tourists, rates are only about half that.

Expatriates are likely to receive an accommodation allowance, and some employers provide free accommodation. For those who have to find their own, the annual rent for a small one-bedroomed Manhattan apartment will be around $38,000.

Many people who work in New York prefer to live outside Manhattan. Find out about schools, shops, clubs and amenities in whatever suburb you choose. Elsewhere in the country, rents vary considerably – in Houston, Texas, for example, they are less than half New York levels.

When renting accommodation, it is usual to be asked for a month's rent in advance and another on deposit. Check the lease for such points as air-conditioning, services, garbage disposal, etc – many blocks have garbage chutes – and security arrangements. The latter may come as a shock to those accustomed to the relative safety of European cities. Flats in New York City, for instance, usually have stout front doors made of heavy wood or metal, and multiple locks. Theft and more violent crimes are not uncommon and doors should be locked when you go out and at night. This even applies to the more expensive apartments that employ a porter or security guard. As for streets, they are not as unsafe as is sometimes suggested, but reasonable care has to be exercised in avoiding walking at night in badly lit or deserted ones.

Don't expect to get any domestic living-in help. You can probably get a daily for about $10.00 an hour, and you can hire a babysitter from $5.00 to $6.00 an hour from several agencies. A domestic, living out, would come to about $850 per month for a 40-hour week. The Yellow Pages of the telephone directory in New York are infallible guides to the kind of domestic and other services you may need.

The electricity supply is generally 110–120 volts, AC 60 cycles. Flat two-pin plugs are normal.

You will find everything you could conceivably need in the shops, stores and supermarkets of the main centres and on the outskirts of the towns. Shopping hours are normally from 9.00 am to 5.00 to 6.00 pm, with late shopping one or two evenings a week. Most shops are open on Saturday and some on Sunday. Drugstores sell not only medicines but a wide range of household goods, ice creams, toys, cosmetics, etc and have coffee and snack bars. They stay open late.

Medical treatment is of a very high standard, but is extremely expensive. If possible, people are advised to get full medical insurance for themselves and their families before departure. However, many European insurance companies no longer offer cover for expatriates and their families in the USA; instead, they advise that insurance should be arranged with a US company such as the Blue Cross.

Even for a short stay, insurance is essential. The cost of a minor operation – such as an appendectomy – is likely to be over $5,000.

Nursery school groups can be found in most American centres. In Manhattan and other New York districts these are run by International Play Group Inc and many other groups for children from two years up to school age.

All children between 6 and 16 must attend school. The school year lasts from September to June. The system comprises public schools – there are about 90,000 in the whole country with over 50 million pupils – and there are 12 grades, 1–6 elementary, and 7–12 in secondary or high school. After the twelfth grade the pupils will probably go to college. Schools are operated by boards of education and are free.

There are fee-paying private schools and a number of boarding schools, modelled on the UK pattern, where tuition and boarding fees are usually fairly high. There are international schools in New York (the United Nations) and Washington. The UN school takes children from kindergarten to high school age and sometimes can take in children whose parents are not UN officials. Instruction is in English and French.

The Americans have taken to the air as naturally as our great-grandfathers took to rail. Flying is the most efficient and speedy (and relatively cheap) way of getting round this vast country. All the main cities are connected by internal flights and there are frequent 'shuttle' services between some cities (eg New York to Washington, New York to Boston and San Francisco to Los Angeles). New York has two international airports and one domestic. Helicopter services are often available, as well as private plane hire.

There has recently been some revival of the railways. Long-distance coaches (usually air-conditioned) are the cheapest way of travelling, if you can stand the boredom.

There are underground trains or 'subways' in New York, Boston and Philadelphia. The famous cable cars in San Francisco are now back in service. New York city bus services are regular and frequent – you need the exact fare. Cars can be rented from hire firms at airports, hotels and agencies. Few New Yorkers drive their cars in the city because of the traffic jams and parking problems, conditions which are found in all major cities.

Driving is on the right. An international or UK licence is valid for one year, but it is advisable to get an American licence from the state department of motor vehicles – after a test. Most highways and super-highways have several lanes, and lane discipline is very strict as is the enforcement of speed limits.

Many expatriates buy a new or used car locally and re-sell it when they leave. A medium-priced car costs around $12,000. The American Automobile Association (AAA) is an extremely helpful organisation for motorists.

Thanks to films, TV programmes and the intensive coverage of presidential elections, most British people have a pretty fair picture of the USA and the American way of life, even if they have never been there. Much of it may be an exaggerated if not distorted picture, but it does convey the sense of hustle and bustle in the big cities and gives some idea of the tensions of daily life.

The Americans are informal. They will probably call you by your first name on sight and outside Washington there is little protocol. Business is often conducted over meals, and working breakfasts are fashionable. There is no strict etiquette to be followed and most appointments are made over the phone. Clothing is very much as in the UK, but remember that the American summers are hotter and the winters colder, so dress appropriately. Remember too that most houses and offices are centrally heated and air-conditioned.

American hospitality and generosity is proverbial and you may find yourself exhausted by the social round. The licensing laws vary in different states. In general, bars are open nearly all hours. In their houses, Americans tend to eat late in the evenings and to have several drinks before dinner – a circumstance that has been the downfall of many a jet-lagged visitor.

There is always plenty to do in the cities, which have entertainments, theatres, opera, ballet, cinemas, museums and art galleries. TV is ubiquitous (there are over 1000 TV stations) and there is a wide choice of channels. There is naturally less in the way of cultural activity in the smaller towns and in the mid-West, which are far removed from the cosmopolitan atmosphere of New York and San Francisco.

Opportunities for open air and indoor sports abound, and many are offered by clubs and societies. Many American take long weekends at the coast or lakeside, swimming, boating, fishing, etc. There is skiing in the winter in New England and in the Rockies and plenty of scope for mountaineering, camping and touring. In the summer months many American offices close early on Fridays to allow staff to get away for long weekends. In New York and in other large cities quite a lot of people rent summer houses in the country or at the beach.

Asia

South East Asia: Some Notes on Etiquette

It used to be said that Britain and America were two countries divided by the same language: meaning that things which appeared similar were often very different under the surface. This is even more true of South East Asia, where the cities, at any rate, have an increasingly western appearance that nevertheless masks profound cultural differences between Asians and Europeans. The tendency is for expatriates to feel that these can be overcome by observing the ordinary niceties of social behaviour, Western-style, but these do not always translate themselves readily. In the West, for instance, it has become customary for business dealings to be conducted relatively informally – indeed informality has become almost a style in itself. In the East, a good deal of ceremony is still observed and the more important the negotiations, the more ceremony will be attached to them. This is related to what people in the East would call 'face'.

The notion of 'face' is prevalent throughout Asia and it is a difficult term to translate. It may be, as in the instance above, the dignity of an occasion or it may be, more often, simple human dignity. The reluctance to violate your own sense of 'face' may cause a subordinate who disagrees with you to disobey your instructions, having apparently agreed to follow them. The way to deal with such a situation is not to take issue with him or her in public but to sort it out in circumstances where no loss of face is involved for either party. This has to be done with a great deal of tact – the western notion of frankness is largely unknown to people in the Far East, who are apt to regard it merely as rudeness.

Another rich area of potential misunderstanding lies in the use of body language. As in the Middle East, it is generally considered impolite to take or offer things with the left hand, though at meals dishes can be passed with the left hand, provided it is supported by the right. Oriental people are also very wary of effusive displays of affection. Even old friends should be greeted with a certain amount of gravity and reserve. Those same qualities should also mark your relations with subordinates – pointing at people with your finger or beckoning them by use of the finger is regarded as the height of bad manners. Indeed, many finger gestures are regarded as obscene, as is making points by pounding the open palm with the fist.

The Asian culture, wherever you go, is in fact one that is very nervous about familiarity and treats as familiarity many modes of behaviour that we would regard as fairly normal.* This also extends to the use of Christian (or proper) names. The Chinese style, incidentally, is for the surname to come first, the middle name second and the equivalent of the Christian name last. Thus a Chinese person with a name such as Goh Kee Seah, would be Mr Goh, not Mr Seah.

Another way in which Asian culture differs from ours is in the importance attached to luck. Again it is important to respect this because to dismiss it as superstition would be a grievous offence against the concept of face. It can, of course, work to your favour; for instance it is considered bad luck if the first person into a shop each day leaves without making a purchase. In those shops where bargaining is part of normal transactions, this can lead to the often expressed sentiment of 'special price, just for you' indeed having some meaning. Normally you will usually find that after prolonged bargaining you have ended up paying about the same as in a department store.

A further point about shopping: Asians are, in general, slighter than Europeans, so you would be well advised to stock up on clothes before you leave.

Brunei

Background

Brunei is a small, prosperous sultanate on the north coast of Borneo which became an independent state in January 1984. It is about the size of Norfolk and is bounded on three sides by the Malaysian state of Sarawak. The fourth side is bounded by the China Sea and it is on this narrow coastal strip that the main towns are located. The rest of the country is tropical rain forest. Brunei's 69 per cent Malay, 18 per cent Chinese and other indigenous population numbers 249,000, over 50 per cent of whom live in and around the capital, Bandar Seri Begawan. There is a large expatriate community with a sizeable British element. The official religion is Islam and the influence of the religious element is increasing. Brunei has very close ties with Britain, including defence.

The economy

Brunei has one of the highest standards of living in South East Asia with

* An excellent account of this whole issue is given in a book called *Culture Shock* by Jo Ann Craig, published by Times Books International of Singapore.

a per capita income of no less than US$14,000 and low inflation. Almost all its wealth comes from oil and gas, but the government has encouraged the use of oil money to foster the development of secondary industries and services such as fishing, agriculture, education and communications. Its revenues, mainly from oil, far exceed government expenditure, even though that revenue has declined with the drop in oil prices. Its foreign currency reserves are about half those of Japan.

Exchange rate: BS2.97 = £1.

Personal finance and taxation

Salaries are upwards of 50 per cent higher than the UK equivalent and usually carry such fringe benefits as subsidised or free housing, an education allowance for children, paid home leave, free medical attention, a car or an interest-free loan to buy one and an end-of-service bonus. There is no personal tax in Brunei. There is also no restriction on remittances.

Working conditions

Entry and exit visas are not necessary for UK nationals. *Employment* and *residence passes* have to be obtained on behalf of expatriates by their employer but they are not usually difficult to obtain for UK nationals. The following is a benefits package advertised for a number of jobs in Brunei:

> In addition to the tax free salary, benefits include a 25 per cent gratuity, and annual bonus equivalent to one month's salary (tax free), generous subsidised housing, free economy class air passages, children's education allowance and holiday visit passages, generous paid leave, interest-free car loan and free medical attention.

Living conditions

The vegetation, climate and general atmosphere of the country is typical of tropical regions of South East Asia, with high humidity and a temperature that rarely falls below 70°F and rarely rises above 90°F. New houses are being developed and accommodation is constantly improving. If you can get one, a government bungalow is excellent. Rent is charged at 10 per cent of your basic salary. Normally the houses are fully furnished and air-conditioned.

Even with air-conditioning, however, the humidity gets at things like hi-fis, cameras and leather goods, so it is probably not worth while bringing treasured possessions with you or spending a lot of money on buying high-quality items locally, though they are available at reasonable prices. Equally, you will certainly need light-weight clothes and allow for plenty of changes. Again, these are available locally, but do not rely on getting them off-the-peg as oriental sizes are much smaller than European ones.

Local tailors are cheap and skilful: they will run up a dress for B$15–30, exclusive of materials. One item that is not available locally, though, are shoes and sandals of size 10 or 11 for men and 7 or 8 for women, so you should take several pairs with you.

Good, full-time servants are hard to find but most expatriates manage to find an *amah* (domestic help) to assist with the household chores for a couple of hours a day, and probably to babysit. Filipino servants are available, but the problem here is that the employer is bound by contract to pay for a flight home every two years.

Many expatriates find servants a help on shopping expeditions, particularly in the local markets where fresh fish is excellent, if no longer a cheap buy and fruit and vegetables are both delicious and reasonably priced. The latter should be washed, though, and care is also advised with drinking water in November and December.

Obviously you will need a car and a good choice is available locally. Japanese cars, which once dominated the South East Asian market, are now in competition with European models – because of the appreciation of the yen. Petrol is cheap.

Most expatriate children of secondary school age go to boarding schools in the UK, although facilities for secondary education do exist in Brunei. There are several good nursery schools as well as three good primary schools, of which the International School is the most popular.

State medical services are free, except for hospitalisation in which case a modest range of charges is applied. Standards are reputed to be high, but there are also private medical facilities for those who prefer them.

Recreational facilities are quite good, especially for water sports, with private clubs for sailing, golf and tennis. Two of the larger ones are for Shell employees, but non-Shell people are sometimes allowed to join. There are English and American films as well. Both Brunei and Malaysian colour TV can be received. TV sets and VCRs are best bought in Singapore or Brunei, as British sets will not work without adaptation. Many of the programmes are in Malay but the range of Australian, British and US programmes is improving. Videos have been regarded as a great boon to expatriates, because Brunei has very little to offer in the way of night life.

The People's Republic of China

Background

China is one of the world's largest countries geographically, stretching over 4800 km from east to west and 4000 km from north to south. That obviously gives it a very varied climate – subtropical in the south and hitting very cold conditions (–15°C) in the north. The coastline extends from North Korea down to Vietnam in the south, but there are also 20,000 km of boundaries: the Soviet Union, India, Nepal, Burma and Laos are all China's neighbours.

In addition to its sheer topographical size, China is also the world's most populous nation. Its population is over 1000 million, even though only 10 per cent of the land is cultivated. What there is, is very fertile. It follows, though, that China is highly urbanised and indeed the cities are very large – Shanghai, for instance, has 12 million people and Beijing 10 million.

China's history in the past 40 years has been truly extraordinary. Unified after the war by Mao Zedong, it has effectively gone through several revolutions since then. Essentially, these were government controlled, or at least government inspired events: the Great Leap Forward, the Cultural Revolution and the present experiment with a mixed economy, which gradually followed the ousting of the Gang of Four in 1976. The leader who emerged from all these events – and undoubtedly the guiding force behind the drive towards economic development along largely western-derived lines – was Den Xiaoping. Most Western observers were astonished by 1989's demonstrations and subsequent massacre in Tiananmen Square. This was followed by a purge of dissidents, as conservatives increasingly gained the upper hand.

At the time of writing, the leadership question is still open – Deng Xiaoping has resigned from office, but while he is alive (currently 86) he retains much of his former influence.

Exchange rate: Yuan 8.93 = £1.

The economy

The economy has run into serious difficulties, with inflation in 1990 of over 17 per cent and industrial output stagnating; the immediate outlook is gloomy. It is at present unclear whether the economic liberalism of the past few years, with its encouragement of private enterprise and joint ventures with foreign companies, will continue.

Personal finance and taxation

All foreigners whose employers are domiciled in China are liable for tax. Only business trips of under 90 days' duration are exempted if the employee is on an overseas payroll. Average expatriation tax would be 10 to 13 per cent. There are also indirect taxes on foreigners in that they have to pay for many goods and services with foreign currency certificates; these can, however, be used anywhere in China. Normal Chinese currency can be used to buy things or meals in places frequented by the Chinese themselves.

Working conditions

Office accommodation is scarce and very expensive. Most foreign companies at present have their offices in hotels. It has been estimated by the *China Business Review* that it costs a company around £400,000 a year to keep a small one-man office in China. Business hours are from 8 am until midday and 2 pm until 6 pm. Saturday morning working is also usual.

Living conditions

Most expatriate business people have to live in hotels, though some expatriate housing is available in Shanghai and Beijing (Peking). Accommodation in general is in very short supply, but at least it is now possible to stay in reasonably priced Western-built hotels. Another indication of the general improvement in conditions is the price of Western-style food; the average meal for two in the coffee shop of a Western hotel costs about £8 and a meal with wine in a French-style restaurant can be had for around £30.

Chinese restaurants, of course, are inexpensive and the food is generally excellent. Western goods can now be bought in numerous supermarkets in Beijing; there are also a few supermarkets in Shanghai. You should bring electrical goods with you and, of course, cars. These are virtually unobtainable in China though you can now get spares for some Japanese makes. Both cars and spares are subject to high rates of duty.

If you have a car it is becoming increasingly possible to get around. You need a permit to travel but these are generally granted without difficulty. The main problem is finding accommodation when you get to your destination. It is obviously a great advantage to be able to speak a little Chinese in such circumstances - and for business purposes as well - and some determined expatriates report that the standard Mandarin is not as difficult as it looks. While virtually impossible for the foreigner as far as reading and writing is concerned, it is apparently feasible to learn how to speak it well enough to get by in basic terms.

Although there are expatriate communities in the main centres, there is very little in the way of entertainment to be found in China. There is an International School in Beijing and American Schools in Guangzhou and Shanghai.

Hong Kong

Background

Hong Kong is not, as some people think, a unitary place, but a group of small territories and islands with a total estimated population officially given as 5.6 million. However, the significant elements are: Hong Kong Island itself which is about 13 km across and 8 km wide at its maximum;

Kowloon peninsula which lies on the mainland, a few minutes' ferry ride from Hong Kong Island; and behind this, the New Territories, which form an area almost half the size of Greater London. They include some arable land, but most of it is too hilly to be capable of much in the way of either urban or agricultural development. The lack of space for development makes the continuing influx of refugees from China and Vietnam a serious problem but, in the light of the Tiananmen Square massacre and continuing uncertainty about China's future policies, there are grave doubts about 1997. Emigration has risen sharply, although it seems that the people of Hong Kong are keener on emigrating to Canada, Australia and the USA than to Britain. The British government's grudging quota of 50,000 passports for 'key workers' is unlikely to be filled – by 1 December 1990 only 3000 Hong Kong Chinese had applied for entry to Britain under the scheme. Perhaps they were deterred by the uproar among conservative right-wingers, Norman Tebbit included, when the scheme was announced, and felt that they did not want to live in such an overtly racist country.

Hong Kong is a Crown colony (though the word 'colony' is no longer officially used), administered by a Governor, an Executive Council and a Legislative Council, but all this will change in 1997 when Britain's lease runs out. Under an agreement signed in September 1984, the colony will then revert to Chinese sovereignty, but under special conditions which should give it a considerable autonomy, including the freedom to operate a free enterprise capitalist enclave within the Communist system for a further 50 years. An important aspect of this is for Hong Kong to remain an international financial centre, outside the Chinese tax system and with a freely convertible currency. There will also be an elected element in the Legislative Council which will then, of course, be run by Chinese rather than British appointees.

Exchange rate: HK$13.04 = £1.

The economy

Apart from its importance as a financial and banking centre (no fewer than 136 banks and 300 insurance companies are incorporated there and it now ranks as the world's third most important financial centre after London and New York), Hong Kong's economy is bound up principally with the manufacture of consumer goods and light engineering products. In the former sphere textile processing is paramount and employs around 25 per cent of the total labour force in a staggering total of over 15,000 factories. In the latter area the most important export earner is the electronics industry, making both industrial equipment and such consumer goods as transistors and pocket calculators. This is followed by the plastics industry, where the manufacture of toys is the most important activity. Over 1800 factories are engaged in toy manufacture. Watchmaking is perhaps the most important of the aggregate of other light industries in which Hong Kong is involved. The colony is now the biggest exporter of watches in the world, but actually the biggest foreign exchange earner after textiles is tourism, although Hong Kong has little to offer other than a good climate, an admittedly fascinating (though perhaps no longer characteristic) glimpse of Chinese life and its status as a duty-free port, which means that some goods – especially cameras, watches, electronic equipment, etc – can be bought fairly cheaply there.

Inflation is around 10 per cent.

Personal finance

There are no exchange controls in Hong Kong and money is fully remittable into and out of the colony. Broadly speaking, an expatriate employee in the private sector should expect to be earning 40 to 50 per cent more than his gross UK pay. On top of this an expatriate employee should expect to get free or heavily subsidised accommodation and medical and dental attention, an education and holiday visits allowance for his children, and possibly further fringe benefits such as a car, servants and a good gratuity at the end of his contract. Public sector salaries are paid in Hong Kong dollars.

Income and other taxes

Tax is charged on all income arising in or derived from Hong Kong, and goes up by steps of 3 per cent to a theoretical top rate of 25 per cent on incomes after deductions of allowances for self, wife and children. However, without any deduction of allowances, the maximum tax payable in practice is 15 per cent, although accommodation, when provided or subsidised by an employer, is regarded as taxable income up to a maximum of 10 per cent of total earnings. Another factor to take into account is that Hong Kong has no double taxation agreement with the UK, so income derived from there while one is resident in Britain would be liable to tax in both countries. Conversely, however, income derived from abroad while one is resident in Hong Kong is not taxable. Clearly, the need for good tax planning advice for expatriates there is imperative.

Interest payable on foreign currency deposits placed with financial institutions carrying on business in Hong Kong is exempt from tax, as is interest on deposits in Hong Kong currency placed with such financial institutions.

Working conditions

Hong Kong's largely Chinese population (98 per cent) is impressively intelligent, skilled and hard-working, so opportunities for expatriates are limited. There is, however, a short-term demand for lawyers, accountants, management consultants and training specialists. It is the policy of the Hong Kong government to recruit locally whenever possible. Details of teaching, academic and technical jobs are advertised in the appropriate sections of the UK press; otherwise, in the case of government jobs, enquiries about vacancies should be directed to the Appointments Division, Hong Kong Government Office, 6 Grafton Street, London W1X 3LB. Non-government employers looking for British personnel would advertise through UK newspapers, offering contract terms of from one to four years, and various fringe benefits in the way of subsidised housing, medical facilities, education allowances, paid home leave and end of contract gratuity. There may, however, be snags about switching jobs once you are in Hong Kong, because the availability of highly qualified Chinese personnel means that employers there do not necessarily have to extend fringe benefits in order to fill a vacancy.

Living conditions

The feature of Hong Kong life that strikes a newcomer most forcibly is the population density, impressive even by Asian standards. The 1986 census recorded a population density for Hong Kong Island of 91,700 persons per sq km. So Hong Kong is no place for people who feel the need for wide open spaces or who are bothered by crowds. Yet it is by no means squalid. In fact its health record is good: public places are unusually clean and Chinese shopkeepers seem to be adept at making the most cramped premises look organised and tidy. Obviously, though, space is at a premium and this is reflected in rents which in the case of luxury accommodation in a desirable area can be over HK$1 million per annum. But smaller flats can be rented for HK$200,000 per annum upwards. Most companies, however, provide free or subsidised accommodation. The latter is also the practice of the government, which charges its employees 7.5 per cent of salary for rent. The climate of Hong Kong – warm and humid for most of the year but with a brief cool winter – makes air-conditioning and some heating facilities a necessity.

Hong Kong is no longer a cheap place to live, particularly if you rely on imported and frozen goods in European style supermarkets. Shopping for food in local markets can be rewarding since prices are subject to some seasonal fluctuation, although perhaps the main advantages over supermarkets lie in variety and interest rather than price. Restaurants are excellent and quite cheap if you like Chinese food. European style hotel meals, on the other hand, are rather expensive.

The following are typical prices:

	HK$
Bread (1 kg)	9.00–13.00
Butter (250 gm)	7.40
Instant coffee (250 gm)	64.00
Tea bags (250 gm)	35.00
Milk (1 litre)	14.50

Eggs (12)	10.00
Beef steak (1 kg)	100.00
Whisky (75cl)	110.00
Beer (large bottle)	6.00

Servants can be obtained in Hong Kong, but despite the general availability of people they are not particularly cheap, and full-time ones are hard to find. An *amah*, fulfilling the functions of that forgotten species, the maid, would expect to earn HK$3000 a month, with an annual bonus of a month's salary, but a more likely option is hourly help.

Public transport and taxis are inexpensive but apt to be overcrowded, and most expatriates have cars, which in many cases are not these days provided as a perk that goes with the job. There are no straight roads in Hong Kong and distances, in any case, are short, so a big car is a status symbol which also attracts a higher rate of registration tax and annual licence fees. UK driving licences are valid for a stay of up to a year, but can be exchanged for a local licence without a test. Bringing a new car into Hong Kong is hardly cheaper than buying one locally; however, good second-hand cars are reported to be readily available. With electrical goods, however, the problem is that British equipment has to be adapted to Hong Kong's system (200V at 50 cycles). Household electrical goods cost only slightly less than in Britain in spite of the colony's duty-free port status. Experienced residents maintain, however, that it is possible to get shopping bargains in Hong Kong, and recommend a book called *The Complete Guide to Factory Bargains* by Barbara Goetz, which lists places where 'overruns' of things made for the US market can be obtained very cheaply.

Education in Hong Kong can be a problem and expatriates are advised to make arrangements for schooling as soon as they get there, or before. Before arrival it is worth notifying the Education Department (295 Lee Gardens, 3F, Hysan Avenue, Hong Kong), or the English Schools Foundation (GPO Box 11284, Hong Kong) to ask about places. This is because most of the schools cater for the predominantly Chinese population, so the medium of instruction is either Chinese or, if in English, with the emphasis on English as a foreign language. There are several independent schools offering a UK curriculum, at both primary and secondary level.

Geography dictates that recreation facilities in Hong Kong are rather limited, but there are good local clubs.

Japan

Background

This mountainous island country is the most crowded on earth, and 121 million people are crammed into an area the size of Britain. The capital, Tokyo, has a population of nearly 12 million, and is the university centre. It is on the east coast of Honshu, the largest of the four main islands (the others are Hokkaido, Shikoku and Kyushu); the area comprising Osaka, Kobe, Kyoto, Nagoya and Tokyo is almost entirely built up. To the west across the Sea of Japan is Korea, and to the east the Pacific Ocean.

Japan lies at the north eastern end of the monsoon area. It has a temperate climate with four distinct seasons and, except in the north, winters are mild. It is subject to typhoons in September which bring torrential rains and violent winds. Average humidity is between 57 and 82 per cent. The country is subject to earthquakes, and new buildings are constructed to minimise damage.

Japan's history has been greatly influenced by China (whence the script derived) and has been marked by alternating periods of absorption and repulsion of foreigners, their religions, customs and inventions; the present time is a period of absorption. Buddhism and Shintoism are the dominant religions, emphasising respect for family and traditional values; their physical manifestations are seen in the shrines and temples up and down the country.

The language is written in characters (a combination of phonetic syllables and ideographs). Expatriates are employed mainly by multinational companies, but for employment with a Japanese organisation, social intercourse, and cultural integration, a knowledge of Japanese is essential.

The emperor Akihito, is head of state. The diet (parliament) has two houses, of which the dominant is the House of Representation. The ruling centre-right LDP (Liberal Democrat Party) has been in power for the past 35 years.

Exchange rate: Yen 253 = £1.

The economy

Despite Japan's almost total dependency on imported energy, the country remains one of the world's economic superpowers. Japan's readiness to adapt to new technology has been one of the secrets of its success, and the latest sign of this is that it is now the world's largest user of industrial robots. In spite of that, the unemployment rate is a low 2.5 per cent. Inflation is also relatively low at around 3 per cent. Continuing economic growth has led to a situation where Japan's per capita GNP exceeds that of the USA; more importantly, Japan is now the world's biggest creditor nation, and the USA the world's largest debtor.

Japan is a highly industrialised country, only 17 per cent of which is cultivable. Fish rather than meat is the main source of protein in the diet.

Personal finance and taxation

An expatriate executive will need double his UK salary to live at his normal standard, entertain as his job will require, and provide UK schooling for his children. Tokyo has consistently been one of the world's most expensive cities and a senior expatriate executive should strive for US$180,000–$230,000, plus 15–20 per cent overseas loading. Japanese indigenous salaries, once relatively low, are also now in the upper quartile and well above UK levels. It is advisable to arrange for some salary to be paid elsewhere to ease the tax burden and facilitate the transfer of funds to the UK.

The Japanese tax system is very complicated, but expatriates do have a concession inasmuch as they are taxed only on income arising in or remitted to Japan. The top rate (for national income tax) is 50 per cent, a typical expatriate would pay something between 30 and 50 per cent.

Working conditions

The majority of expatriates working in Japan are employed by foreign companies, particularly as representatives; otherwise, the main source of employment is as a teacher of English language. EFL teachers are likely to be recruited by the British Council. Bona fide students in Japan can appeal for permission to work a limited number of hours per week (teaching EFL); pay is from £16 to £25 an hour. Some language schools underpay their full-time staff. Even a primary school teacher should be earning at least £16,000 a year, bearing in mind the cost of living.

Employment patterns in Japanese firms differ from those in the West – recruitment is on traditional paternalistic lines from families with loyalty to the company – and a knowledge of Japanese would be a prerequisite.

Holders of UK passports require no visas for tourist visits under 60 days, which period may be extended to a maximum of 180 days at the discretion of the authorities. A *working visa* is required by those who have already obtained a post, which takes up to eight weeks once all the necessary documents have been presented. Information is available from the Visa Section, Japanese Embassy, 43–46 Grosvenor Street, London W1. Temporary work is not permitted, but if when visiting as a tourist you receive a written offer of a permanent post, a working visa may be obtained by leaving the country and applying from outside (Korea, for example).

Booklets outlining Japanese business practices and attitudes are available for businessmen from the Japan Trade Centre, Leconfield House, 6th Floor, Curzon Street, London W1Y 7FB, and may be useful for other visitors.

Living conditions

Tokyo is currently the second most expensive city in the world (Tehran is the most expensive). With the exception of cars and public transport, everything in Japan costs much more than in the UK. Rents of up to 1 million yen a month for furnished Western-style flats in central Tokyo are not uncommon. Japanese-style flats are more reasonably priced. Accommodation is cheaper in the suburbs and the average Japanese expects to spend two hours a day travelling to and from work.

Measurements are metric; the electricity supply is 100V, 50 cycles AC in eastern Japan including Tokyo, and 60 cycles in western Japan, including Nagoya, Kyoto and Osaka. Hotels generally provide sockets for both 110 and 220 volts.

Expatriate wives may find life difficult because of the position of women in society, where they are expected to be self-effacing. A wife's role might be confined to formal entertaining at home, of which there is a great deal, to promote her husband's interests. Much business is done as a result of socialising, and membership of a club (usually golf, but not exclusively devoted to it) is essential; the fees are exceedingly high (around £3000 a year is not uncommon) and usually form part of the remuneration package. Many expatriates belong to the Tokyo America Club, where annual fees are much lower – but the entrance fee is around £5000. A Japanese wife may not ease the path of the expatriate executive, unless she is from a certain class. A successful businessman needs to be at least 45 (no one younger cuts much ice in commercial circles) and to maintain the 'right' life-style.

The expatriate who will be staying longer than a year may bring in household effects, including a car and/or boat, duty free within limits considered reasonable by the customs. The car (or boat) sales receipt must be presented to show that the vehicle has been in use for more than one year before its arrival in Japan. An international driving licence is valid for one year, after which a Japanese licence must be obtained. This involves both practical and written tests, which may be taken in English. Traffic drives on the left, and tolls are payable for motorway use. The volume of traffic is immense, but Japanese drivers are patient and disciplined, and accidents are consequently few.

Signposting is inadequate (supposing one can read them) and a compass might be useful. A Toyota Carina 2000 would cost around 2 million yen.

A full-time maid would cost around 35,000 yen per week; cleaners and babysitters are paid about 1000 yen per hour.

Medical insurance for employees and their families is provided either by a government-managed scheme or a health insurance society. There are a number of English-speaking doctors in major cities, and Western brands of drugs are available.

There are many schools for English-speaking children but they are not geared to UK education. Most expatriates leave their children to be educated in Britain.

Some typical costs are:

	Yen
Sugar (1 kg)	290
Instant coffee (250 gm)	2040

Whisky (75 cl)	3100
Beer (50 cl)	280
Cigarettes (20)	260
Rice (1 kg)	600
Chicken (1 kg)	920
Steak (1 kg)	10,000
Eggs (12)	275
Butter (250 gm)	430
Petrol (1 litre)	137

Office hours are usually from 9 am to 5 pm, banks 9 am to 3 pm Mondays to Fridays and 9 am to noon on Saturdays; many companies operate a five-day week. Shops and department stores are usually open on Sundays and public holidays, but most other businesses are closed then. There are 12 public holidays a year.

Four English language newspapers are published daily: the *Japan Times*, the *Daily Yomiuri*, the *Ashi Evening News* and the *Mainichi Daily News*. A useful publication for intending expatriates in Japan is *Living in Japan*, published by the American Chamber of Commerce in Japan, 7th Floor, Fukide Building no 2, 1–21 Toranomon, 4-chome, Minato-ku, Tokyo 105.

Malaysia

Background

Malaysia is a federation of 13 states which fall in two separate geographical entities: peninsular Malaysia (the Malaya of colonial days minus Singapore) and East Malaysia which consists of Sabah and Sarawak and forms a wide strip on the northern half of what used to be Borneo Island. Peninsular Malaysia is about the size of England. East Malaysia is rather larger in area. However, a great deal of the interior in both cases is extremely mountainous and much of the coastline is swampy. East Malaysia is separated from the peninsula by about 750 km of the China Sea.

The total population of Malaysia is about 16.5 million, of whom 13.7 million live in the peninsula. The largest city in the latter is Kuala Lumpur and nearly 2 million people live in and around it. In East Malaysia, Kuching (500,000) and Sibu (250,000) are the main centres. Chinese form well over 30 per cent of the racial mix and Malays about 55 per cent. The rest are Asians, small tribal groups like Dayaks and expatriates. There is a good deal of rivalry between the tough, energetic Chinese (who have tended to dominate commerce and banking) and the Malays. Bahasa Malaysia is the official language and a knowledge of it would be useful to anyone going to live there for a long period, although English is widely spoken and understood.

The government is democratically elected and is headed by a titular monarch who is also elected, but only by his fellow hereditary rulers. Malaysia is politically stable but the influence of Moslem fundamentalists is said to be growing alarmingly.

Exchange rate: Malaysian Ringgit (more generally called Malay dollar) $4.62 = £1.

The economy

Malaysia is a fertile country. Its economy has traditionally been associated with growing rubber and timber and these are still important products, particularly because of the impact of oil price rises on the synthetic rubber industry. Malaysia is also one of the few remaining sources of tropical hardwoods, grown mainly in East Malaysia. Oil palm is the most rapidly expanding new crop and Malaysia is now the world's leading exporter of oil palm products. Food crops are also grown extensively and the country is 90 per cent self-sufficient in rice. Recoverable gas reserves, however, have been found on a very large scale indeed and these have spurred industrialisation at a growing pace.

The other resource with which Malaysia is traditionally associated is tin, and though facing competition from synthetic substitutes, Malaysia is the West's leading supplier of this metal. The exploitation of bauxite, natural gas and copper ore reserves is growing in importance and the Federation also has oil in modest quantities.

The most rapidly expanding sector of the economy, however, has been manufacturing and the government is actively encouraging the development of small-scale, labour-intensive industries which will even out discrepancies in regional development. Both the manufacture of a wide range of consumer goods and the development of processing associated with the tin and rubber industries fall under this heading.

Personal finance

Broadly speaking, an expatriate should expect to be earning about 50 per cent more than his gross UK salary, taking the value of fringe benefits into account. Free or subsidised accommodation and medical care, a car, financial assistance with education and paid home leave every second year are usually provided. Expatriates on contract employment may freely remit money out of the country, though formal permission must be obtained from the Controller of Foreign Exchange for sums over M$2,000,000

Taxation

Tax is levied on a PAYE basis on any income accruing in or derived from Malaysia; benefits in kind, excluding free medical treatment and the payment of passages home, are counted as part of chargeable income. Deducted from chargeable income are a broad range of allowances for a wife, dependent children, contributions to pension schemes and part of the cost of educating dependent children outside the Federation. The rate of tax on expatriate salaries would begin at 30 per cent and reach a maximum of 40 per cent on salaries of over M$100,000. The government is encouraging companies to establish their South East Asian headquarters in Malaysia, and expatriates employed in their regional office for a short period (182 days or less) are exempt from Malaysian income tax.

Working conditions

No one may enter Malaysia to take up employment without a *work permit* and this can only be obtained by the employer. Dependants need a dependent pass and must also obtain permission from the immigration authorities if they wish to take up any kind of paid employment. Separate passes are issued for peninsular Malaysia, Sabah and Sarawak and they are not interchangeable.

The working week is usually Monday to Friday, 8.30 am to 4.30 pm, Saturday until 2.30 pm, but in some states the Moslem week, Saturday to Wednesday, or Thursday morning, is kept; most Malays are Moslems.

Living conditions

The climate is tropical, hot and humid, varying little (except in the highlands) from a mean of 80°F. Seasons are more related to rainfall than to temperature. Rain, which amounts to 100 inches a year, falls in short, drenching thunderstorms: about 60 per cent of it from November to March. Conditions, it will be seen, are apt to be rather trying, but air-conditioning is provided nowadays in most homes and offices. Lightweight clothing is a necessity, but is readily available and relatively cheap.

Accommodation has become somewhat easier to find and prices have been steady. Monthly rents for a large house are about M$4000 to M$6000 in the Kuala Lumpur area but a good deal lower outside the principal towns. However, in most cases housing is provided as part of the contract. Where furniture and appliances are supplied as well, it is worth finding out in advance just what they consist of, so that the cost of shipping or purchasing locally can be allowed for in assessing the value of the remuneration package. Usually, cutlery, glass, linen and kitchen utensils are not provided, but household effects can be brought in free of duty if the house owner has had them for more than three months. They can, however, be purchased locally and though they will be more expensive than in the UK, it may be advisable to do this because of shipping delays. UK electrical equipment is suitable for Malaysian conditions (230V at 50 cycles AC). The cost of electrical equipment is comparable with UK prices.

Food prices are higher. As in the case of many other developing countries, those who are not too dependent on European style foods (cornflakes for breakfast, and the like) will find it cheaper than those who are. Some characteristic 1990 prices are:

	M$
Steak (1 kg)	25.00
Chicken (1 kg)	5.00
Butter (1 kg)	10.00
Bananas (1 kg)	1.50
Coffee (ground) (500 gm)	17.00
Oil (1 litre)	5.50
Sugar (1 kg)	1.60
Tea (500 gm)	17.00
Potatoes (1 kg)	3.00
Milk (1 litre)	2.60
Eggs (12)	2.30
Oranges (1 kg)	4.50
Bread (loaf)	3.00

Most expatriates get domestic help for household chores. A full-time servant in Kuala Lumpur earns about M$500 per month, plus one month's bonus annually, and wages tend to be lower elsewhere.

A private car is considered a virtual necessity and the general opinion is that it is better to buy one of the makes that is locally assembled than to import a car: spares are easier to get hold of, mechanics are more familiar with the cars and they are better suited to local conditions. Moreover, there is an import duty of 100 to 350 per cent on cars. In the light of this, employers should be prepared to supply a company car, and as an expatriate employee you can reasonably expect that a car will go with the job. If it does not, you will find that a model in the medium price range will cost about M$45,000. Petrol is cheaper than in the UK. It is advisable to take out a comprehensive insurance policy because local driving standards are poor. You will need to have a Malaysian driving licence, but a UK licence can be exchanged for a local one without taking a further test if done within three months of arrival.

Organised leisure in Sabah and Sarawak is limited to the main centres, but there is a wide choice of clubs of all kinds in the peninsula. Facilities for local leave are excellent, both in the hills and at the seaside, where some of the world's few remaining great unspoiled beaches are to be found.

Malaysia's climate is obviously apt to present health problems for those who cannot take long spells of uninterruptedly hot, humid weather. However, the principal disease hazard, malaria, has been largely eliminated, though it still exists in some rural areas. (Yellow fever and cholera injections are required before you enter the country, and your doctor will advise you on other precautions.) Most expatriates receive free medical treatment in some form or other, either as government employees or as part of the remuneration package. Otherwise, this is a potentially major expense to be budgeted for or insured against. First class hospital accommodation alone – apart from actual treatment – costs up to M$800 a day. Malaysia is very strict about drugs and trafficking in hard drugs carries the death penalty. If you are bringing medicines with you, make sure they are prescribed and labelled.

The schools situation in Malaysia is awkward for expatriates. It is difficult to get into state schools because Malaysian children have priority, and in any case the curriculum is really designed for the indigenous population. There are a number of fee-paying schools catering for expatriate children, although only one, the Uplands School in Penang, offers boarding *and* a UK curriculum. However, it is still common for the children of expatriates, particularly in the older age groups, to attend boarding school in the UK.

Singapore

Background

The Republic of Singapore consists of a main island and a group of islets; it lies off the southern tip of the Malay peninsula, but is close enough to be connected to it by a causeway across the Straits of Johore. In total area it is about the size of the Isle of Wight. It has a population of about 2.6 million, 76 per cent of whom are Chinese, 15 per cent Malay, and the rest Indian or European. The official languages are Malay, Chinese, Tamil and English, but English is the language of administration and business. In spite of its proximity to Malaysia, Singapore is a quite separate state. Its government, though democratically elected, could be described as a benevolent dictatorship and has been in power since 1959. Ideologically it practises a form of pragmatic socialism and is favourably disposed towards business while having many of the characteristics of a welfare state. Criticism of the government is unwise and political opposition is very much circumscribed. In fact, though, the government is generally popular and has been extremely efficient in managing the economy while enacting far-reaching measures to improve health, housing, social benefits and education. Singapore is regarded as being one of the most politically stable areas of South East Asia.

Exchange rate: Singapore $2.97 = £1.

The economy

Traditionally Singapore, with its geographical position at the crossroads of many international trade routes, its fine natural harbour and its excellent port facilities, has served as the principal entrepot for South East Asia. It is also an important base for companies operating oil exploration and refining services. To a large extent this continues to be its role, but the government, conscious of the fact that this makes the economy somewhat too dependent on outside forces, has strongly encouraged the development of manufacturing industry. In particular, the government has fastened on to the opportunities created by the 'second industrial revolution' of the new technology. It has deliberately fostered a high wages policy to force manufacturers to move from labour intensive to capital intensive activities, particularly in view of the fact that Singapore suffers from labour shortages. However, this policy has had the effect of pricing many Singapore goods out of export markets and their replacement by products from the country's Asian competitors; the rate of growth is now lagging behind that of South Korea and Taiwan. Singapore traditionally had one of the lowest inflation rates in the world, but the rate has now risen to the relatively high level of 4 per cent.

Manufacturing industry in general has grown rapidly in recent years, sometimes at phenomenal rates. Textiles, printing, electrical goods, electronics, plastics, building materials and foodstuffs are all active sectors. The main slow-down has been in heavy industry. Singapore also continues to be an important financial and banking centre, and, as elsewhere in Asia, tourism is a rapidly growing industry.

Personal finance

Managers of medium-sized companies might expect to earn £40,000–£50,000 a year plus fringe benefits such as free or subsidised housing, home leave, free medical treatment, school fees and a car. There are no restrictions on the amount of money that can be taken out of the country.

Taxation

Individuals resident in Singapore for tax purposes are liable to Singapore personal income tax charged on a sliding scale on income derived in or remitted to Singapore. Accommodation provided by the employer and certain benefits in kind are taxable, but not capital gains. Tax is levied at progressive rates from 3.5 to 33 per cent. There is tax relief for up to three children, but none thereafter – part of Singapore's policy of keeping down family numbers.

Employment exercised for a period or periods which together do not exceed 60 days in a calendar year is exempt from tax.

Working conditions

The British expatriate community is quite large – between 7000 and 8000.

Jobs are advertised in the appropriate sectors of the overseas press and are usually on a contract basis with a salary plus fringe benefits as indicated in the personal finance section. The major Singapore professional bodies are affiliated to, or otherwise closely connected with, their UK counterparts. People going to work in Singapore must have an *employment pass* which has to be obtained by the prospective employer. Dependants must also obtain a pass which has to be applied for by the employer.

Living conditions

Singapore is less than 100 miles from the equator and is hot and humid for most of the year. Air-conditioning is standard equipment in an executive-level house or flat, but light-weight clothing is also essential. A good cotton, off-the-peg dress costs about S$150. Evening dresses would cost upwards of S$150 if locally made – much more if imported. Ladies' locally made shoes cost from S$95. A man's locally made tailored suit can be ordered at about S$400. Singapore abounds in small shops and stalls selling consumer durables of all kinds. However, unless you are accompanied by a Singapore citizen or are very good at bargaining you will probably find it no more expensive to shop at a department store like Tang's in Orchard Street, Singapore's main thoroughfare.

Accommodation in Singapore is becoming cheaper and easier to find and is well below the Hong Kong levels. Hotels can cost around £70 a night and although previously it was possible to reduce hotel prices by haggling (due to over-supply), this is no longer the case. This is also becoming true of rents. A three-bedroomed unfurnished apartment would cost S$3000 per month and upwards to rent. A luxury apartment with such amenities as a shared swimming pool would come to S$4000–£5000 a month. However, rents are considerably cheaper outside the more popular residential districts. There, a flat can be obtained for as little as S$1000 a month. It is also possible to buy property, but there are restrictions on non-citizens doing so, except in the case of flats in high-rise buildings and condominium units. Accommodation is generally let unfurnished, but household appliances are slightly cheaper than in the UK – you can buy a large colour TV for S$900. The electricity supply is 230V, 50 cycles AC. Three square pin plugs are common. Except in department stores, bargaining for expensive items is worth while.

Singapore is self-sufficient in many foods and it is possible to eat fairly cheaply if you buy local products. Prices vary considerably from month to month, but here are some characteristic prices:

	S$
Milk (1 litre)	2.80
Margarine (500 gm)	4.00
Oranges (1 kg)	3.20
Steak (1 kg)	20.00

Potatoes (1 kg)	3.00
Eggs (12)	2.10
Corn oil (2 kg)	8.00
Wine (75 cl)	20.00

Tropical fruit is delicious and quite cheap; so are Chinese restaurants, although eating out European style is expensive. On the other hand, you can buy a delicious Chinese meal from a clean government-inspected street stall for under S$6.00.

Domestic servants are now much harder to find because of Singapore's low unemployment rate. An *amah*, fulfilling the functions of a maid (cooking, cleaning and babysitting) will earn around S$400 a month. On top of this, the employer has to pay 10 per cent of her wages to the Central Provident Fund and, if the servant is foreign, S$120 per month tax. It is advisable to arrange workmen's compensation insurance for domestic staff such as *amahs*, drivers and gardeners. For Filipino maids, personal accident insurance is compulsory and you may also have to provide medical insurance, annual air fares home and a bond for the Immigration Department.

The importing of cars is discouraged, and there is a duty of 45 per cent on imported cars on top of a basic additional registration fee of 175 per cent of the value of any new car, imported or otherwise. Thus it is not advisable to bring a car into Singapore from abroad, even though buying one locally is very expensive. Second-hand cars are advertised for sale in the *Straits Times.* The government is trying to limit car ownership on the island, both by fiscal policies and by placing restrictions on the use of cars in the central business district. On the other hand, both taxis and public transport are correspondingly inexpensive, and indeed are among the world's cheapest.

Leisure activities and participation in sport in public places are reasonably priced but membership and entrance fees at private clubs are in some cases very expensive. Top of the league is the Singapore Island Country Club, with four magnificent golf courses and an Olympic size swimming pool. Although membership fees are high, many foreign based employers will pay these on behalf of their senior expatriates.

As far as private entertainment is concerned, expatriates should be aware that there is strict censorship on moral as well as political grounds in Singapore. For instance, videotapes brought into the country have to be submitted to the board of censors.

Singapore has a good health record and the government wages a somewhat draconian cleanliness campaign, which includes hefty fines for dropping even a bus ticket in the street. There are no free medical facilities but treatment in government clinics is very cheap, though most expatriates prefer to use private doctors, who charge between S$25 and S$50 (specialists S$45–$80), depending on their qualifications and what sort of treatment is involved. Surgeons' and obstetricians' fees start at around

S$2000 and a private room in a hospital costs about S$175 a day. Medical fees, or insurance premiums to cover them, are often, in the case of expatriates, met by employers.

As in many other jobs overseas, education can be a problem, and arrangements to send children to local schools should be made as soon as possible. Government schools are very cheap, with only nominal fees for the children of Singapore residents. There are three good English private primary schools; the Singapore American School which takes all ages up to 18, and the United World College of South East Asia (which has facilities for A level teaching). There is also an excellent university in Singapore, at which the standards of entry and the level of the courses are equivalent to UK universities. Fees vary depending on the nature of the course being taken.

Australasia

Australia

Background

Australia is the world's largest island and smallest continent. It has an area approximately equal to the continental USA and a population of about 15.7 million people. It is a highly urbanised society: 70 per cent of the population live in the 10 largest cities, and more than 6 million live in Sydney and Melbourne. Inland (up to 500 miles from the coast) there are many pleasant rural cities and towns; the remainder of the continent tends to be very sparsely populated and arid.

Australian government is modelled on the Westminster parliamentary system and, broadly speaking, operates at two levels – State and Federal. Although considerable overlapping of responsibilities occurs, State legislature concerns education, health, justice, roads and railways, housing and agriculture while the Federal government covers matters of national importance: defence, foreign affairs, taxation, social services, etc. This system sometimes results in a conflict of political interest, between Central and State Governments which may have different elected majorities. (Incidentally, the Liberal Party in Australia corresponds more to the Conservative party in the UK while the Labour party is somewhat to the right of its counterpart here. The Australian Democrats are broadly similar to the UK Liberal Democrats.) In spite of these rivalries, Australia is politically very stable. The present Labour government, led by Bob Hawke, came to power in 1983 and was re-elected in 1984, 1987 and 1990.

Exchange rate: A$2.14 = £1.

The economy

The Australian economy has never fully recovered from the long-term effects of the stock market crash of 1987. Over the past three years the boom that preceded this event has gradually unravelled, bringing down many large and small companies with it, as well as a number of financial institutions. At the same time, there has been a sharp downturn in one of Australia's primary industries, agriculture. Wool, sheep and cattle prices have all been depressed in 1990–91 and farm incomes are officially expected to fall by 50 per cent – though on the positive side, this means that some farm products, like meat, are amazingly cheap by European standards. (On a personal note, in Australia last Christmas the writer paid $10 for a whole sheep – the money was for the cost of killing it, not for the animal itself!) From a macro-economic view, a further positive side is that Australia is largely self-sufficient in oil and has huge mineral reserves. Its long-term economic future must be good.

The extractive industries, which account for about three quarters of the country's exports, are largely carried on in remote areas. More visible are the big, sprawling cities where services and manufacturing are the main activities but in this other economy high wages and long distances from both internal and export markets have reduced the competitiveness of Australian goods. More than two-thirds of Australian export earnings still come from commodities, especially wool, wheat, sugar, beef, coal and metals. The country's vulnerability to international markets was demonstrated over the last three years by Australia's huge trade deficit, one of the highest among developed countries. In part this is due to a reduction of protective tariff barriers which had previously protected Australian manufacturers from international competition.

The low value of the Australian dollar (it has been as low as A$2.50 to the pound during the last year) has not helped the economy as much as was expected. In fact the main result has been an influx of investment in property, particularly by the Japanese, whose presence in Sydney and Queensland is beginning to be very noticeable. A boom in tourism has also begun, although it suffered from the general downturn in tourism in 1990.

The government is maintaining a cautious line on immigration policy, but the intake has gone up slightly and in 1988–89 140,000 were admitted. Preference is given to people with direct and close family connections, skilled and business migrants and others accepted under refugee or special humanitarian programmes. As part of the selection process, a points system is used to determine an applicant's employment and economic prospects, based on such factors as age, education and skills. There is a strong bias in favour of immigrants with engineering qualifications. Teachers with maths, science or language degrees are also high on the list of preferred immigrants, as are people prepared to settle in country areas. Business migration proposals have to be realistic and backed by substantial personal investment – a minimum of AS500,000 is required. Additional information can be obtained from the Australian High Commission in London or the Australian Consulates in Manchester and Edinburgh.

Personal finance

Public sector salaries are graded according to seniority and qualifications. For graduate and professional-level jobs, these grades run in bands, beginning at around A$28,000-plus at the lowest level and reaching

A$70,000–$80,000 in areas such as engineering and geology, which demand specialist and much sought-after skills. In a country where the average weekly earnings are around A$600, however, this may not seem particularly attractive. University vocations may seem a better bet. A professorship carries a salary that compares with managerial jobs – around A$67,000. School teaching is also comparatively well paid. A qualified graduate teacher with experience could expect to earn in excess of A$28,000. A skilled worker could, without overtime, earn in excess of A$30,000. Middle management jobs would command a salary of A$40,000-50,000. Professional jobs vary widely but doctors and dentists could expect to earn in excess of A$120,000. Senior secretarial salaries are about A$22,000 on average (depending on experience).

Taxation

Income tax is levied on a PAYE system against individuals whose source of income is derived from salary or wages. The scheme is known as standard rate taxation. Tax rates vary between 20.5 per cent and a top marginal rate of 47 per cent.

Unearned income (dividends, interest, etc) of minors is subject to special rules. Taxable income is derived by subtracting allowable expenses, eg subscriptions to professional journals, trade union subscriptions, from total income. There is also a system of rebates which are deducted from tax payable and include dependent spouse and concessional rebate. Concessional rebate includes expenditures on life assurance and pension contributions, medical and related costs, children's education expenses and rates and taxes on principal residence. Most are subject to an upper limit. The effect is that a married man with two children earning A$80,000 per annum would pay about 37 per cent income tax.

In addition, a family allowance is paid monthly to all resident families which include either children under 16 or full-time students aged 16–25. There is no VAT, though non-essential goods are subject to indirect taxation.

A universal health insurance scheme, Medicare, provides residents with protection against hospital, medical and optical costs. Contributions to the scheme are 1.25 per cent of taxable income (with low-income cut-off points).

Working conditions

At executive and professional levels international standards and conditions of work apply. Holidays are normally four weeks a year and some firms pay a holiday bonus. There is also often a form of sabbatical leave after 10 years' service with a company. Flexible working hours are quite common in Australia, particularly in the public sector. The chief difference in working conditions between Australia and other countries is that the concept of status related to specific jobs – and even more, social and workplace behaviour associated with it – has to be discarded. Any tendency to 'give yourself airs' is fatal!

Australian employers will not usually recruit from a distance, but it is possible to get a good picture of the sort of employment opportunities available from Australian newspapers and particularly from the Australian migration authorities. In general the demand is for specific skills and professional or managerial qualifications (in, for example, computer work). Most British professional qualifications are recognised in Australia, but it is necessary to show documentary evidence of having obtained them.

Living conditions

Australia has often been presented in this country as being a rather uncouth place with a nice climate. Though the latter is still true (no state capital averages less than five and a half hours of sunshine a day) Australia is, in spite of its reputation, a very civilised place in which to live. It has excellent wines, varied and sophisticated restaurants and surprisingly good cultural amenities. The major newspapers are as good as any UK daily but British and American books cost approximately twice as much as in the country of origin. They are not subject to import duty, however, so if you are keen reader, it is a good idea to have an account with a British book shop.

Manufactured goods are expensive. Current (1991) prices include the following:

	A$
Refrigerator	750
Washing machine	850
Electric steam iron	90
Vacuum cleaner	370
Colour TV (22-inch screen)	1000

This may suggest that it is worth while taking domestic appliances with you, but be careful. Electrical goods should be checked with the maker to see if they would work in Australia, because the voltage systems differ. Gas appliances are particularly tricky because of differences in pressure and gas composition. A car, essential in Australia, is best bought there. Prices for four-door standard saloons are in the region of £10,000. Japanese cars are widely considered to be 'best buys'. If you import a car you will have to make sure that it meets the safety regulations of the state to which you are going. You can drive on a British licence for the first three months. After that you will have to take a local test, but this will only be an oral one if you already hold a British or international licence.

Food, allowing for seasonal variations, is varied and fairly reasonable.

Indeed, recent surveys suggest that in this respect Australia is cheaper than the UK.

A good up-to-date source of information on prices (as well as other facts about Australia) is a magazine available at Australia House Migration Office called *Australian Outlook*, which gives the following prices:

	Sydney *A$*	*Melbourne* *A$*
Petrol (1 litre)	0.69	0.65
Flour (2 kg)	2.25	2.39
Rump steak (1 kg)	11.63	11.68
Margarine (500 gm)	1.44	1.48
Detergent (1 litre)	4.08	4.15
Milk (1 litre)	1.14	0.92
Potatoes (1 kg)	0.93	0.84
Bananas (1 kg)	2.88	2.83

Fruit and vegetables vary with the season and according to the climate of the state, but can be very cheap at the appropriate times of year. Prices vary from state to state. In ascending order of cost the ranking is, roughly, Melbourne, Adelaide, Brisbane, Perth, Sydney, Canberra, Hobart, Darwin.

Education begins at the age of five or six (depending on the state) and is compulsory up to age 15 or 16 (depending on the state). The school session starts early in February, not September as in the UK. Tuition is free in government schools, but parents generally have to provide uniforms, books and other materials, though such items can be claimed against income tax, up to a maximum of A$250.00 per child. As many as 25 per cent of pupils, however, attend private schools, particularly in the latter years of secondary education. Fees are reasonable (and subject to tax rebates) because these schools are aided by government grants.

There are no tuition fees for university-level education, which is very well provided for in all states. The equivalent of three GCSEs and two A levels (or three As and one GCSE) would qualify for admission to an Australian university. Most Australians take a pass degree rather than honours. Standards are similar to those in the UK.

The sources for finance and house purchase are principally savings banks and building societies. Repayment periods run at between 15 and 25 years and mortgage repayment rates average around 25 per cent of income. (There are also special state schemes for families on low incomes.) As a rule the lender will provide around 75 per cent of the lender's valuation of the property (not market value) and no distinction is made in this respect between old and new houses.

The availability of houses and flats, both for rent and for sale, varies widely from state to state. Although it varies from town to town the weekly rental of an unfurnished three-bedroomed flat in a decent area can be as high as A$400 a week. To buy a quality house in a good area in most cities will cost from A$250,000 upwards (except in Sydney where house prices tend to be 20–21 per cent higher than elsewhere in the country). A good up-to-date guide on house purchase and price levels in Australia is available from the Commonwealth Bank of Australia, Aldwych House, 71–91 Aldwych, London WC2B 4ES.

New Zealand

Background

New Zealand is not, as many people seem to believe, next door to Australia, but some 1200 miles away. It is a country about the size of Italy, mostly very beautiful, mountainous and with marvellous facilities for every kind of outdoor life. It has a population of around 3.3 million, of whom nearly 75 per cent live in the North Island, specifically around the main cities: Auckland, Wellington and Hamilton. There are quite marked differences of climate between Auckland, situated in a very mild part of the North Island, and smaller cities like Dunedin or Invercargill in the South Island, where winters can be decidedly cold.

The population is largely of British descent – New Zealand has not attracted European settlers from other countries to the same degree as Australia – and about 12 per cent of the total are Maori. Of late, there has been some rise in racial tension, spilling over from a growing politicisation of the Polynesian population generally. Externally, the outstanding political event of the last decade was the sinking of the Greenpeace yacht *Rainbow Warrior* in Auckland harbour by French saboteurs, thus crystallising New Zealand's stand against French nuclear tests in the Pacific and leading to a ban on all nuclear ships, including those of the US Pacific Fleet.

Exchange rate: NZ$2.86 = £1.

The economy

Agriculture is still the major factor here and accounts for the majority of New Zealand's exports. Cattle, sheep, fruit and arable farming are much in evidence on both islands. Forestry is also important and is one of the growth points of the economy; tourism equally so. New Zealand has little in the way of mineral resources, but a big offshore oil and gas exploration programme is under way and quite a lot of gas has been discovered. The country also has plentiful resources for the production of hydro-electric power, some of which comes from the fascinating thermal region around Rotorua on the North Island.

Manufacturing employs some 25 per cent of the labour force, but one of the peculiarities of the industrial scene in New Zealand is the large number of very small firms. Over 60 per cent of the manufacturing output comes from factories employing fewer than 10 people. The home market is not big enough to generate many large-scale enterprises. This does not make for efficiency or low costs, but may in the end turn out to be socially and ecologically beneficial, on the 'small is beautiful' principle.

New Zealand has an unemployment rate of approximately 14 per cent and the economy has been in recession since the 1987 stock market crash. Inflation is currently running at around 5 per cent. Although the economy has had a low growth rate for some years, there is a continuing demand for technological and applied scientific skills.

Personal finance

Salaries in New Zealand are unlikely to be a prime attraction. In the public sector, according to seniority and qualifications, they can go up to NZ$40,000–$50,000, about the same as that for a senior university lecturer. A university professor's salary is around NZ$60,000–$75,000. This is about the same as a good managerial salary, although these can go as high as NZ$80,000 and more. Professional salaries for architects, engineers, accountants, etc are roughly equivalent to senior academic salaries on average. Obviously a successful professional man can earn a lot more: a figure of NZ$100,000 has been quoted as the earnings of a successful lawyer. In a more clearly defined area, that of nursing, a registered nurse would earn around NZ$24,000 – slightly more than a senior secretary.

Taxation

Tax is deducted on a PAYE basis. The basic rates of income tax are as follows:

Taxable income *NZ$*	*Basic tax rate* %
First 30,875	24
Over 30,875	33

Tax credits ('Family Support') are given to families with one or more dependent children. In addition there is a goods and services tax, similar to VAT, of 12.5 per cent.

Working conditions

The New Zealand 'welfare state' included far-reaching health and social security benefits to cover illness, unemployment, superannuation etc but in an effort to cut state spending the new National Party Government has announced sweeping cuts to these.

Under a reciprocal arrangement with the UK health care (including hospitalisation) is available to residents who go to live in New Zealand and have made the necessary NHI contributions here.

New Zealand is not an economically dynamic country, and job opportunities are limited outside a well-defined range of agricultural, technological, accounting and medical skills. Since 1974 *work permits* have not been readily given unless you have a firm offer of employment and accommodation and this in a category deemed by the New Zealand Department of Labour to be 'in high demand'. The list of occupations that fall into this category is available from the Chief Migration Officer at the New Zealand High Commission, New Zealand House, Haymarket, London SW1. Applicants also generally have to be under 45. There are no restrictions about taking money in or out of the country.

Living conditions

New Zealand has less to offer in the way of night life than its Tasman neighbour, Australia. Unless you are enamoured of the great outdoors you are liable to find it rather boring. On the other hand, the general level of affluence is high. Food, as might be expected, is somewhat cheaper than in the UK, but most household and manufactured goods cost somewhat more. Overall, the cost of living is about the same as in the UK. Whether or not you take to New Zealand depends very much on your life-style. If you like a rather conservative, comfortable way of life you will find it suits you very well; and, of course, the opportunity for outdoor life is much greater and much cheaper than in Europe. At the same time, hotels and the standard of food and wine in restaurants have improved immeasurably in recent years.

Some typical 1990 prices are given below:

	NZ($)
Mince (1 kg)	8.00
Lamb (leg) (2 kg)	6.70
Butter (500 gm)	2.20
Bread (1 kg)	2.50
Sugar (1 kg)	1.50
Eggs (12)	2.90
Wine (750 ml)	8.00–20.00

There are virtually no restrictions on bringing personal effects into the country; most electrical equipment will work in New Zealand (except TV sets), but some items may require a transformer to reduce voltage. British TVs have to be adapted as frequencies and systems differ, but it is possible to buy a suitable export model before your departure. A VHF modulator is required for video viewing on a normal NZ TV set. Cars are also expensive in New Zealand, but there are some special conditions for bringing them in and you would be well-advised to make sure that your shippers are acquainted with them; or you can check with the New Zealand High Commission. UK licences are accepted for the first year of your stay, after which you have to take a test to obtain a New Zealand licence. Although New Zealanders drive on the left and road rules are essentially the same as in the UK it would be advisable to check out the New Zealand road code – there are differences – especially in the give-way rules.

Primary school education begins at age five, but there is also an excellent network of pre-school education for three-year-olds upwards. Education is compulsory from 6 to 15 and tuition is free, though parents are expected to pay for uniforms, the wearing of which is customary. There are also private schools, mostly conducted by religious bodies. University entrance qualifications correspond to those in this country and tuition is free to those who reach top-level entrance qualifications. A cash allowance is payable to students living away from home. There are university scholarships for the brightest students and these carry somewhat higher financial benefits. At the other end of the scale, students who have got in on somewhat lower qualifications are eligible to receive a grant, but not full remission of fees.

The typical New Zealand house is a bungalow, serviceable and with a nice garden, but low on individuality and aesthetic appeal. Rented accommodation is hard to obtain and quality houses are scarce and expensive to buy. The principal lender is the government's Housing Corporation, and though their loans carry a low rate of interest and a long repayment period, they restrict lending to first-time buyers in low income groups, which excludes many expatriates. (The national average house price is around NZ$110,000, but prices in Wellington and Auckland are considerably higher.)

A minimum 20 per cent deposit is always payable. A useful list of current lenders and interest rates is available from New Zealand House.

Papua New Guinea

Background

Papua New Guinea lies 100 miles north of Australia and has a land area of 461,700 square kilometres. The country comprises the eastern part of the main New Guinea Island and about 600 smaller islands, of which the largest are New Britain, Bougainville and New Ireland. It is geographically very diverse, with a massive mountain range running east-west on the main island and large areas of tropical rain forest around its fringes. Some areas, particularly in the south, receive 200 inches of rain a year, among the world's highest.

The population is estimated at 3.5 million, of whom about 10 per cent are non-nationals, principally Australians, Chinese, Indians, Africans and South-East Asians. The capital is Port Moresby (population 132,000) and the other major towns are the main port and commercial centre of Lae on the north-eastern coast, Madang, Rabaul and Goroka.

The official language is English, but in addition to Melanesian Pidgin and Hiri Motu, both of which are widely spoken, there are over 700 other languages – about half the world's total.

Papua New Guinea has been an independent state since 1975, when power was finally transferred from Australia. There are 19 provinces, each with a provisional government that is more or less autonomous in local matters. The central government is democratically elected, has one chamber and acknowledges Queen Elizabeth II as head of state, represented by a Governor General.

Exchange rate: Kina 1.59 = £1.

The economy

The country's principal products are copper, gold, coffee, cocoa, timber and copra.

Oil and natural gas have been found in the Southern Highlands and there are large offshore gas reserves, but these are yet to be fully exploited. Overall the economy is fairly sound and stable. However, crime is becoming a serious problem, particularly in Port Moresby; its main cause is migration from rural areas of young people, who then cannot find work in the city. Inflation is around 5 per cent. Many of the rural areas have no cash economy, but agriculture is estimated to account for one-third of total GNP and there are huge untapped forestry resources. The country remains heavily dependent upon Australian economic aid.

Personal finance and taxation

Wage-earners with only one source of income have tax deducted automatically from their pay, after deductions for dependants. Tax rates on the salary levels expatriates might expect to earn would be in the region of 35–45 per cent.

There should not normally be problems with the remittability of currency from Papua New Guinea.

Working conditions

It is necessary to hold a *work permit* in order to gain permission to reside in the country. This is obtainable before arrival, either through the Department of Labour and Industry or through the employer. In addition, all foreign nationals must have a valid passport and visa before entering Papua New Guinea.

Many expatriate posts in the country are in government employ, and are well advertised in the UK, typically in the *Guardian*. Salaries are quite high, but the qualifications and experience demanded are equally so.

An advertisement for civil servants at what would be administrative level in the UK offered salaries in the range of £30,000 plus with an annual gratuity of 25 per cent of salary and the following conditions of service:

Gratuity 24 per cent of salary taxed at 2 per cent
Three-year contract with possibility of renewal
Fares to be paid to and from Papua New Guinea
Settling in allowance
Six weeks' annual leave
Leave fares to home country once during the contract
Almost rent-free accommodation
Generous educational subsidies for dependants
Inflation adjustment.

Living conditions

The climate is typically tropical and cool cotton clothes are normal year-round wear. The Highlands are cooler. Port Moresby has a dry season from May to November, the opposite of Lae's. Malaria is a problem in many areas, although Moresby is now relatively safe. Health problems have now been replaced by the usual Third World domestic and personal security ones. Violent crime is a particularly serious issue and houses should be well protected.

Travel within the country is usually impossible by road (except from Lae to the principal Highland towns). Consequently, air is the normal medium for transport and Air Niugini flies to all the major centres and to many small towns; other carriers include Talair, Douglas Airways, Bougair and several other charter firms. Hire and radio cars are available in the main towns but bus services are still inefficient. There are some scenic highways, of various quality.

Although reasonably well-supplied with hotels and boasting a few good restaurants, Port Moresby has little to offer by way of night life. What there is centres around the hotels, and is generally Australian in flavour.

It is easy to get domestic servants, but it is wise to check references and make an initial provisional arrangement, as there are many urban drifters. Pay is usually around K30 a week and it should be agreed at the start how many relatives and others will be sharing it with the servant actually hired.

Imported food is expensive, but local produce is plentiful, varied and quite cheap.

Some typical 1990 living costs are:

	K
Sugar (1 kg)	1.20
Eggs (12)	2.60
Butter (500 g)	1.40

Rice (1 kg)	0.70
Bread	1.30
Cooking oil (1 litre)	2.60
Bacon (1 kg)	14.00
Chicken (1 kg)	4.00

Accommodation is hard to find, and annual rents range from around K4500 for a one-bedroomed flat to K14,000 for a four-bedroomed house. Port Moresby has a good water supply and in all the main centres there is safe drinking water and electricity. The telephone service is excellent but all mail must be addressed to PO boxes. There is no mains gas supply.

Cars may be admitted duty free if they have been in the owner's personal use for 15 months before taking up residence in Papua New Guinea. A new Japanese saloon car (eg the Toyota Corolla 1.6) costs around K16,500.

The education system is good, and there is a university with 3000 students at Port Moresby and a University of Technology at Lae. The language of instruction is English. There are a number of International Schools which follow a broadly New South Wales, Australia curriculum, but many expatriates send their children abroad for their education.

Further Information

Principal Sources

We are indebted to a great many sources for the information in this book, but the following – not arranged in order of merit – were the ones we found particularly useful.

Business Profiles. Individual booklets issued by the British Bank of the Middle East, a part of the Hong Kong Banking Group. They cover many of the Middle Eastern Countries. They are aimed at both companies and private individuals and contain some useful information on living conditions.

Prices and Earnings Around the Globe. An excellent comparative survey of a wide variety of costs and earnings in some 50 countries. Issued every three years by the Union Bank of Switzerland.

Expats International (29 Lacon Road, London SE22 9HE, tel: 081-299 4986) publish a useful monthly newsletter, *Home & Away*.

Hints to Exporters. Issued by the Department of Trade and Industry. Intended mainly for business visitors, but contains useful data on things like holidays, hotel addresses, business etiquette, climate at various times of the year, etc.

The Multinational Employer (DCR Enterprises, c/o Simplex, St Clare House, 30–33 Minories, London EC3N 1DD) gives information and advice on tax, law, exchange rates, salaries, employment opportunities and working conditions.

Special supplements on various countries included in quality newspapers and periodicals. These mainly contain very general business information, but often have data of interest to intending expatriates.

The monthly *Resident Abroad* covers both life-style and money. It is published by Financial Times Business Information, 102–108 Clerkenwell Road, London EC1M 5SA.

Barclay's Country Reports, covering more than 20 OECD countries, are available from the Librarian, Economics Department, Barclay's Bank plc, PO Box 12, 1 Wimbourne Road, Poole, Dorset BH15 2B. Also available from Barclay's are over 100 ABECOR country reports, produced by an association of European banks.

Many pamphlets and books have been published about Europe, especially since Britain joined the EC. EC material can be obtained from the London office, or HMSO. Foreign embassies based in London will also have material of value for expatriates intending to live and work in the country which they represent. Their addresses are given in the *London Diplomatic List*, available from HMSO.

Useful Addresses

Anderson Sinclair & Co
The Leatherhead Institute
High Street, Leatherhead
Surrey KT22 8AH
Tel: 0372 379345
(Financial advisers specialising in expatriate investment and tax problems.)

British Association of Removers
3 Churchill Court
58 Station Road
North Harrow
Middlesex HA2 7SA
Tel: 081-861 3331

British Council
65 Davies Street
London W1Y 2AA
Tel: 071-930 8466

British Medical Association
BMA House
Tavistock Square
London WC1H 9JP
Tel: 071-387 4499

BUPA International
Imperial House
40–42 Queen's Road
Brighton BN1 3XT
Tel: 0273 23563

Centre for International Briefing
Farnham Castle
Farnham
Surrey GU9 0AG
Tel: 0252 721194

Centre for Information on Language Teaching and Research
Regent's College
Inner Circle
Regent's Park
London NW1 4NS
Tel: 071-486 8221

Citicorp Insurance Brokers Ltd
St Clare House
30–33 Minories
London EC3N 1DD
Tel: 071-488 1388

Conrad Languages
Premier House
77 Oxford Street
London W1R 1RB
Tel: 071-434 0113

Council of British Independent Schools in the European Communities (COBISEC)
Secretariat
c/o The British School of Brussels
Chaussée de Louvain
Tervuren B3080
Belgium

Department of Social Security
Overseas Branch
Benton Park Road
Newcastle upon Tyne NE98 1YX
Tel: 0632 857111

DHL International (UK) Ltd
Orbital Park
178–188 Great South West Road
Hounslow
Middlesex TW4 6JS
Tel: 081-890 9393
(Provides world's largest air courier service, with pick-up and delivery.)

Education and Guardian Advisory Services Ltd (EGAS)
11 Seaton Avenue
Mutley
Plymouth
Tel: 0752 261229

Employment Conditions Abroad Ltd
Anchor House
10 Britten Street
London SW3 3TY
Tel: 071-351 7151

Europea – IMG Ltd
Expatriate Health Care
Provender Mill
Mill Bay Lane
Horsham
West Sussex RH12 1SS
Tel: 0403 51884

European Council of International Schools (ECIS)
21B Lavant Street
Petersfield
Hampshire GU32 2EL
Tel: 0730 68244

Exeter Hospital Aid Society
5 & 7 Palace Gate
Exeter EX1 1UE
Tel: 0392 75361

Expats International
29 Lacon Road
London SE22 9HE
Tel: 081-299 4986

Financial Intermediaries Managers and Brokers Regulatory Association (FIMBRA)
Heartsmere House
Marsh Wall
London E14 9RV
Tel: 071-538 8860

Gabbitas, Truman & Thring Education Trust
Broughton House
6 Sackville Street
London W1X 2BR
Tel: 071-734 0161

Independent Schools Information Service (ISIS)
56 Buckingham Gate
London SW1E 6AG
Tel: 071-630 8790

International House
106 Piccadilly
London W1V 9FL
Tel: 071-491 2598
(Principal source of information on ELT/TEFL opportunities abroad.)

International Training and Recruitment Link
51A Bryanston Street
London W1H 7DN
Tel: 071-706 3646

Kibbutz Representatives
1a Accommodation Road
London NW11 8ED
Tel: 081-458 9235

Overseas Development Administration
Abercrombie House
Eaglesham Road
East Kilbride
Glasgow G75 8EA
Tel: 0355 8444000

PPP
Phillips House
Crescent Road
Tunbridge Wells
Kent TN1 2PL
Tel: 0892 512345

Resident Abroad
102–108 Clerkenwell Road
London EC1M 5SA
Tel: 071-251 9321

Ross Institute of Tropical Hygiene
Keppel Street
Gower Street
London WC1E 7HT
Tel: 071-636 8636

Royal College of Nursing
20 Cavendish Square
London W1M 0AB
Tel: 071-409 3333

Royal Society of Arts
John Adam Street
London WC2N 6EZ
Tel: 071-839 1691

School of Oriental & African Studies
External Services Division
Malet Street
London WC1E 7HP
Tel: 071-637 2388

Universal Aunts Ltd
PO Box 304
London SW4 0NN
Tel: 071-371 9766

The Visa Shop
1 Charing Cross Underground
London WC2 4NZ
Tel: 071-497 2590

Voluntary Service Overseas
317 Putney Bridge Road
London SW15 2PN
Tel: 081-780 2266

Women's Corona Society
Commonwealth House
18 Northumberland Ave
London WC2N 5BJ
Tel: 071-839 7908

World-wide Education Service (WES)
10 Barley Mow Passage
Chiswick
London W4 4PH
Tel: 081-994 3622

Further Reading from Kogan Page

Blackstone Franks Guide to Living in Portugal, David Franks, 1990

Blackstone Franks Guide to Living in Spain, 2nd edition, Blackstone Franks 1989

Daily Telegraph Guide to Buying a Property in France, 2nd edition, Philip Jones 1991

Daily Telegraph Guide to Changing Your Job After 35, 6th edition, G Golzen and P Plumbley 1988

Daily Telegraph Guide to Living and Retiring Abroad, 5th edition, Michael Furnell, 1991

The Educated Executive, Harold Taylor, 1991

The Mid Career Action Guide, Derek and Fred Kemp, 1991

Moving Up, Stan Crabtree, 1991

Index of Advertisers

Hong Kong Schools p.292
Women's Corona Society p.130